D0983901

# Springer Series in Language and Communication 13

Editor: W. J. M. Levelt

# Springer Series in Language and Communication

Editor: W. J. M. Levelt

Traute Taeschner

# The Sun is Feminine

A Study on Language Acquisition
in Bilingual Children

With 18 Figures

Springer-Verlag
Berlin  Heidelberg  New York  Tokyo 1983

Dr. Traute Taeschner

Istituto di Psicologia, Università di Roma, Via del Castro Pretorio, 20
I-00185 Roma, Italy


*Series Editor:*

Professor Dr. Willem J. M. Levelt

Max-Planck-Institut für Psycholinguistik, Berg en Dalseweg 79
6522 BC Nijmegen, The Netherlands

ISBN 3-540-12238-9 Springer-Verlag Berlin Heidelberg New York Tokyo
ISBN 0-387-12238-9 Springer-Verlag New York Heidelberg Berlin Tokyo

Library of Congress Cataloging in Puplication Data. Taeschner, T. (Traute), 1950- The sun is feminine.
(Springer series in language and communication ; 13) Bibliography: p. Includes index. 1. Language
acquisition. 2. Bilingualism. 3. Interference (Linguistics) I. Title. II. Series: Springer series in language
and communication ; v. 13.   P118.T28   1983   401'.9   83-525

Typesetting: K + V Fotosatz, 6124 Beerfelden
Offset printing: Beltz Offsetdruck, 6944 Hemsbach. Bookbinding: J. Schäffer OHG, 6718 Grünstadt
2153/3130-543210

*To my husband,*
*with love*

# Preface

Lisa is 4 years and 5 months old and Giulia 3 years and 4 months. One morning, the girls' father is taking them to nursery school.

**L:** ... *è bravissima, ha riscaldato l'auto. E' bravissima, vero?*
In praising the sun for having warmed up the car, Lisa has referred to it in the feminine gender, as in the German *die Sonne.* Her father corrects her by using the masculine gender.
**F:** *E' bravissimo. E' il sole.*
**L:** *E' un maschietto, il sole?* (Is the sun a little boy?)
**F:** *E' maschile.* (It's masculine.)
**G** [determined]: *E' una femmina!* (No, it's a girl!)
**F:** *Forse in tedesco.* (Perhaps it is in German.)
Giulia is left disoriented, speechless.

This book is devoted to language acquisition in children who have been exposed to two languages since birth.

It has often been said that the study of simultaneous bilingualism is the "most fertile ground" for the formulation of general theories on language acquisition processes, and indeed, most of the studies on early bilingualism aim in this direction. But in a sense this book serves the reverse purpose. Using the results of psycholinguistic research as a basis, I have sought to understand the peculiarities of the process of language organization in the child who faces the problem of learning two languages when other children are learning only one. Thus, the recurring theme of my study is the diversity of bilingual as opposed to monolingual acquisition.

In writing this book, I have tried to balance the needs of the specialist with those of the reader who is approaching the subject for the first time. I hope that the parent desirous of bringing up his child bilingually will find answers here to some of the questions raised by his project.

I have examined several of the fundamental aspects of speech. In Chap. 1, I briefly discuss the results of the most important research in the field of simultaneous bilingualism and outline the methods I used in my research. The development of lexicon is analysed in Chap. 2 in the attempt to ascertain whether bilingual subjects acquire the two lexical systems at the same time, whether this acquisition calls for particular strategies on the child's part, and whether the lexicon of the bilingual child is quantitatively similar to that of the monolingual child. Chap. 3 is a description of sentence structure development beginning with the initial two-word combinations and proceeding to the more complex structures, which gradually achieve the adult level. In Chap. 4, I have analysed the development of several morphological and syntactic aspects, some of which are the same in the bilingual's two languages, and some of which are very different. Chap. 5 is devoted to interferences between languages in child speech. In Chap. 6, I have taken a look at some very important aspects of the upbringing of my bilingual subjects by relating the actual conditions in which these children had contact with each language to their ability to express themselves in each of them. The reader interested in immediate information about my subjects' environment might want to read Chap. 6 after Chap. 1. Finally, in Chap. 7, I have related all of these aspects of the process of speech acquisition in the bilingual child to one another.

This book was made possible by the stimulus, advice and criticism I received from many friends and colleagues. My first thanks go to my professor, Renzo Titone, who has not only always believed in my work, but who also patiently read and criticized the entire manuscript. I am deeply indebted to Virginia Volterra, who followed each step of the study with enthusiasm and extreme care, never hesitating to give her best effort and advice. The criticism of Vittoria Giuliani, Claudia De Lemos and Elisabeth Bates was no less important, and contributed greatly to the clarification of several theoretical aspects. I would also like to thank Domenico Parisi, Edward Klima, and Pier Marco Bertinetto for their comments on some of the chapters, as well as Norbert Dittmar for his advice during my stay in Heidelberg. Paola Bonetti's help was also very valuable, because as she read the Italian version of the book aloud with me, I was able to understand some of the secrets of the language more clearly. Finally, I would like to express my gratitude to my daughters Lisa and Giulia, who provided the inspiration, motivation and data for my study.

For the entire period in which this research was carried out I was affiliated with the Institute of Psychology of the CNR in Rome, whose technical and financial support I gratefully acknowledge.

My thanks also go to the Alexander von Humboldt Foundation of Bonn for its financial support during my stay at the University of Heidelberg.

Rome, January 1983                                        *Traute Taeschner*

# Note to the Reader

In keeping with general convention in the literature on child speech, the ages of the children studied here are given in numerals in the following order: years, months, days (e.g., 3;8,10).

Lisa and Giulia, the names of the two principal subjects of this study, are abbreviated **L** and **G**, while **M** and **F** stand for their mother and father.

The children's utterances were translated literally when it proved necessary to do so in order to demonstrate certain principles. This often resulted in ungrammatical English.

# Contents

# 1. An Overview of Research on Bilingualism

Giulia (1;11,0, i.e., 1 year; 11 months, 0 days old) is helping her mother tidy up. She looks at an umbrella and takes it in her hand.

**G:** *L'ombrello no-o-o-!* [to mean one doesn't play with the umbrella].
**G** [looking at her mother]: *Hut no, nein.* (Hat no, no!)
**M:** *Das ist kein Hut, das ist ein Regenschirm.* (That isn't a hat, it's an umbrella.)
**G:** *Ein Legenschirm, no!* (An umbrella, no!) And she leaves the umbrella in its place.

Lisa (3;2) hears her mother telling her father that if he had wanted to, he would have learned some German by now. Lisa turns to her father.

**L:** *Papà, dì: Ja!* (Papa, say: Ja!)
**F:** *Ja.*
**L:** *Hast du gehört, Mami? Papi spricht Deutsch!* (Did your hear Mommy? Daddy speaks German!)

Giulia (3;3) complains to her mother because Lisa (4;4) said to her:

**L:** *Ti spacco la testa.* (I'll break your head.)
**G:** *Wenn Lisa mein Kopf kaputt macht a sagt mein Gehirn? Wo ist mein Haus?* (If Lisa breaks my head, what will my brain say? Where's my house?)

When Lisa is 3 years and 7 months old, her father finds the door open for the $n^{th}$ time.

**F:** *Mi sembrava! La porta aperta!* (I thought so! The door's open.) [Lisa closes the door.]
**L:** *Ho chiuso!* (I've closed it!) [Her mother speaks to her.]
**M:** *Was hast du gemacht?* (What have you done?)
**L:** *Für Papi gesagt.* (I said it for Papi.)
**M:** *Willst du nicht auch für Mami sagen!* (Won't you say it for Mami, too?)
**L:** *Ich hab die Tür zugemacht.* (I've closed the door.)

Marta, Giulia and Lisa are playing together. Lisa is 8, Giulia is 7, and Marta is $6\frac{1}{2}$ years old.

**M:** Giulia, are you Italian or French? (Giulia's last name is Francese, which means "French" in Italian.)

**G:** No! German! And Italian! And a little Brazilian, too! (Giulia's grandparents live in Brazil.)

**M:** Well, I told my Mommy that you speak French.

**G:** Marta, what are you talking about? Are you crazy? I don't know French! My name is Francese. But I only know German, Italian and a little Portuguese, too.

**M:** But did you speak English first?

**G:** No, I spoke German first!

**M:** Oh. [Lisa arrives.]

**M:** Will you teach me your language?

**L:** What, German?

**M:** Yeah.

**L:** Okay. I'm the teacher. Come here, come here. [Lisa takes Marta into the other room. Giulia stays behind.]

**L:** Okay. "Play" is *spielen* in German. SPI-E-LEN. In German, "ei" is pronounced "ī." "Flying" in German is *fliegt*. Say it: *fliegt*.

**M:** Flikete.

**L:** No! *Fliegt,* gt, gt.

**M:** Flikete.

**L:** Okay. Remember that: *fliegt*, gt, gt. In German, "the" is *die*. It's spelled "ie," but it's pronounced "e."

**M:** Oh, yeah? [She laughs.] I don't understand anything!

**L:** How can I teach Marta German if she still doesn't even know how to read and write? Listen, Marta. After you learn German, you have to pay me.

**M:** Yes.

**L:** Two thousand lire? Twenty thousand? Fifty thousand?

**M:** That's just a bit too much.

**L:** Eighty thousand?

**M:** That's too much! Ten thousand.

**L:** Okay. Now Marta, you have to buy a third-grade notebook with lined paper, and I'll give you some cards.

Camilla and Lisa, both 7 years old, are playing together. Lisa says something to her mother in German, and Camilla listens.

**C:** Are you speaking English?

**L:** No, German.

**C:** Oh! That's another language I don't know.

## 1.1 The Definition of Bilingualism

The brief episodes described above have given the reader an initial idea of the linguistic production of bilingual children. Examples such as these raise a series of questions. For instance, can bilingual children really manage to learn two different languages well? Or do they not give the impression of speaking less correctly than monolingual children? Doesn't learning two languages require such an enormous effort that language acquisition is retarded? Is merely speaking with the child in both languages enough to enable him to achieve bilingualism easily? In a different vein: How will the child's monolingual playmates react? Will they reject or accept him?

These are only a few of the questions being examined in the field of bilingual education and this particular type of language acquisition. My aim in this book is to answer many of these questions by examining language acquisition in children who have had continuous relations with two different languages throughout their childhood. I have deliberately not given consideration to language acquisition in children who have only briefly, perhaps while spending a vacation abroad, come into contact with a foreign language, or children who have acquired their second language after being already quite familiar with the first, perhaps as a result of a move from one country to another. The latter type of acquisition is called consecutive bilingualism and the former simultaneous bilingualism.[1]

In distinguishing between simultaneous and consecutive bilingualism [Mc Laughlin, 1978, p. 8], the difficulty lies in establishing the age at which it may be said that the child has acquired a language. For instance, if a $2\frac{1}{2}$-year-old English child moves to France and then begins acquiring both French and English, can this be said to be a case of simultaneous bilingualism? Obviously, the term "consecutive bilingualism" implies that at least the fundamental structures of the first language have already been acquired before the child begins the second language ("first" and "second" refer here to chronological order). If this is not the case, then it is impossible to speak of consecutive language acquisition, and we must use the term "simultaneous acquisition," in which there are two first (or native) languages, neither of which may be called the second language.

---

1 According to McLaughlin (1978, p. 9), a distinction can be made between the acquisition and the learning of a second language. In acquisition, both children and adults pick up the language through their natural environment, without necessarily having any formal instruction. Learning a second language, on the other hand, implies formal instruction, feedback, the correction of errors, and the teaching of rules in an artificial linguistic setting. Similarly, Schönpflug (1977) distinguishes between natural and guided acquisition of the two languages (*gelenkter und natürlicher Zweitsprachenerwerb*). However, these are both cases of consecutive bilingualism. In simultaneous bilingualism, we can distinguish between acquisition, which takes place during the first six or seven years of life, and learning, which begins when the child starts school.

Generally speaking, we may accept McLaughlin's [1978] arbitrary division, on the basis of which the term "simultaneous" is given to all bilingual subjects who have begun having steady contact with two languages before the age of 3 and "consecutive" is used to refer to all those who have their first contact with a second language after that age. Naturally, this does not mean that a 3-year-old child has completely mastered his native language. It merely means that his knowledge of his native tongue is such that any bilingualism which begins henceforth cannot be considered simultaneous.

The simultaneous bilingual has two native languages, but this does not mean his competence is identical in both. Usually one of the two dominates over the other. As we shall see, this depends greatly upon the opportunities the child has had to speak each language. Because contact with the two languages is never constant or equal, it would appear to be extremely difficult, if not impossible, to become "equilingual", i.e., to have the same competence in both languages [Titone, 1972; Taeschner, 1976; McLaughlin, 1978].

Should the term "true" in reference to a bilingual be used only for the simultaneous bilingual, because only he is as competent in both languages as a native speaker? Or can the term be used for people who can understand a second language perfectly without being able to speak it? At what point does a person become bilingual? Is a minimal knowledge of the second language sufficient, or does one need to have wide knowledge in order to be considered bilingual?

The precise definition of bilingualism and of the bilingual person is a constant preoccupation of the field, as can be seen in the books and numerous articles on the subject. Some authors consider a person to be bilingual if he knows only a few words of a second language, while others only use the term for those who speak two languages as well as native speakers. Naturally, this brings up the problem of what is meant by the competence of the native speaker, as it is well known that competence among the native speakers of any language varies widely. According to MacNamara [1967], the bilingual is anyone who possesses to a minor degree even one of the skills listed in Table 1.1.

Ervin and Osgood [1954] felt it best to distinguish between what they called compound and coordinate bilinguals. The distinction is based principal-

**Table 1.1.** Matrix of language skills [MacNamara, 1967]

| Encoding | | Decoding | |
|---|---|---|---|
| Speaking | Writing | Hearing | Reading |
| semantics | semantics | semantics | semantics |
| syntactics | syntactics | syntactics | syntactics |
| lexicon | lexicon | lexicon | lexicon |
| phonemes | graphemes | phonemes | graphemes |

ly on the semantic aspect of language. The compound bilingual is one who attributes the same meaning to corresponding words in the two languages. Ervin and Osgood maintain that this correspondence is the result of having learned the second language in school, translations, etc. Coordinate bilinguals, on the other hand, are able to give different or partially different meanings to corresponding words. Ervin and Osgood assume that this ability to distinguish is due to the different situations in which the individual has come into contact with the two languages. For instance, one language might be used at school with friends and another at home with one's parents.

According to Brooks [1960, p. 40], "bilingualism is an individual's ability to express himself in a second language, while faithfully using the concepts and structures of that language, rather than paraphrasing those of his own." On the other hand, Mackey's [1956] proposal is to get away from the generalities of a concept which sees bilingualism as no more than an equal command of the two languages. He suggests that a better idea might be to analyze the various aspects of the problem, which would also make it possible to draw up a systematic classification of the intricacies implied in the use of two or more languages. Instead of drawing up such a complex classification, I have based this study on the definitions put forth by Haugen and Weinrich. According to Haugen [1956, p. 10], bilingualism means that "the speaker can produce complete, meaningful utterances in the other language." Weinrich [1974, p. 3] considers bilingualism to be "the practice of using two languages alternatively." Although they may seem arbitrary and equivocal, these definitions nonetheless make it possible to exclude all those who are only able to say a few words in a second language. The children studied for this work did not read or write before six years of age, but they spoke and understood both languages, and as they grew, they were able to extend this ability to include sentences and complete discussions.

In defining what a bilingual is, it is best not to make too many requirements, as, for example, nativelike competence. Nor should one use such adjectives as "true" or "false" to describe bilinguals. What one must certainly do is to recognize the gradual nature of any person's ability to express himself in one, two, or more languages. Like the monolingual, who may be good or bad at understanding and speaking his own language, the bilingual may be quite good in one language and only fair in the second, fair in both, or excellent in both. In fact, as Malherbe said [in Arsenian, 1945, p. 72], "bilingualism is a continuum from one to one hundred"; I apply this to monolingualism as well.

## 1.2 Previous Research

As regards the choice of subjects to be observed, studies on child bilingualism have for the most part been carried out along three lines:

a) observation of a large number of children of roughly the same age at a precise point in the process of language acquisition.

b) observation of various groups of children whose ages differ by precise intervals. For instance, when the first group is 18 months old, the second is 21 months, the third 24 months, and so on. With this method, it is possible to study the entire range of evolution in a shorter period of time. The technique used in these two types of study is generally that of the test or guided observation [see Roeper, 1972; Grimm, 1973].

c) observation of the process of language acquisition in a small number of children over a period lasting from 6 to 12 months to a maximum of 13 or 14 years. Such studies, for which researchers generally use a diary or a tape recorder or, more recently, a videotape machine, are normally called longitudinal studies (because they require an extended period of time), or case studies (because they are based on the intense observation of a few individual cases).

The study described here was carried out according to the third procedure; in it, a small number of children were observed for more than four years.

In the following, several studies of simultaneous bilingualism are described and a summary given of their principal results. These studies, which were conducted independently of one another, have led to conclusions which have often been of great interest but are sometimes patchy, and they deal with a very heterogeneous range of topics. Furthermore, the quality of these research projects varies greatly, with some of them having an almost impressionistic quality due to their use of anecdotes, while others are more rigorous and scientific. Nonetheless, all of them use the methodology in gathering data which is described in point c above. While numerous longitudinal studies could be cited which have been conducted on language acquisition from birth, not many more than twenty deal with simultaneous acquisition (see Table 1.2; for another list of the studies on simultaneous bilingualism, see McLaughlin [1978, p. 87]).

The first study to deal specifically with simultaneous language acquisition was conducted by the French linguist Jules Ronjat [1913], who successfully brought up his son Louis speaking French and German. Ronjat closely followed the *une personne, une langue* principle suggested to him by Maurice Grammont [in Ronjat, 1913, p. 3]: "Nothing has to be taught to the child. You must simply speak to him, when there is something to be said, in one of the two languages that you want him to learn. But there is a key factor, and that is that each language must be represented by a different person."

Thus Ronjat spoke only French with his son, while his wife spoke only German. Apart from the family servants, the child came into contact with his grandparents and aunts and uncles, and they all spoke either French or German. But the predominant factor was the constant relationship between the respective parent and his or her language.

**Table 1.2.** The principal longitudinal studies on simultaneous bilingualism (taken from McLaughlin [1978, p. 87] and updated to include more recent studies)

| Author | Languages | Age of child during study | Number of children |
|---|---|---|---|
| 1. Ronjat (1913) | French, German | First 5 years | 1 |
| 2. Pavlovitch (1920) | French, Serbian | First 2 years | 1 |
| 3. Hoyer & Hoyer (1924) | Russian, German | First year | 1 |
| 4. Smith (1935) | English, Chinese | First 4 years | 8 |
| 5. Emrich (1938) | German, Bulgarian | First 3 years | 1 |
| 6. Leopold (1939 – 1949b) | German, English | First 2 years and $2-12$ years | 2 |
| 7. Burling (1959) | Garo, English | 1 year, 4 months $-$ 2 years, 10 months | 1 |
| 8. Imedadze (1960) | Russian, Georgian | 11 months $-$ 3 years | 1 |
| 9. Raffler-Engel (1965) | English, Italian | First $4\frac{1}{2}$ years | 1 |
| 10. Murrel (1966) | Swedish, Finnish, English | 2 years $-$ 2 years, 8 months | 1 |
| 11. Rüke-Dravina (1967) | Swedish, Latvian | First 6 years | 2 |
| 12. Mikés (1967) | Hungarian, Serbo-Croatian | First 4 years | 3 |
| 13. Tabouret-Keller (1969) | French, German (Alsatian dialect) | 1 year, 8 months $-$ 2 years, 11 months | 1 |
| 14. Oksaar (1970) | Swedish, Estonian | 2 months $-$ 3 years | 1 |
| 15. Swain (1973) | English, French | 3 years, 1 month $-$ 3 years, 10 months | 1 |
| 16. Volterra & Taeschner (1975) | German, Italian | $1-3$ years | 2 |
| 17. Bergman (1976) | English, Spanish | 10 months $-$ 2 years, 5 months | 1 |
| 18. Calasso & Garau (1976) | English, Italian | First 5 years | 1 |
| 19. Bizzarri (1977) | English, Italian | First $3\frac{1}{2}$ years | 2 |
| 20. De Matteis (1978) | German, Dutch, Italian | $1-2, 6-7, 7-8, 8-9$ years | 4 |
| 21. Redlinger & Park (1979) | German, Spanish; German, English; German, French | $2-3$ years (study conducted over a period of $5-8$ months) | 4 |
| 22. Cunze (1980) | German, Italian | First $5\frac{1}{2}$ years | 1 |

Ronjat based his data on accurate daily observation. Louis began speaking at the age of about 13 months, but he only became aware of the existence of two different languages at about 21 months. From the very beginning, the two systems of articulation were distinct, and phonetic development was parallel. The child's contact with the two languages was not always the same, and this was reflected in his speech. At 20 months, although his pronunciation was typically French, he nevertheless used more German words, placing more French words into German sentences than vice versa. At 26 months, following an increase in his contact with French, his use of the two languages was almost the same. At 33 months his use of French had jumped noticeably ahead of his use of German, and at 43 months the two languages were once again at the same level.

In the end, Ronjat's son spoke both languages like native-speaking children. When he had to accustom himself to a new maid who spoke, for example, German, while her predecessor had spoken French, the child needed a few days to identify the language, but after that he never made a mistake. Moreover, he never translated; rather, he automatically spoke the language of the person with whom he was talking. He spoke the one or other of the languages depending upon who had inspired him and who was going to be listening.

After observing the considerable difficulties encountered by another bilingual child whose parents had not been consistent in applying the "one person, one language" principle, Ronjat concluded that giving the child the opportunity to relate a specific person constantly to each language greatly facilitated bilingual acquisition.

The Serbian linguist Pavlovitch [1920] arrived at the same conclusion after having studied the development of his son, who grew up in Paris as a Serbian – French bilingual. The child, whose mother was Serbian, heard only Serbian spoken up to the age of 13 months, and thus his first words were also in that language. After this stage, however, a close family friend came to know him and spent several hours a day speaking only French to him. Gradually, the child was also exposed to other people who spoke French, and thus he learned that language as well.

Pavlovitch concluded that the child had attained complete acquisition of vocalization in both languages as if he were a native speaker; he had no foreign accent in French, nor were inhibitions or interferences ever observed. Until the age of 21 months, he used fewer French words than he did Serbian words. According to Pavlovitch, the child did not realize until he was about 2 years old that he was speaking with two different linguistic codes. Until that time, he was in effect only speaking one language and using the corresponding words of the two languages as synonyms but not as parts of two specific systems. Later, he ceased to confuse the two languages with one another and kept them separate at all times. Pavlovitch attributed the child's ability to keep the two languages separate to the fact that he associated each of them with a different person. Although he had realized that both of his parents understood and even spoke French, he always spoke to them in Serbian.

The studies carried out by Hoyer and Hoyer [1924], Smith [1935] and Emrich [1938] were less detailed than those of Ronjat and Pavlovitch.

Hoyer and Hoyer observed their son's phonological development in a situation where he heard his mother speak Russian and his father German.

They discovered that some of the sounds produced by the child in his first year of life reflected those of the languages he heard, whereas others did not.

Smith [1935] studied the linguistic development of eight North American children who had lived for many years in China. The data upon which her study was based were supplied in the diary kept by the children's mother. It contained various kinds of information, such as a list of words the children knew at the age of 1, the date their first true words were uttered, and accounts of minor episodes which for one reason or another interested the mother enough to include them in the diary.

Despite the lack of systematic data with which to work, Smith did obtain several interesting results which have recently been confirmed in other studies. In the beginning, the children used many phrases consisting of words from both languages, but as they grew older, these structures decreased in frequency. Furthermore, Smith noticed that when each adult spoke to the child in only one language, the child received the languages along two separate channels and thus was greatly assisted in acquiring the languages and learning early to distinguish one from the other and treat them as two distinct systems.

Emrich [1938] in McLaughlin [1978] observed the linguistic development of a young girl whose parents spoke German to her and whose nurse spoke Bulgarian during a period when the family lived in Bulgaria. The child's linguistic development followed the usual pattern: she easily understood both languages, learned a great deal of the phonology of both, and began to develop German and Bulgarian vocabularies. Unfortunately, Emrich allowed herself to be too strongly influenced by the German philosophy then in vogue in many countries and carried to an extreme in Germany. Schmidt-Rohr [1933] stated, for example, that a child must retain his native language in its entirety or he will lose his nationality. Weisgerber [1933] felt that bilingualism was harmful to the individual, and argued that people are not, after all, required to have two religions. Thus, according to Emrich, the girl's difficulties in reacclimating upon her family's return to Germany were caused by her bilingualism, despite the fact that her German steadily improved.

Up until this point, almost all studies on bilingualism from birth had been conducted in Europe. But in the thirties, contributions in this field began to come from North America as well, in the work of Smith and above all Leopold.

Leopold's sizable monograph [1939] gives a detailed description of the language development of his daughter Hildegard. He spoke German and his wife English with her. The Leopolds kept two diaries of their child's development. One dealt with linguistic aspects and contained phonetic transcriptions and a record of the new words and phrases uttered by Hildegard; these were entered in the book immediately after she produced them. The other was a record of the child's general development.

Hildegard's diaries cover the period from her birth to the age of 7, with additional observations extending to the age of 14. They also contain data on the couple's second daughter, Karla. But the data on Karla are not extensive, and serve principally as a comparison.

In Hildegard's first two years, Leopold did not find phonemic disharmony in the acquisition of sounds due to bilingual presentation, probably because the child had not yet learned the fundamental phonological differences between English and German. Words which for adults are unquestionably correspondent in the two languages did not have this aspect in Hildegard's language. For example, the words *bitte* and "please" had two very distinct uses: "please" was used in formal situations, and *bitte* was familiar. It was only at the age of about 20 months that Hildegard began to give signs of using true equivalence. But these equivalent words were short lived, and the German words were replaced by English ones, because she moved into a phase where English dominated. Indeed, Hildegard's last intensive contact with German was from the age of 11 months to 14 months, when she went to stay in Germany. After that, she returned to the United States, and her father once again became the only person who spoke to her in German. Although Leopold never stopped addressing her in German, English took over and the child quickly began to replace her German words with their English equivalents. This occurred in the very period when she began using equivalent words, which was at about 2 years of age. Hildegard's understanding of the two languages was perfect, but her production was definitely English after that. This situation prevailed until the age of $4\frac{1}{2}$, at which time she returned once again to Germany for 6 months. Unlike comprehension, linguistic production is quite difficult, and the child managed to save herself this trouble by speaking almost exclusively in English.

Burling's study [1971] is short, but interesting, because it involves the acquisition of a language that is not European. Burling observed the linguistic development of his son Stephen from the age of 16 months, when he moved from America to India, until the age of 34 months, when they moved back. The child's predominant contact was with the Garo language, as his father was the only person who spoke English with him. Consequently, the child spoke less English than Garo, in which he developed most of his syntax and morphology. He used a multitude of constructions in Garo, often inserting English words into them; in English, he used fewer words and constructions. "This assimilation of English words into Garo was characteristic of his speech for as long as we were in the Garo Hills" [Burling, 1971, p. 179].

For some words, Stephen did not have the equivalent in the other language; in other cases, he had acquired the words at the same time and said them one after the other, as in: "milk-*dut*." Burling considers such a pair firm proof of true equivalence.

Burling noticed that some elements of the English phonetic system developed after the corresponding elements had developed in Garo. At the beginning, Stephen used a series of Garo phonemes in English words. By the age of 33 months, he could distinguish between the vowels, but not yet between the consonants of the two languages.

Burling, in addition, makes a critical observation regarding average sentence length [see Brown, 1979]. He considers the number of words in a sentence to be of relatively small importance in the analysis of a child's speech development. In his view, the ability to make substitutions, i.e., to use the same structure with different words, is of greater importance than the use of long sentences such as "What are you doing?" Stephen memorized such sentences in their entirety but then did not use the individual words separately.

Murrel [1966] observed the linguistic development of his daughter Sandra, who spent her first two years of life hearing Finnish, Swedish, and to a lesser extent English. By the age of 26 months, Sandra was using a series of words in all three of these languages, as well as several Swedish – Finnish and Swedish – English equivalents and equivalents in all three languages. When the family later moved to England, the child soon lost her Finnish and spoke only Swedish and English. She then progressed rapidly in English, while her Swedish gradually weakened, so that by the age of 33 months only traces remained.

During those seven months, Murrel observed several cases of interference between English and Swedish in the child's speech, both in phonology and vocabulary. Furthermore, the sentences showed no regularity of word order, and several morphological elements were lacking.

Imedadze [1967] systematically observed a bilingual Russian – Georgian child from the beginning of active speech up to the age of 4. His aim was to determine whether it is possible for two languages to function autonomously in the speech of a child who learns them contemporaneously. A further goal was to discover the nature of the interaction between the two languages. The child was brought up under the "one person – one language" system, with his father and mother always speaking Georgian to him and his grandmother and his nurse addressing him only in Russian. Imedadze observed a first stage in which there were no equivalents; the first ones, however, appeared fairly soon. Unfortunately, Imedadze did not provide quantitative data, i.e., data on how many pairs of equivalents were used and how many words were without equivalents. The first equivalents were pronounced by the child one after the other, as though they were one unit.

According to Imedadze, identical and dissimilar grammatical rules were learned simultaneously, but the latter were expressed incorrectly in one of the two languages. For example, sentences which require the dative case in one language and the accusative in the other were first expressed in the accusative in both languages and only later in the dative in the language which called for it. This means that in the beginning only one syntactic rule was applied to both languages, and that the different rules were distinguished only later.

According to Mikés [1967], some semantic relations of differing morphological – syntactic difficulty in the two languages are not acquired at the same time. In studying the linguistic development of two Serbo-Croatian – Hungarian girls, Mikés noticed that they expressed the locative in Hungarian, which calls only for the case inflection, at an early age. In Serbo-Croatian, on the other hand, which calls for the case inflection and a locative preposition, they did not learn to use it until a much later age.

Tabouret-Keller's study [1969] is an exception among case studies for two reasons. The first reason is that Eve, the child studied, was not the child of linguists, psychologists, or even intellectuals. Her father worked in a potassium mine and her mother was a housewife, and thus she lived in a middle-to-low cultural milieu, rather than the usual high one. The second reason is that while most studies had taken as their subject of observation the bilingual living in a monolingual community, Eve was a bilingual subject living in a bilingual community: she lived in Alsace, where both French and an Alsatian dialect are spoken. According to Tabouret-Keller, Eve's case was a more faithful reflection of the average bilingual, while the other studies on bilingualism should be considered isolated cases, not to be generalized. It must be remembered, however, that it is no longer an exception to belong to an intellectual family, if the term "intellectual" is taken to apply to those who have had some form of higher learning. The same may be said of bilingual families who live in monolingual communities; this is a group which is constantly growing. Furthermore, Tabouret-Keller's study does not reveal any great difference between Eve and the subjects of other studies (as, for example, Leopold's daughter Hildegard or Ronjat's son Louis) which would justify making generalizations based on the one case and not the others.

Eve's speech was observed and recorded between the ages of 20 months and 3 years. A tape recorder was not used; notes were taken based upon observation of the child as she interacted with her natural environment. In transcribing Eve's phrases, Tabouret-Keller used the phonetic alphabet. When Tabouret-Keller was not present, Eve's mother provided assistance by recording data.

Eve's parents spoke both languages, using both indiscriminately within the course of a single conversation but never within a single sentence. Up to the age of 3, the girl's dominant language was French, and her lexicon amounted to about 500 words. Eve used the dialect equivalent for only 50 of these.

Eve's vocabulary in the dialect consisted for the most part of adjectives, adverbs, prepositions and pronouns, while her French lexicon was comprised mainly of nouns and verbs. For this reason, Tabouret-Keller concluded that the child commanded only one semantic system, the vocabulary of which consisted in part of French words and in part of words from the dialect.

In a series of more recent studies, Bizzarri [1977, 1978a], El-Dash [1978, 1981] and Cunze [1980] analyzed the speech of their bilingual children, who spoke English and Italian, English and Portuguese, and German and Italian, respectively. All of these researchers came to the same conclusions as Tabouret-Keller. They discovered that there were more words in a given language without equivalents in the other language than there were with, and also that certain grammatical categories appeared more frequently in only one of the two languages.

Tabouret-Keller concluded her work with the statement that Eve's speech reflected the modes of speech in her environment. She added that her study of Eve's language acquisition had established the fact that language development has the same characteristic features in bilingual children as it does in monolingual children, with respect to vocabulary as well as to grammar.

As regards the age at which the young bilingual begins to realize he is dealing with two different languages, a question raised by Stern and Stern [1928] in the fourth edition of their classic work on early speech, Tabouret-Keller observed that Eve became aware that she was speaking two different languages much later than the children studied by Leopold, Ronjat and Pavlovitch. The cause of this delay can be traced to Eve's different linguistic environment, in which the two languages were neither kept so clearly distinct nor constantly associated with a specific person, as was the case in the other studies.

According to Bizzarri [1977], the child who begins speaking at a late age realizes that he is dealing with two different linguistic codes from the moment he begins to use his first words. Bizzarri's study on the Italian – English language development of her two children presents a variable which had not appeared in previous studies on early bilingualism. One of the children, Nicola, started speaking late, and his speech development proceeded slowly at first. At the age of 26 months, he used only about 15 words, and at 31 months his vocabulary had increased by only 50 words. This increase was parallel in the two languages. His sentences were short and lacked morphosyntax. Later, towards the age of 36 months, Nicola began using morphosyntax and quickly made up for the time lost; this development occurred in both languages contemporaneously.

With the help of diaries and monthly tape recordings, Calasso and Garau [1976] observed the motor and linguistic development of Garau's bilingual Italian – English daughter. They compared her development with the results described in Lenneberg's motor and linguistic behavior tables [1971]. Calasso and Garau concluded that their bilingual subject had passed through the same stages as those described by Lenneberg for monolingual children, and furthermore that with respect to the size of her vocabulary in her dominant language, their subject was well in advance of Lenneberg's averages, while in her weaker language she fell within the range of average achievement.

Raffler-Engel [1965] asserted that her son behaved like all the other children she knew in Florence who were born into Italian – English families. He understood English, but his answers to people who spoke to him in English were usually in Italian. "His desire to improve his English is almost non-existent, and evidences itself only when the child is placed under pressure by his surroundings. This occurs, for example, when English is his only means of communication" [Raffler-Engel, 1965, p. 176]. Raffler-Engel noticed that her child's interest in his English picked up considerably after a trip to Germany, where at the age of 4 he played with several American children every afternoon. He began asking to know the name of new objects in English as well, because "otherwise he wouldn't be able to talk to his American friends" [Raffler-Engel, 1965, p. 176]. He often asked, "What is this called in English?" When his mother no longer answered, the child answered his own questions, creating a fantasy word which was nevertheless perfectly consistent with the English phonological system in sound and intonation. The child's enthusiasm for English disappeared when he began attending a nursery school where all the children spoke Italian.

Raffler-Engel considers the study of early bilingualism to be a good way to conduct psycholinguistic analysis. On the question of whether phonology is autonomous with respect to morphological elements, she says, "The structure of speech is not monolithic; thus, the desire to distinguish between two levels, one phonological and the other morphological and semantic, is not merely a point of theory: it actually does correspond to psycholinguistic reality" [Raffler-Engel, 1965, p. 179].

In support of this statement, Raffler-Engel points to her observations on the speech development of her son from birth to the age of $4\frac{1}{2}$, during which time the child was addressed by his mother in Italian and by his father in English. Because of his professional situation, the father spent little time with his son during his first year of life, and as a consequence the child spoke only Italian until the age of 1. Nevertheless, the boy's parents spoke to each other in English, and thus the child should have had the chance to hear that language, too. Raffler-Engel had "the impression that in all cases where the child was unaware that he was mixing morphologies, he was aware of the phonological differences. It is in fact on the basis of this factor that he determines whether the language is Italian or English" [Raffler-Engel, 1965, p. 179]. As an example of this mixing of morphologies, Raffler-Engel gives the sentence: "*No, io non spredo*" (with the English verb "to spread" conjugated as if it were an Italian verb); this was her son's response when asked by his father to spread out the bowling pins some more.

I am of the same opinion as Raffler-Engel regarding the child's early phonological differentiation between the two languages, and I agree that this skill differs from the ability to distinguish between morphologies. Syntax, morphology, semantics and phonology are different aspects of a single linguistic phenomenon; each of these aspects requires different skills. However, I do not believe that Raffler-Engel's child was unaware of the morphological aspect when he said, "*Io non spredo*". He even managed to conjugate the English verb using the typical Italian ending "o" for the first person singular present indicative.

Oksaar [1971], who reported examples similar to Raffler-Engel's, held that her son, an Estonian – Swedish bilingual, was capable of understanding morphological aspects when he began adding Estonian suffixes to Swedish words. For example, at 30 months, the child said, "*Nenne taha ema hälsama*" [Oksaar, 1971, p. 343]. Roughly translated, this means, "Nenne wants to go say hello to mamma". The child took the Swedish infinitive *hälsa* and added the suffix belonging to the Estonian equivalent, *teretama*.

Oksaar's primary interest is speech acquisition in general, and not the specific problems of bilingualism. Still, because the subject she observed was her son Sven, who learned Estonian at home with his parents and Swedish with his friends and the other people with whom he came into contact, Oksaar included the variable of bilingualism in her studies on speech development in early childhood. She observed that Sven's use of the one or other language depended strongly on the language spoken by the person with whom he was having the verbal exchange. If, for instance, he was at home speaking with his mother (i. e., in an Estonian environment) about something a Swedish friend had said, he used Swedish. When he spoke in a monologue before going to sleep, he usually started out in Estonian and then, if he happened to mention a Swedish person, continued in Swedish. In Oksaar's view, this means that initially, the different languages are linked to people (one person, one language): *"Es lernt verschiedene Systeme, ein bestimmtes sprachliches Verhalten für bestimmte soziale Kontakte"* (He learns different systems and specific linguistic behavior for each social contact) [Oksaar, 1971, p. 352].

In her studies, Oksaar did not find evidence of phonological interferences between the two languages, a fact which shows that an early and continuing distinction was made between the two different systems. Even in phonological aspects which are typical of only one language, no interference was noted. For instance, the consonants and vowels in Estonian have three different lengths: short, long, and extra-long. There are no such differences in Swedish. Nevertheless, Sven developed them early in Estonian, even before he had completely developed the vowel and consonant system. Moreover, he never pronounced Swedish vowels and consonants with the Estonian system of differing lengths.

On the other hand, Rüke-Dravina [1965, as quoted in McLaughlin, 1978, p. 83] found phonological confusion in the speech of two Swedish – Latvian girls who were learning to use the Latvian rolled apical *r* and the Swedish uvular *r* at the same time. Rüke-Dravina noted that the uvular *r*, which they learned first, tended to take the place of the rolled apical *r* in the other language. Phonological interferences occurred more often in words with the same form in both languages.

De Matteis [1978] conducted a one-year study on his four Dutch – German – Italian trilingual children aged 2, 7, 8, and 9. He found that the children acquired two or more phonetic systems at the same time. However, De Matteis remarked that one child, although he spoke all three languages, applied German phonetics to the other two because German was the dominant language.

According to Bergman [1976], the bilingual child realizes from the very first phrases that he is speaking two languages. Bergman used a tape recorder and a diary to gather data on the speech of her bilingual English – Spanish daughter Mary from the age of 10 to 27 months. Her work brings to light once again the fundamental importance of context in the simultaneous acquisition of two languages. Bergman believes that each language develops independently in the bilingual child and that interferences are not necessarily a part of the simultaneous acquisition of two languages, but are, instead, the result of a certain kind of linguistic environment in which the child's interlocutors do not keep the two languages clearly separated or in which the adult's speech perhaps deviates from the norm.

Swain [1973] made bimonthly tape recordings of the speech of a bilingual French – English child, Michael, from the ages of 37 to 46 months. A series of structural interferences were observed in Michael's use of the two languages. For instance, his English questions, "That's what? It's what?" corresponded to the French construction *C'est quoi?* However, this type of interference decreased gradually, giving the impression that the child had begun with one structural system for both languages and then slowly built up a double system. The same conclusions were reached by Volterra and Taeschner [1978] in a study of the word order in several types of sentences used by Lisa, a bilingual Italian – German child. Her speech contained orderings of words which either corresponded to neither of the two languages, or to only one of them. It was not until later that the child began to develop a distinct order for each language just as she had previously developed distinct vocabularies.

The distinction between two vocabularies and two syntaxes is not made at the same time. The child learns first to differentiate between the two vocabularies and only later to distinguish between one syntax and the other. This problem was studied more recently by Redlinger and Park [1980], who gathered data on the spontaneous speech of four children between the ages of 2 and 3, basing their research on 30- to 45-minute tape recordings made every 3 weeks for a period of from 5 to 9 months for each child. Two of the children spoke French and German, one Spanish and German, and the other English and German. As a starting point, Redlinger and Park used two different approaches developed in previous research. Some authors, e.g., Leopold [1939 – 1949b], Imedadze [1967], Oksaar [1971], and Volterra and Taeschner [1978], maintain that the child possesses only one linguistic system for the two languages at first and then gradually distinguishes between the two systems later. Others, such as Padilla and Liebman [1975], Bergman [1976], and Lindholm and Padilla [1978] have suggested that the bilingual child is able to keep the two systems separate from the very first stages of linguistic development.

Redlinger and Park believed that a study of mixed speech within single sentences could give solid support to one of these two theories. They conducted an analysis of their subjects' utterances, comparing the sentences in which the children used two languages with those in which they used only one. Their results confirmed the theory that only one system exists at the beginning. The four children were studied at a period which is, as will be seen in Chap. 2, particularly crucial in bilingual vocabulary development. They used many mixed phrases when they were small, but this use gradually diminished as their linguistic development progressed. The presence of many mixed phrases at the beginning of bilingual development seems to reflect the child's general inability to differentiate between the two codes.

The studies briefly described here have presented various aspects of great interest in research on bilingual acquisition. In some of these areas, there is considerable agreement among researchers, while in others opinions diverge. Let us take a look at the first category.

a) None of the researchers mentions difficulties in comprehension. On the contrary, those who have taken this aspect into consideration have explicitly stated that the children understood both languages well.

b) No author reported examples of words which were equivalent at the beginning of the lexical development of the children observed. Although these researchers come from every part of the world and have dealt not only with different languages, but also with children who have grown up in different environments and begun to speak at different ages, they all agree that from the very beginning of speech development, the child has only one lexical system.

c) None of the authors found that the development of bilingual children was any different from that of monolingual children. While it is true that few parallels have been drawn, it is equally true that these parallels reveal a strong similarity between the two types of development.

d) All of the authors emphasized the fundamental role played by linguistic context and linguistic interaction in the process of acquiring two languages from birth.

As for the areas where differing results have been reported by the researchers I have mentioned, the following may be said:

a) Some authors maintain that lexical interference exists from the very beginning. A few others have found that this type of interference occurs only during the initial period, in which the child does not yet distinguish between the two languages, and that it then disappears.

b) Opinions are also divided on the issue of phonological interferences. Some researchers have observed phonological interference in their children's speech, while others have noted that phonology was used to keep the two languages distinct, and that the sounds of one language were therefore never mixed with those of the other.

c) Another area of discord has been that of linguistic production, i. e., the speech of the children. Some children were able to speak both languages, while others could understand both but speak only one. Thus, from this point of view, a bilingual upbringing was successful for some and unsuccessful for others.

The research described in this book belongs among the group of studies mentioned above insofar as it analyzes the same problems with the help of the same techniques. But while the areas of study are the same (vocabulary development, sentence development, morphosyntactic aspects, interference), I have tried not only to amplify the results reached thus far, but also to analyze speech from the point of view of bilingual development. Furthermore, I have endeavored to compare the development of the two languages in the bilingual and then to compare this development with that of monolingual children.

In addition, the book focuses upon various aspects of the children's upbringing. Their social and linguistic environment is described, followed by a description of their parents' strategy in bringing up their children bilingually.


## 1.3 Description of the Present Research

Data was gathered on the spontaneous speech of two bilingual Italian – German girls, Lisa and Giulia. Their mother is a Brazilian of German origin who spent her childhood in a German – Portuguese community in southern Brazil and thus grew up a bilingual herself. She heard Portuguese spoken by her neighbors and at school, and although she heard as much German as Portuguese around the neighborhood, any language other than Portuguese was forbidden at school, and thus she was not exposed to German there. However, German was the only language she spoke with her parents and relatives.[2] Lisa and Giulia's father is an Italian and has always spoken his native language with them. Their mother has never spoken anything but German to them since the time they were born.

Lisa and Giulia live in Rome with their parents. They have no other relatives in this city, as their father's family lives in northern Italy and their mother's family in Brazil. Their contact with their relatives is thus limited to occasional visits, and they see their father's family more often than that of their mother. Rome is a monolingual city, but many foreigners live there, and the girls have some friends who speak German and many who speak Italian. In their neighborhood, in nursery school and then in elementary school, they have come into contact exclusively with Italian.

Data on Lisa's and Giulia's speech was gathered from the moment they began to utter their first words, in Lisa's case at about 18 months and in Giulia's at about 11. The data was gathered in bimonthly tape recordings,[3] once each with a German and an Italian speaker.[4] In some of the recordings only one of the girls spoke to the adult, while in the remaining cases both girls

---

2  Blumenau, the city under discussion, was founded in 1850 by German immigrants who kept their language for another century. But since the generation of the sixties, only a small minority of the children who start elementary school are bilingual or monolingual in German. Funke [1902] and Lenard [1970] have written two very interesting books on the customs, language and way of life of the Germans in southern Brazil.

3  Ochs tried [1979b] to standardize a transcription method for such recordings which would make it easier to compare the data gathered throughout the world. Ochs was assisted in this task by the works of Bloom et al. [1974], Reilly et al. [unpublished], Sachs et al. [1974], Ochs and Schieffelin [1979], and Scollon [1976].

4  Data was gathered until Lisa was 5 and Giulia 4. After that, data was gathered occasionally until the girls reached the ages of 8 and 9 respectively.

**Table 1.3.** Tape No. 32c, recorded on April 13, 1976. The participants were Lisa (3; 9, 27) and her father. The language spoken was Italian

| Lisa | Father | Context |
|---|---|---|
| | | Lisa and her father are playing on the rug with small varicolored wooden triangles, cubes and cones. They are building a village. |
| | Sembrano tende, come hai detto prima. (They look like tents, like you said before.) | |
| 1. Sì. (Yes.) | | |
| 2. Vedi. Le tende fanno così. Fanno le tende però. Le tende sono così. Dal mare si fa e qui c'è il mare e c'è l'asciugamano. Vedi per proteggere le ... le ... le ... (See, tents do this. But they are tents. Tents are like this. They come from the sea and the sea is here and there's the towel. See, to protect the ... the ... the ...) | | Lisa takes a piece of wood and puts it aside. Then she places a second and a third piece near it. She doesn't look at her father while she is describing her movements. |
| | | She looks at her father, then at the other pieces. She is looking for something. |
| | Per proteggere le? (To protect what?) | |
| 3. Le ... le ... ecco ... due ... metto nell'asciuga-mano, vero? (The ... the ... there ... two ... I'll put in the towel, right?) | | |
| | Queste cosa sono? Tende per andarci sotto? (What are these? Tents to go under?) | |
| 4. Ma non c'è la porta per entrare. (But there's no door to go through.) | | She looks at the piece they're talking about and then examines it closely. |
| | Eccola qui, questa è la porta, ci sone anche le finestre, vedi. (Here your are. This is the door. There are windows, too. Look.) | Her father takes a piece of wood shaped like a house, with the doors and windows painted white and red. Lisa points to different pieces and names them. |

**Table 1.3** (continued)

| Lisa | Father | Context |
|---|---|---|
| 5. Sì, vedi. Quest'è Mammi, quest'è Papi, quest'è Giulia e quest'è Lisa. (Yes, see! This is Mommy, this is Daddy, this is Giulia and this is Lisa.) | | |
| | Stai giocando? (Are you playing?) | Lisa takes plastic triangles and gives each house a triangle. |
| 6. E questi? No c'entra. (And these? It doesn't fit.) | | |
| | Non c'entra e va bene. No fa niente. (It doesn't fit and that's okay. It doesn't matter.) | |
| 7. Facciamo così. (Let's do this.) | | |
| | Facciamo così, guarda. Mettiamo due insieme per vedere cosa succede. (Let's do this. Look. Let's put two together and see what happens.) | |

were recorded speaking to one or more other people. The other speaker was in the vast majority of cases the mother, but sometimes the father, and occasionally a friend or relative. The recordings averaged 45 minutes each. During vacations, which usually lasted 2 months in the summer and 1 month in the winter, Lisa's and Giulia's speech was recorded less regularly. The recordings were transcribed very carefully, with particular attention given to the context in which the statements were made. The speakers' actions and gestures were described, as were the objects to which they referred. The transcripts were not phonetic; rather, they reflected the way in which the children spoke. One example of such transcripts can be seen in Table 1.3.

For comparisons with Italian and German monolingual children, I used data gathered by means of the same techniques in monthly recordings. The data on Italian children was supplied by the CNR Institute of Psychology in Rome and collected by V. Volterra, F. Antinucci, and P. Tieri. The data on German children was supplied by M. Wintermantel of the University of Heidelberg as part of her longitudinal study, and by myself in research at the same university. A list of the children who made this study possible is given in Table 1.4.

In addition to the above-mentioned tape recordings, Lisa and Giulia's mother kept a diary in which she made notes on all trips taken by her daugh-

**Table 1.4.** Children about whom data was collected

| Child | Language(s) | Age of child when data was gathered |
|---|---|---|
| Lisa | German, Italian | 18 months – 6 years |
| Giulia | German, Italian | 11 months – 5 years |
| Claudia | Italian | 15 months – 33 months |
| Sara | Italian | 23 months – 31 months |
| Francesco | Italian | 16 months – 44 months |
| Oliver | German | 28 months – 40 months |
| Jana | German | 25 months – 37 months |
| Mara | German | 42 months – 48 months |
| Julia | German | 44 months – 50 months |
| Malte | German | 47 months – 51 months |
| Florian | German | 49 months – 55 months |
| Verena | German | 49 months – 55 months |
| Adrianna | English, Italian | A single test at 28 months |
| Giulia Milli | English, Italian | A single test at 20 months |

ters, their attendance at nursery school, the visits they received from Italian and Brazilian friends and relatives, the time spent with their mother, and a series of episodes she felt to be interesting. These episodes were recorded immediately after they occurred and in chronological order. The words and sentences spoken by the children were not modified, enriched or interpreted. An example of such an episode can be seen in the following:

Giulia (1;2,23) brings her mother a cushion which is usually on the seat of a chair.
**G:** *Sitzi.* ( =*sitzen*, the verb "to sit")
**M:** *Brav Giulia, sitzi machen.* (Good Giulia, make sit down.)
Giulia puts the cushion back on the chair and says *sitzi* several times. Then she points to Lisa's bicycle seat.
**G:** *Sitzi, sitzi, sitzi ...*

Naturally, data gathered by means of such techniques can serve only as a sample of a child's speech. I hold it nonetheless to be sufficiently encompassing to serve as a basis for the type of analysis made here.

# 2. Word Acquisition

The German-speaking mother in a bilingual German – Italian couple gave up the idea of speaking to her child in her own language because he still had not begun talking at the age of $1\frac{1}{2}$. Up until that time, she had spoken to him in German, while his father had addressed him exclusively in Italian. They consulted a pediatrician and accepted his advice that German be eliminated. The pediatrician was certain that the child's delayed linguistic development was due to his having been exposed to two languages. Two months after the "treatment" had begun, the "miracle" occurred, and the child began to speak.

Many monolingual parents whose children have not begun speaking until shortly before their second birthday have also been perplexed, worried, and somewhat disappointed. But they were luckier, because no pediatrician told them to keep quiet in order to resolve the problem.

When a situation seems unusual, it is understandable for parents to feel uncertain about their child's pseudodelay. But while many children do begin to speak at the age of about 14 or 16 months, just as many others do not begin until they are 18 or even 30 months old. The fact of the matter is that studies on early speech still have not established where the boundary lies between normal and delayed periods for the beginning of real speech in normal children.

But such a situation is only seemingly unusual, because the world contains at least as many bilinguals as monolinguals. Our insecurity about bilingualism probably stems from the assumption that A plus B is twice as difficult as A or B. Thus, one is either well acquainted with A (or B) or one is poorly acquainted with both A and B. It would seem improbable that one could be well acquainted with both A and B; at the very least, it would be an exception. This assumption is put forth continually. A group of speech researchers was commenting on the case of X, a monolingual child who at the age of 27 months still spoke only a dozen or so isolated words and never combined them in phrases, but who had a rich collection of gestures, was very sociable, and communicated vivaciously in complicated interactions. One of the researchers said that the children of a friend of his had exhibited the same linguistic development. But then he added, "You can't compare X with them, though, because they're bilingual, and it's a 'known' fact that bilinguals begin speaking later".

It is very easy to blame bilingualism for crimes it has not committed. One mother told another that her 8-year-old daughter had had trouble reading a book by Rodari because, for example, it contained words such as "jail", "jailor", and "jailbird", while her daughter was used to only "prison", "prisoner", and "prison guard". The other mother answered, "Yes, but she's bilingual". When the question was put to an elementary-school teacher, the answer was quite different. "Rodari is rather difficult to understand. He uses a very rich vocabulary, and all children have a hard time getting to the message underlying his stories. He's a children's author who is more popular with adults than children".

In the following pages, we will seek to determine whether these assumptions are still justified after a careful analysis of the bilingual child's vocabulary. We will examine Lisa's and Giulia's vocabularies to discover whether they acquired the German and Italian vocabulary systems in parallel fashion and whether specific strategies were necessary to acquire them. We will also seek to establish whether the children's vocabularies were quantitatively comparable to those of monolinguals.

The monolingual child usually uses only one word to refer to an object or event, while the bilingual child uses two words which are often quite different from one another phonetically. The bilingual child must have at least two symbols to communicate, while the monolingual child needs only one.

The acquisition of interlingual synonyms is a fundamental aspect of the bilingual vocabulary. These synonyms have been called equivalents in order to prevent them from being confused with synonyms which exist within one linguistic system. We will also apply the term "equivalent" to sentences, for example: *Ich möchte heute Maria besuchen* and "I would like to visit Maria today".

It should be added here that each word is part of an entire pragmatic-semantic field and that the equivalents often refer to related fields. As Jespersen [1953, p. 47] correctly states, "Even when the literal meaning can be considered the same, the associations suggested by the words vary from one language to another." [1] In the case, for instance, of the English-speaking adult who is learning a second language by the translation method, the foreign word *Baum* takes on all the semantic connotations of the word "tree" (see Ervin and Osgood [1954]).

The child who lives from birth in an environment where he hears two languages does not acquire equivalents in this manner, but rather in two fundamentally different ones. The child learns the word *Baum* in one context and "tree" in another. In other words, the child has two pragmatic-semantic fields at first, and only later, in a process of generalization which will be discussed, is he able to make the connection between the two fields and understand that "tree" and *Baum* are equivalents. In the second type of learning process, the two words are offered to the child in the same context, so that the child has two equivalent words for one pragmatic-semantic field from the outset. Thus,

---

1 This difference applies not only when the languages are different, but also within one language when it is spoken in different areas.

unlike the situation described above for the adult, this is not a case of giving a new label to a field that is familiar and well absorbed, but of learning and experiencing two different linguistic symbols simultaneously. When we speak of equivalence in this study, we are always referring to one of these two processes, which are the result of two different kinds of contact with the language.

In the following we will analyze the acquisition of this system of equivalents, which forms the foundation of the bilingual child's lexical repertoire.

## 2.1 The First Stage: The Bilingual Child Has No Equivalents

In our brief introduction to studies conducted on bilingualism, we saw that researchers were essentially in agreement that the initial lexicon of the bilingual child has no equivalents, despite the fact that such equivalents are constantly being supplied by the people who speak to the child. However, the authors stop at this observation, without inquiring into the manner in which this system takes shape.

In Volterra and Taeschner [1978], this period was designated as the first stage, with the second stage beginning when the child starts to produce equivalents. In this chapter, I will demonstrate once again the validity of this classification by examining closely what happens after the child begins to increase his use of two words for a single event or object. An analysis of Lisa's and Giulia's speech shows that they had one lexical system consisting of words from both languages, with the terms used in one language having no equivalent meaning corresponding to the terms in the other[2].

The words that the girls used during this period are listed in Tables 2.1, 2. The fact that these tables contain so few equivalents is of great significance. If the contexts are more carefully analyzed, it becomes apparent that the girls did not appear to consider these words equivalents. An example of this can be seen in the words *dà* and *daki* ("to give").

Lisa used the word *daki*   – to thank someone
                            – when giving someone something
                            – when she wanted to receive something from someone.

Towards the age of 22 months, Lisa began using the word *dà*, but not in all the contexts in which she used *daki*. She used the Italian word *dà* only when she was giving something to someone.

---

2 Many of the hypotheses and conclusions put forth in this chapter are taken from Volterra and Taeschner [1978].

**Table 2.1.** Words from both languages used by Lisa in the first stage (1;10). Where necessary, the correct German or Italian is given in parentheses. Words for which Lisa knew the equivalent in the other language are listed on the same line and in italics; the translation follows in brackets. The term "neutral" is used for all words which are the same in sound and meaning in both languages

| Italian words | German words | Neutral words |
|---|---|---|
| aaino (bavaglino) | Aie (Seife) | baubau/wauwau |
| aaila (aereo) | Beine | bu (rumore) |
| belle | Bobo (Bonbon) | bata (basta) |
| bui (buio) | Bu (Buch) | caca |
| cucutetè | Guguck da | cocò |
| coa (ancora) | Blle (Blume) | Dodo (Rodolfo) |
| chiai (occhiali) | Baum | Giulia |
| chiaie (chiavi) | Bauch | lata/lade (ciocolato) |
| *chechea* (acqua) [water] | *Wasser* | Lalla (Daniela) |
| chi è | Chku (Schuhe) | Lia (Lisa) |
| *cotto* (biscotto) [cookie] | *Keks* | miao |
| cata (cane) | haia haia (schlafen) | Mamma |
| caa (cara) | ist | mu |
| chie (scrivere) | Keh (Käse) | Nanna (Anna) |
| chiu (chiudere) | Kita (Kinderwagen) | popò |
| chio (anch'io) | Koka (Kartoffel) | Papa |
| cotta (scotta) | nyam-nyam (essen) | tatau (ciao) |
| carta | Puppe | tum (cadere) |
| dito | Taila (Tasche) | totò |
| da (dare) [give] | *daki* (danke) | Paola |
| *là* [there] | *da* | tic − tic |
| laila (lascia) | Titi (Brust) | tata |
| latte | Tuta (Lutscher) | onc − onc (maiale) |
| lata (l'altra) | upa (hochgenommen werden) | palle/balle |
| Nonno | | |
| Nonna | | |
| no | | |
| *sti* (si) [yes] | *ja* | |
| tona (viziatona) | | |
| tia (zia) | | |
| ti (tirare) | | |
| tu | | |
| totto (cappotto) | | |
| otto (rotto) | | |
| tita (matita) | | |
| qua/qui | | |
| pappo (tappo) | | |
| più | | |
| pila | | |

Some examples (1;9, 1;10):
**L:** *Daki Buch.* [Her mother has just given her a book.]
**L:** *Daki* [giving her mother a pencil].
**L:** *Dà* [giving her mother a piece of candy].
**L:** *Daki* [giving a piece of candy to guests].
**L:** *Mamma tita daki.* [She wants her mother to give her a pencil.]

**Table 2.2.** Words from both languages used by Giulia in the first stage (1;6,15). Where necessary, the correct German or Italian is given in parentheses. Words for which Giulia knew the equivalent in the other language are listed on the same line and in italics; the translation follows in brackets. The term "neutral" is used for all words which are the same in sound and meaning in both languages

| Italian words | German words | Neutral words |
|---|---|---|
| acqua | auch | Auto |
| ada (guardare) | aizi (anziehen) | Anna |
| api (aprire) | Bonbon | bata (basta) |
| ancoa (ancora) | Baum | bum |
| baba (barba) | Baby | caca |
| bua | Bauch | babau |
| bimba | Buch | Chichi |
| bella | bitte | dodo (Rodolfo) |
| balla | badi-badi (baden) | Mami |
| buonnatale (il tavolino | baite (arbeiten) | Nado/nase |
| suo) | | |
| cane | Beine | |
| cate (carta) | dicke | Oi |
| *cotta* (scotta) [it burns] | *heiss* | Pipì |
| cara | Donn (Donner) | Paola |
| *dazie* (grazie) [thank you] | *danne* (danke) | Papi |
| da (dare) | guguck da | tatau (ciao) |
| *tutto-tutto* [all] | *alle-alle* | tite |
| *fatto* [done] | *feitich* (fertig) | tati |
| cotto (biscotto) | Hale (Haare) | Taute (Traute) |
| mela | haia haia (schlafen) | |
| *là* [there] | *da* | |
| Nonno | kalt | |
| Nonna | Kuchen | |
| *no* [no] | *nei* | |
| pela (pera) | kin-kinny (trinken) | |
| pettapetta (aspetta) | Käse | |
| più | komm | |
| palle | Milch | |
| pane | Nenni | |
| panna | Puppi | |
| qua | sitzi-sitzi (sitzen) | |
| tato | wo | |
| tovato (trovato) | upa (hochgenommen werden) | |
| toia (togliere) | nyam-nyam (essen) | |
| zita | | |
| zia | | |
| uva | | |
| *sì* [yes] | *ja* | OK |

The relationship which existed between *dà* and *daki* in Lisa's speech can be represented pictorially in the following form:

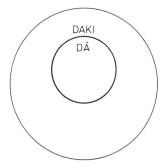

This is, in other words, the kind of relationship which usually characterizes the synonyms of one lexical system. *Daki* appears to have a much more general meaning than *dà*.

If we examine *da* and *là* ("there"), we see that Lisa made an even greater distinction between the German word and the Italian word in this stage. I believe, in fact, that Lisa used *là* for objects which were not present or visible at the time of speech, and *da* for things which were.

Lisa (1;10) comes in from the balcony and approaches her mother.
**L:** *Meow, meow. Là meow.*
**M:** *Wo ist meow?* (Where is the cat?)

Lisa pulls her mother onto the balcony.

**M:** *Wo ist meow?* (Where is the cat?)
**L:** *Da ist meow.*

The relationship between *da* and *là* in Lisa's speech might be represented as follows:

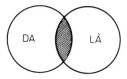

Thus, these words are not synonyms but are related by hyponymy.

The other words written in italics differed from each other in frequency of use. Lisa's *cotto*, *chechea*, and *ja* were used quite often, while there were only a few incidents where she used the corresponding *Keks*, *Wasser*, and *sti*.

Giulia often used *no*, *dazie*, and *OK*, while *nei*, *danne*, and *sì* or *ja* were rare.

Giulia said the *scotta-heiss* ("it burns — hot") couplet together, suggesting a compound word. Thus, when she approached the burner or the radiator, Giulia (1;4) said, *"Cotta heiss cotta heiss cotta".* [3]

It should be remembered here that examples of synonyms can also be found in the speech of monolingual children of the same age. Similarly, the bilingual may also know more than one word to designate a single event or object. For example, after finishing her food, for which she was always praised by the whole family, Giulia usually pointed to her empty plate and said, *"Fatto, tutto-tutto, alle-alle, feitich."* (Done all, all, finished.) However, this does not mean that the words of bilingual children at this stage are not in reality part of a single lexicon. In practice, the child understands two languages, but he has only one; it is not completely identifiable with either of the two, but has its own particular system composed of words from both.

## 2.2 The Second Stage: The Child Begins to Build a System of Equivalents

In the second stage, Lisa and Giulia began to use numerous equivalents. While the earlier tendency had clearly been not to have word equivalents, starting with a certain age they began to use them with great frequency.

In order to gain a better understanding of this increase in word equivalents in Lisa's and Giulia's speech, we conducted a lexical analysis in which the words in the girls' speech were grouped into the traditional categories of nouns, verbs, articles, adjectives, prepositions, adverbs, pronouns, and conjunctions. [4] The words were listed in the order of their appearance and compiled as shown in Table 2.3.

When the child began to give a name to an object for the first time, this name was then considered to have appeared, regardless of which language the child was speaking. When the child then gave a name to the same object in the other language, an equivalent was considered to have appeared.

In this way it was possible to ascertain the age at which the children began using certain words and their equivalents. This was not merely a word count designed to show how many words the children used in each language. Rather its purpose was to discover when and to what extent these words were equivalent. The use of the various categories helped to give a clearer overall picture

---

3 *Heiss* (*caldo* = "hot") and *scotta* (*brennt* = "it burns") have been considered equivalents because they are both words which are always used by adults to indicate danger through heat, such as from burners, hot water, radiators, etc. The girls' mother did not say, *"Achtung, es brennt"*; she said, *"Pass auf, das ist heiss"*. And their father did not say, *"Attenzione è caldo"*, but instead, *"Attenzione che scotta"*.

4 These equivalents refer only to literal correspondence and do not take into account all of the various meanings which each word may have.

**Table 2.3.** An example of the way in which vocabulary was listed (from the data for Giulia: nouns). The words are presented in the order of their appearance. Equivalents and the time of their appearance are given to the right

| Word | Age at which word appeared | Age at which equivalent appeared | Equivalent |
|---|---|---|---|
| Acqua (water) | 1;5 | 1;8 | Wasser |
| Coda (tail) | 1;5 | 1;9 | Schwanz |
| Beine (legs) | 1;5 | 1;11 | Gamba |
| Uva (grapes) | 1;5 | 2;8 | Trauben |
| Chiavi (keys) | 1;6 | (no equivalent as of 2;4) | |
| Haare (hair) | 1;6 | 1;11 | Capelli |
| Bimba (little girl) | 1;6 | 1;9 | Kind |
| Carta (paper) | 1;6 | 2;3 | Papier |
| Mani (hands) | 1;6 | 1;10 | Händchen |
| Milch (milk) | 1;6 | 1;11 | Latte |

of the words the girls used. However, not all of the words used by the children were taken into consideration. I excluded all proper names, cases of onomato-poeia, and words that were very similar, if not identical, in the two languages, such as *Nase – Naso* ("nose").

This analysis reconfirmed the existence of a first stage as described in Sect. 2.1. Thus, Giulia, who began speaking at about 14 months, only began definite production of equivalents at about 20 months. In the same way, Lisa, who began speaking at about 19 months, began to use numerous equivalents at about 26 months. As can be calculated from Table 2.4, the first stage lasts for an average of 6 months, with slight variations from category to category and child to child. During this period, the children acquired a vocabulary of about 65 to 85 words, and only after this stage began producing equivalents frequently. Articles, prepositions and conjunctions have not been included

**Table 2.4.** Time lapse between initial word acquisition and the appearance of equivalents

| Category | Child | Age at time of acquisition | | Age when equivalent appeared | | Time interval in months |
|---|---|---|---|---|---|---|
| Noun | Lisa | 1;7 | | 2;0 | | 5 |
| | Giulia | | 1;2 | | 1;9 | 7 |
| Verb | Lisa | 1;7 | | 2;3 | | 8 |
| | Giulia | | 1;2 | | 1;8 | 6 |
| Adjective | Lisa | 1;9 | | 2;5 | | 8 |
| | Giulia | | 1;4 | | 1;8 | 4 |
| Adverb | Lisa | 1;7 | | 2;3 | | 8 |
| | Giulia | | 1;5 | | 1;8 | 3 |
| Pronoun | Lisa | 2;3 | | 2;9 | | 6 |
| | Giulia | | 1;9 | | 2;2 | 5 |

in Table 2.4, because there were too few examples and they are acquired very gradually. Moreover, these categories appear at an age when the child has already passed into the second stage.

During the second stage, the child learns the equivalent of words which he has been using for quite some time. Thus, for example, when Giulia was 21 months old, she began using equivalents for words she had begun saying in one language or the other as much as 3 months before. Naturally, there are a few examples of word-pair equivalents which appeared at the same time. These are very few in number compared with the total number of word-pair equivalents which appeared at different times. It would seem, therefore, that the child learns first to use a word well in one language to refer to specific events or objects, and only after having used it for a certain period of time begins to use its equivalent also.

The equivalents increase gradually, following a curve similar to that of new acquisitions. The only difference is that the former curve begins at a later date. Furthermore, from a quantitative point of view, the values of the equivalent curve are always lower than those of the curve for new acquisitions (see Figs. 2.1 – 8).

Even when the child is well into the second stage and uses a considerable number of equivalents, he continues to acquire more new words than equivalents,[5] at least at the age level used as a basis for the lexical tables (for Lisa

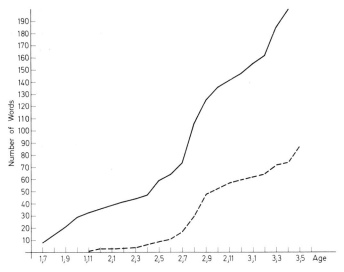

**Fig. 2.1.** Curves for Lisa's initial acquisition of nouns (———) and the appearance of their equivalents (– – –)

---

5 "New" is used here to mean words that denote objects or events which have never been named before.

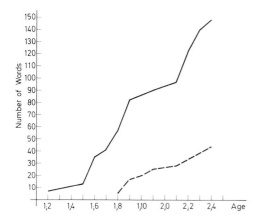

**Fig. 2.2.** Curves for Giulia's initial acquisition of nouns (———) and the appearance of their equivalents (– – –)

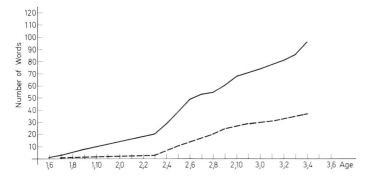

**Fig. 2.3.** Curves for Lisa's initial acquisition of verbs (———) and the appearance of their equivalents (– – –)

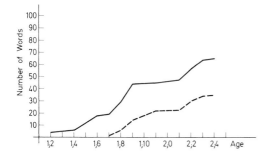

**Fig. 2.4.** Curves for Giulia's initial acquisition of verbs (———) and the appearance of their equivalents (– – –)

from 1;6 to 3;6 and for Giulia from 1;2 to 2;4). When the count for these tables was interrupted, the girls did not yet command the equivalents for the words they had learned most recently, while they did use the equivalents for words learned in the earlier months. Gradually, the empty spots in the "equi-

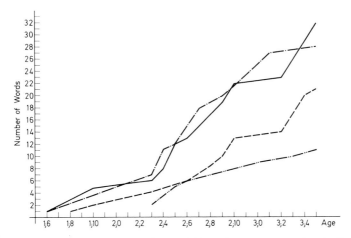

**Fig. 2.5.** Curves for Lisa's initial acquisition of adverbs (———) and adjectives (– · – · –) and the appearance of their equivalents (– – – and – ·· – ·· – ·· respectively)

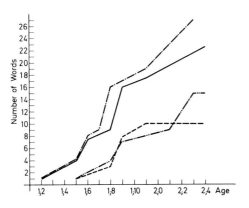

**Fig. 2.6.** Curves for Giulia's initial acquisition of adverbs (———) and adjectives (– · – · –) and the appearance of their equivalents (– – – and – ·· – ·· – respectively)

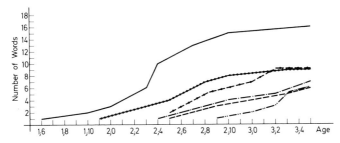

**Fig. 2.7.** Curves for Lisa's initial acquisition of conjunctions (– · – · –), pronouns (———), and prepositions (•••••••) and the appearance of their equivalents (– ·· – ·· – ··, – – –, and •–•–• respectively)

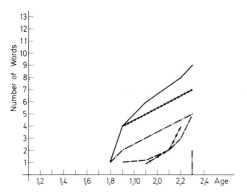

**Fig. 2.8.** Curves for Giulia's initial acquisition of conjunctions $(-\cdot-\cdot-)$, pronouns (———), and prepositions (•••••••••) and the appearance of their equivalents $(-\cdot\cdot-\cdot\cdot-,\quad ---,\quad$ and ━━━ respectively)

valent" column were filled. [6] But an examination of the development of Lisa's prepositions and conjunctions or Giulia's articles reveals that the children had all equivalents in these categories. Thus they came to a meeting point between the new-word curve and the equivalent curve, something which was not the case with the other categories. In the process of bilingual acquisition, nouns can naturally be predicted to be the last to obtain a complete set of equivalents, if at all, because they are so numerous.

To sum up, in creating a bilingual lexical system, the child tends not to produce two words for one object or event at the same time. First he acquires one word in one of the two languages, and only when he has mastered it well and used it for a while does he begin to use its equivalent. Furthermore, for the entire period studied here, the number of equivalents is lower than the number of words that denote new objects or events.

This does not alter the fact that the number of words that the child produces in each language, including both new words and equivalents, is essentially the same. Thus at the age of 28 months, Giulia used 420 words, of which 211 were German and 209 Italian. Of the 211 German words, 79 were equivalents and 132 were new words. Of the 209 Italian words, 60 were equivalents and 149 were new. At the age of 34 months, Lisa also used 420 words, of which 193 were German and 227 Italian. Of the 193 German words, 87 were equivalents and 106 were new words. Of the 227 Italian words, 65 were equivalents and 162 were new (see Figs. 2.9, 10).

Thus, approximately one-third of the entire vocabulary is made up of equivalents, while two-thirds are new acquisitions. As will be seen at the end of this chapter, it is in this relation that the bilingual child is able to acquire two lexical systems simultaneously.

At this point it might be interesting to take a closer look at the processes used by the child in producing these equivalents or in managing the two lexical systems, in order to see what later influence, the choice between the two

6 Cunze [1980], who used these principles to analyze the lexicon of her daughter Dunia, obtained results identical to mine, thus providing further evidence of this process of equivalent acquisition.

**Fig. 2.9.** Lisa's vocabulary at the age of 34 months

| Total German words | Total Italian words | Total words |
| --- | --- | --- |
| 193 | 227 | 420 |
| new words | new words | new words |
| 106 | 162 | 268 |
| equivalents | equivalents | equivalents |
| 87 | 65 | 152 |

**Fig. 2.10.** Giulia's vocabulary at the age of 28 months

| Total German words | Total Italian words | Total words |
| --- | --- | --- |
| 211 | 209 | 420 |
| new words | new words | new words |
| 132 | 149 | 281 |
| equivalents | equivalents | equivalents |
| 79 | 60 | 139 |

codes. As I stated at the beginning of this chapter, there are basically two different ways of acquiring equivalents. In the first, the equivalents are learned in different contexts, and in the second, in the same context. Ochs [1979, p. 1, 5] provides a definition of the word "context": "A key concept in pragmatic approaches to language is 'context'. ... The scope of context is not easy to assess and define. ... It includes minimally the language user's beliefs and assumptions about temporal, spatial and social settings; prior, ongoing and future actions (verbal, nonverbal); and the state of knowledge and attentiveness of those participating in the social interaction at hand. ... Not all entities in a physical space constitute context. Rather, context consists of environmental features that form part of the language user's universe".

Following this brief definition of context, we can hypothesize that the process of generalization in which the child realizes that equivalents exist takes place in the second stage, and that there is a difference between cases in which there is only one context for both words and cases in which there are two contexts, one for each word. So far, we have seen that during the first stage, even if the bilingual child uses words from and understands both of the two languages, he does not, in reality, possess equivalents, and thus may not be called truly bilingual. In fact, it is only during the second stage that the child acquires two distinct lexical systems and above all realizes that there are equivalents in the two languages, i. e., now names objects or events at times with words from one language and at times with words from the other.

In order to support this hypothesis further, I performed small trials with two bilingual children of about the same age, Lisa (2;5) and Arianna (2;4), during a period in which they were beginning the second stage of vocabulary development. In these trials I observed the acquisition of equivalents as offered in different contexts as opposed to equivalents offered in the same context.

The first case to be examined here is equivalent acquisition when the words are offered to the child in different contexts. Lisa was taught several equivalent pairs in different situations with different interlocutors in this way.

First it was ascertained that the child was not yet producing the equivalent in question. This was achieved by asking her, "What is this called?" while pointing to an object. Later, Lisa's father taught her the Italian name of the object, and her mother taught her the German name, using a different room and a differently-shaped object for each language. During the trial period, both of Lisa's parents made sure they did not use the word in another context.

By means of this system, it was possible to follow each step of acquisition for several equivalent pairs. It was noted, firstly, that the meaning of the word was not immediately generalized to include its equivalent; this happened only after some time. Secondly, the context in which the word was first learned showed itself to be decisive.

The following shows how Lisa acquired the word pairs *Armadio – Schrank* ("wardrobe closet"), *Specchio – Spiegel* ("mirror"), and *Occhiali – Brillen* ("eyeglasses").

**Word pair:** *Armadio – Schrank*
**Subject:** Lisa
**Present:** Father, Mother, Lisa
**F:** *Lisa, cosa è quello?* (What is that?) [Lisa's father points to the bedroom wardrobe, a big piece of furniture with several doors.]
**L:** *La porta.* (The door.)
**F:** *E' l'armadio.* (It's the wardrobe.)
**L:** *Amadio.*

Two days later.
**Present:** Lisa and her mother. Lisa's mother shows her several wardrobes in a magazine.
**M:** *Das ist ein Schrank.* (This is a wardrobe.)
**M:** *Was ist das?* (What is this?) [Lisa answers several times, always correctly,]
**L:** *Schank.* [Later, her mother shows her the children's wardrobe, which is equally as big as the other, with just as many doors, and Lisa says,]
**L:** *Schank.*

Two days later.
**Present:** Father, Mother, Lisa. Lisa's father points to the bedroom wardrobe and asks her what it is.
**L:** *Madio, amadio.*

The next day.
**Present:** Father, Mother, Lisa. Lisa's father takes her into her parents' bedroom. He hits the wardrobe fairly hard.
**F:** *Cos'è?* (What's this?)
**L:** *Piano!* (Gently!)
**F:** *Cosa è questo?* (What is this?)
**L:** *Madio. Madio.*
**F:** *Dillo bene: armadio.* (Say it right: *armadio*)
**L:** *Amadio.*

Half an hour later, Lisa's mother takes her into the girls' bedroom and asks, pointing to the wardrobe,
**M:** *Und was ist das hier?* (What is this?) [Lisa looks at the wardrobe and then suddenly says,]
**L:** *Madio, madio, madio, Mamma, madio.* [At this point, her mother says the word *Schrank*, and Lisa repeats it without any problem.]

About an hour later they are looking at magazines. Lisa's mother has her bring her the magazine where they saw so many *Schrank*. Lisa gives her the magazine and says,
**L:** *Schank sehn ja?* (See wardrobe, yes?)
**M:** *Ja.* [Her mother opens the magazine, points to a wardrobe and says,]
**M:** *Was ist das?*
**L:** *Schank.*

The next day.
**Present:** Lisa, Father. Lisa's father picks up the magazine, points to a wardrobe and asks Lisa what it is.
**L:** *Schank.*
**F:** *Cosa è questo?*
**L:** *Schank.*
**F:** *Questo è un armadio.* (This is an *armadio*.)
**L:** *Amadio.*

That same evening, Lisa says *armadio* and *Schrank* while looking at both the magazine and the wardrobes in the house. When she goes into the girls' bedroom and her father points to the wardrobe and asks her what it is, Lisa answers, "*Schank*". They go to her parents' bedroom and she says *armadio*, and then, when they return to the girls' room, she says *armadio*.

**Pair:** *Specchio – Spiegel*
**Subject:** Lisa
**Present:** Father, Mother, Lisa. [They are in Lisa's parents' bedroom.]

**F:** *Dove è uno specchio?* (Where is the mirror?) [Lisa points to a small, round mirror. Then her father shows her two different types of mirrors, both of which are in the same room. He teaches her the word *specchio*, which she repeats several times, saying,]
**L:** *Pecchio.*

Two days later.
**Present:** Lisa, Mother. They are in the same bedroom as before and Lisa mentions both mirrors, making a distinction between the big mirror and the small one:
**L:** *Gosa specchio.* (Big mirror.)
**L:** *Ganz kein pecchio.* (Small mirror.)

An hour later, in the bathroom, Lisa's mother shows her a big mirror and says,
**M:** *Das ist ein Spiegel, Lisa, ein Spiegel.* (This is a mirror, Lisa, a mirror.) [Lisa repeats several times,]
**L:** *Biegel.*

That evening, Lisa and her mother are in the the bathroom again. Lisa's mother wants her to learn the word *Spiegel* a little better, so she asks her to say it. Lisa repeats it twice or three times, then suddenly says,
**L:** *Anda Pecchio, anda pecchio, anda pecchio.* (Other mirror.) [She says these six words while looking at the mirror. Then, smiling, she looks at her mother and says,]
**L:** *Tutti specchio.* (All mirror.)

About two hours later, she goes into the bedroom with her mother, who points to the mirror and asks,
**M:** *Lisa, was ist das hier?* (What is this?)
**L:** *Pecchio, gos pecchio.* (Big mirror.) [Then, walking over to the small mirror, she says,]
**L:** *Kein pecchio.* (Small mirror.) [Then her mother takes her into the bathroom and asks,]
**M:** *Lisa, was ist das?*
**L:** *Biegel.*
**M:** *Was ist das?*
**L:** *Biegel.* [They go back into the bedroom and her answer to the same question is:]
**L:** *Pecchio.*

For another month, the child tended to call the mirror in the bedroom *specchio* and the one in the bathroom *Spiegel*. For example, Lisa is in the bedroom:
**M:** *Oder Spiegel.* (Or *Spiegel*.)
**L:** *No, specchio.*
**M:** *In Deutsch sagt man "Spiegel". Man kann "Spiegel" oder "specchio" sagen.* (In German it's *Spiegel*. You can say *Spiegel* or *specchio*.)

**L:** *Nein, Lisa sag "specchio".* (No, Lisa says *specchio.*)
**M:** *Und kann Mammi "Spiegel" sagen?* (Can Mommy say *Spiegel*?)
**L:** *Biegel bagno.* (*Spiegel* bathroom.)

**Pair:** *Occhiali – Brillen*
**Subject:** Lisa
**Present:** Mother, Lisa, Giulia. Lisa has already known the word *"occhiali"* for some time, and she has used it often to designate her father's eyeglasses. Her mother draws a woman wearing eyeglasses on a piece of paper, and next to her she draws more pairs of glasses. She points to these drawings and teaches Lisa the word *Brillen*. Lisa repeats it several times. Then her mother asks her to go into the other room to her father and tell him what's in the drawing.
**F:** *Cosa à questo?* (What's this?)
**L:** *Billen.* [She repeats *Billen* several times, but never says *"occhiali".*]

Later, she sees her father's glasses and says,
**L:** *Occhiali.*
**M:** *Was ist das hier?* (She points to Lisa's father's glasses.)
**L:** *Occhiali.* [Then her mother shows her the glasses in the drawing and asks,]
**M:** *Was ist das hier?*
**L:** *Billen.* [Lisa wants her mother to draw other *Billen*, which her mother does. Suddenly, when her mother has drawn two or three pairs of glasses, Lisa says,]
**L:** *Occhiali, occhiali.* [Her mother shows her the glasses in the previous drawing and Lisa says,]
**L:** *Billen.*

Later, in the presence of her father, she says,
**L:** *Occhiali Billen.*

Afterwards, her mother teaches her that *occhiali di Papi* is equal to *Papis Billen*, because Lisa insists on saying only *occhiali* for her father's glasses, and never *Brillen*.

Half an hour later, her mother asks her again, pointing to Lisa's father's glasses.
**M:** *Lisa, was ist das hier?*
**L:** *Occhiali, occhiali.*
 *Occhialen occhialen.*
 *Occhiali Bille.*

As these examples show, Lisa was able to make generalizations; she could understand that, for instance, *Brillen* is equal to *occhiali*. But in normal use, she was still influenced by the context in which she had learned the word for the first time. She tended to call her father's glasses *occhiali* rather than *Brillen*, regardless of whom she was talking to. It appeared that what distinguished *occhiali* from *Brillen* were the pragmatic conditions which influenced their use, and these coincided with the context in which she had learned these words for the first time. Several recent theories based on the study of the pragmatic-semantic field have given a more precise description of the generalization process which the child goes through in acquiring equivalents [Rosch, 1973, 1978; Fillmore, 1978; Bowerman, 1978; Bamberg, 1979; Lorenzer, 1976]. [7]

On the basis of these types of reasoning, the formation of equivalents in bilingual children can be explained: for every new word that the bilingual child acquires there is a relatively wide set of features, one of which has the property of being a generalizing element. When such an element is found in another word, this word may be considered equivalent. In other words, the child may use the word *specchio* not only for a mirror, but also for a shop window, a shiny table, a silver spoon, etc. if, for example, the "you can see yourself" feature is found in these other objects. The generalizing element is called the prototype here, and the features making up the various nuances which specify the prototype are the pragmatic-semantic field. Thus, for example, we have one pragmatic-semantic field and prototype for the word *Spiegel* and another for the word *specchio*. This twofold quality can be represented graphically as in the diagrams below if the two words have been acquired in two different contexts.

---

7  "Real categories (that is, words which designate concepts in natural languages, 'natural' here meaning the opposite of artificial languages, which are programmed by computer) have a highly elaborate internal structure and poorly defined margins. ... 'Internal structure' means that the categories are composed of a 'central meaning' which consists of the clearest instance (the best example) of the category 'surrounded' by other members of the category. ... The central meanings of the categories are not arbitrary: they are 'given' by the human perceptive system" [Rosch, 1978, p. 112, 113]. Fillmore gives the term "semantic prototype" to the central part of word meaning, which he describes as follows: "Native speakers are equipped with cognitive schemata or images which enable them to judge physical objects and events as 'good' or 'better' representatives of the category. When the speaker is presented with a particular, decontextualized word, he/she uses this knowledge and tries to match the word with prototypical events in which the object or the activity the word refers to could play a meaningful role" [Fillmore, 1978 as quoted in Bamberg, 1979, p. 25]. Fillmore also argues that "it may often be psychologically inaccurate to describe word meanings in terms of sets of features specifying conditions that must be satisfied before the word can be appropriately used." He proposes instead that "the understanding of meaning requires ... an appeal to an exemplar or prototype ... possibly something which, instead of being analyzed, needs to be presented or demonstrated or manipulated" [in Bowerman, 1978, p. 279].

According to Rosch, the prototype or "best example" is formed through (a) "principles of information processing subsequent to experience with a number of particular instances of their categories"; and (b) "frequency of exposure to given instances [that] may make some items salient in a not-yet-organized domain and may influence how that domain comes to be divided" [in Bowerman, 1978, p. 280]. "The interactional setting, i.e., the contextual experience against the shared background of listener and speaker, ... serves as the basis for early word meanings" [Bamberg, 1979, p. 36]. "An *a priori* differentiation between ... pragmatic knowledge and semantic knowledge cannot be inferred; rather, the semantics of first words always have to be considered in pragmatic terms" [Bamberg, 1979, p. 38].

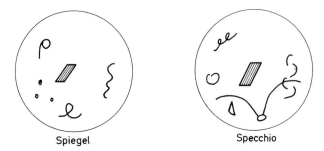

The parallelogram in the center of each circle represents a functional prototype; i.e., the object is used to see oneself.[8] The remaining symbols in the circle to the left represent the features of the context for the word *Spiegel*: the bathroom with the big, frameless mirror, the tiles, the mother, the language used, etc. The symbols aside from the parallelogram in the circle to the right represent the features for the context of the word *specchio*: the bedroom with the small, round, orange mirror, the white beds, the father, the languages used, etc.

As long as the child is not yet using decontextualization to extrapolate the common features of these two words, i.e., the semantic prototype, then *specchio* and *Spiegel* are not considered equivalents. Decontextualization is "a freeing-up process whereby the child can carry out a given conventional symbolic act representationally (in the absence of perceptual support from the

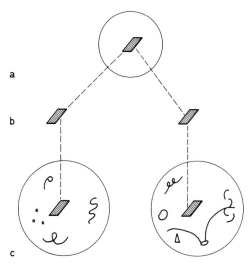

**Fig. 2.11.** (a) Recognition of the identity of two prototypes: process of generalization; (b) prototype extrapolated from the context: process of decontextualization; (c) contextualized experience: pragmatic-semantic field

8 As Bowerman [1978] rightly notes, prototypes may be of a functional nature, as I have suggested here for *specchio* and *Spiegel*, or of a perceptive nature, as I would suggest for the pair *occhiali/Brillen*, which denote two round things found in front of eyes.

referent and its associated context) as well as presentationally (with full contextual/referential support)" [Bates, 1976, p. 1].

The point is that it is not the overall meaning of *Spiegel* that the child considers equivalent to the overall meaning of *specchio*, but only the prototypes. The two pragmatic-semantic fields do not blend, and thus they are not considered equivalent. This process can be represented graphically as in Fig. 2.11.

The fact that the pragmatic-semantic fields remain different for the two words also explains the rigid manner in which each word is kept attached to the original context in which it was acquired before becoming generalized to include the other word. I found the same rigidity in Giulia as in Lisa.

Giulia (2;2)
**Present:** Giulia, Mother
**G:** *Mami, was ist das da?* (Mommy, what is that there?) [pointing to a hair clip.]

**M:** *Das ist eine Klammer.* (This is a hair clip.)
**G:** *Klammer Klammer.* [She repeats the word several times.]

About a month later, her father is putting a hair clip into Lisa's hair. Giulia is off to one side, apparently distracted.
**F:** *Questa è una molletta.* (This is a hair clip.)
**G:** *No! Non è molletta, è eine Klammer!*

Leopold [1949b, p. 44] tells about the first time he read the book *Struwelpeter* (Peter the Porcupine) to his daughter Hildegarde in German: "She tells her mother the stories in English, adorned with a few German words, especially nouns, but also some verbs like *weinen*." But we know from the preceding data that Hildegard already knew and used the English equivalent, "to cry."

The process of generalization is evidently an enormous effort from the cognitive point of view, as these examples permit us to verify. The child must recognize the prototype of a certain word, take it out of its own pragmatic-semantic field, and identify it with (or consider it an equivalent of) the prototype of another word that belongs to the other language and which possesses its own pragmatic-semantic field. This pragmatic-semantic field is an integral part of the meaning of the word.[9]

---

9 It does not appear to me that the choice of a word is determined by the phonological difficulty presented by the equivalents in the two languages, as Celce-Murcia [1975], among others, maintains. Celce-Murcia believes that the bilingual child chooses the word which is easier to pronounce.

Apart from the well-known fact that children are not deterred by the phonological difficulty of complicated words and solve this problem by using such modifications as *chechea* for *acqua*, *tuta* for *Lutscher*, *capse* for *scarpe* and so on, it is the context in which the interaction takes place that gives the child the elements he needs to attribute meaning to certain symbols; thus, the child will only learn words that are encountered in a context meaningful to him.

It is during this period that the child no longer accepts passively, as he once did, the fact that a certain object can be called something different from the name that he gives to it. When he begins to correct the adult, it may be said that the bilingual child is beginning to realize that he is dealing with two different lexicons. Thus, for example, when her mother picks up her shoes and asks, *"Wem gehören diese Schuhe?"* ("To whom do these shoes belong?"), Giulia (1;9) answers, *"Capse, chiama capse"* (*Capse* for the Italian word for shoes, *scarpe*).

It would appear that the bilingual child has passed into that period which Piaget called the first stage of nominal realism. In his 1926 study of the child's spontaneous representations for several events in the physical and psychological world, Piaget examined nominal realism, whose first stage he defined as "the conviction which children have that the name of an object is justified by the physical characteristics of the object itself; that the name originated together with the object itself and cannot be modified or replaced without modifying the object itself."

In the second stage, "the child admits that someone gave the object its name, that the name is not necessarily inherent to the object, and that while replacement of the name might be possible, it should be avoided because it would create confusion and incomprehension in people" [in Benelli, 1978, p. 5].

Piaget bases this distinction on the responses he received from children aged 5 to 11 to the questions: What is a name? How did names begin? How did we find out that the name is what we call it? Where are names? Do clouds know they are called clouds? Has the sun always had its name, or did it exist without a name for a while before it got its name? Why is the sun called the sun? Could Jura have been called "Salève" and the Salève "Jura" at first? [Piaget, 1973, p. 68].

Naturally, smaller children cannot be asked such questions, and thus it is not possible to tap their metalinguistic information. However, it is interesting to observe that towards the age of 2 or 3, the bilingual child behaves as though he were passing through these two stages. Thus, he begins quite early to admit that one object may have two names. For example, it was often observed that Giulia compared two words using sentences such as the following:

**G** (1;9): [Looking at her feet, which she has pulled out from under the blankets, and talking to herself]: *Ah! C'è piedini. Füsse, chiama piedini, chiama Füsse. Füsse anche piedini.* (Oh! They're feet. *Füsse,* called *Füsse. Piedini* called *Füsse. Füsse* also *piedini.*)

Or:

**G** (1;9): *Das hier guida.* (This here drives.) [She points to the man in a toy car.]
**M:**     *Ja, der fährt.* (Yes, he's driving.)
**G:**     *Macht guida, fährt.* (Makes *guida, fährt.*)

Or:

Giulia (1;9) uses only the word *mela* ("apple"), to designate apples and pears in the fruit bowl. Her mother teaches her the corresponding *Apfel* and also the word *Birne* ("pear") to show her that these are two different kinds of fruit. Later, when Giulia refers to apples, she says,

**G:**    *Eccolo a mela, anche Apfel. Vuoi a mela, Apfel.* (Here is *mela*, also *Apfel*. Want *mela, Apfel.*)

Giulia not only repeated words one after the other in one language and then the other, but she did the same with entire sentences. For example:

Giulia (1;9) runs up to her mother, throws herself on her and screams,
**G:** *Giulia alabia! Booo! Tò Tò!* (Giulia mad.) [from the Italian *arrabbiarsi*]
    [She backs off and then charges again, saying,]
**G:** *Giulia böse! Booo! Tò Tò!* [She repeats the game several times.]

Or:

Speaking to her mother about herself, Giulia (1;9) says,
**G:** *No no glos, klein klein.* (No big, small.) [After a short pause:]
**G:** *Nè glande, piccola piccola.* (Not big, small.)

According to Leopold, "bilingualism helps to break the intimate association between form and content. In other words, precisely because of his experience of contact with two different expressions for the same object, the bilingual child somehow manages to understand the conventional and arbitrary nature of words" [in Benelli, 1978, p. 1].

It is during this second period that the bilingual child begins to use equivalents as a strategy to get the adult's attention. For example:

Giulia (1;9) is in the car with her mother and her grandmother.
**G:** *Elato, elato, elato, elato.* [The child wants some ice cream (= *gelato*), but her mother and grandmother pay no attention to her and continue to talk to each other.]
**G:** *Eis, Eis, Eis* ("ice cream" in German). [At this point, her mother and grandmother finally pay attention and get her some ice cream.]
Lisa (2;9) is barefoot.
**L:** *Papi, dove sono la mia pantofole?* (Daddy, where are my slippers?) [Her father is busy doing something else and doesn't answer, so Lisa repeats her question, again with no success. Then:]
**L:** *Dove sono la mia sciappen, eh?* (*sciappen* = *Schlappen* = "slippers")

Not only do children begin to admit that there may be two words for the same thing, but very early we observe the first examples of translation from one language into the other:

**L (2;5):** *La panna da oben, ada.* (The cream up there, look.) (ada = *guarda*)
    [She points to the cream on the sink.]

**M:**     *Ja, die Sahne ist da oben.* (Yes, the cream is up there.)
**L:**     *Dillo, dillo!* (Say it!)
**M:**     *Die Sahne ist da oben.*
**L:**     *No, la panna e là sù.* (No, the cream is up there.)

**G (2;2):** *Metti tavolo di Giulia.* (Put Giulia's table.) [She wants her mother to take the cups that are on her sister's table and put them on hers.]
**M:**     *Wo soll ich's hintun?* (Where should I put it?)
**G:**     *Das da, das da auf Tisch von Giulia.* (That there, that there on Giulia's table.) [She points to her table.]

What is more, Lisa and Giulia began to keep the two lexicons separate in an attempt to relate each language to a precise person. For example:

Lisa (3;3) turns to an Italian friend and says,
**L:**     *Dov'è Kitty?* (Where is Kitty?) [Immediately afterwards, without waiting for the answer, she turns to her mother and asks,]
**L:**     *Wo ist Kitty?*

**G (2;3)** [looking at a small child on the bus]: *Quetto parla no.* (This one speak no.)
**G**     [turning to her mother and pointing at the child]: *Das hier splecht nicht.* (This one speak no.)
**G**     [turning to the child]: *Quetto è buono.* (This one is good.)
**G**     [turning to her mother and pointing to the child]: *Das hier lieb.*

Thus, with reference again to the second stage of nominal realism as described by Piaget, it would seem that since bilingual children cannot help but use two terms for the same concept, their way to avoid confusion and disorder is to create a new reference point, which is the person. That is, the bilingual child begins to organize his speech according to the language of the person with whom he is speaking.

Along these lines, such self-corrections as these were often noticed in Giulia:

**M:**     *Wie ist dieser Bleistift?* (What is this pencil like?)
**G (1;9):** *Pi- ... klein klein.* (Small.)
**G (1;11):** *Den- ... mami lein lein.* (*rein* = "inside" = *dentro*)
**M:**     *Was ist das hier?* (What is this?)
**G (1;11):** *A sca- ... Schuhe a Giulia.* (*Schuhe* = *scarpa* = "shoe")

Cunze [1980, p. 48] gives a wonderful example of this process in her bilingual child, Dunia.

Dunia (1;9) and her father are both putting on their shoes.
**D:** *Due mette.* (Shoes put on.) (*due* = *Schuhe*)
**F:** *Si, Papi ti mette le scarpe. Si chiamano scarpe.* (Yes, Daddy's putting your shoes on. They are called shoes.)

**D:** *Cape mette.* (Shoes put on.) (cape = *scarpe*) [A pause ensues, followed by:]

**D:** *Due iama, Mamma, iama due.* (= *Schuhe chiama*) (Mommy calls *Schuhe*.)

On the other hand, since the two equivalent words are acquired not at the same time but are separated from one another by a certain interval, and remain strongly tied to the context in which they were acquired, the children continue for quite a while to use words from both languages in one sentence:

**L** (2;5): *Spetta, lass zu, Lisa komm ida, bene? Bene!* (*Aspetta* = "wait", leave it closed, Lisa is coming back; *bene* = "okay")

**G** (2;5): *Mami ich will prendere ja?* (Mommy, I want to take, yes?)

Now the other case can be examined, i.e., when the child acquires the equivalents in the same context. For this study, a test was performed with Arianna, a bilingual English – Italian child, in which two adults told her the same story, once in English and then in Italian. In such a situation the child interacts with two people who are speaking two different languages, and learns simultaneously to name objects or events in both languages; the semantic field of both symbols is the same.

In the story Arianna was told, there were several objects with completely new features and names. They were made of multicolored cardboard with a solid base so that they could stand alone. The two adults each told a part of the story, repeating what the other had already said. The objects were moved about during the story as in a puppet show. They were not given real names. To make sure that the child had never heard the words before, names were invented for the new objects. In this way, it was certain that this was the child's first linguistic contact with the words.

The objects were named:  il mipo  = the fooker
                         la blaba = the haytschi
                         i fosi   = the poobles
                         la sura  = the nuggie

The transcription of part of the story as it was told to Arianna is as follows:

**A** = Arianna     **A1** = English-speaking adult [10]
                    **A2** = Italian-speaking adult

**A2:** *Guarda, Arianna, io ho dei bellissimi pupazzi. Questo pupazzo è uno dei mipi.* (Look, Arianna, I have some beautiful puppets. This is one of the mipi.)

**A:** *Si?*

**A2:** *Hmm.*

---

10 My thanks go to Elena Radutzki for her kind collaboration on this experiment.

**A1:** You see? This is called fooker. This is the funniest funniest thing that you've ever seen. Just look at the hair, look at the face! That's probably why it's called fooker!

**A2:** *Non ha veramente dei capelli buffi, questo mipo? Però pensa che questo mipo è tanto, tanto triste, è tristissimo.* (Isn't his hair funny? But just think, this mipo's sad; he's very, very sad.)

**A1:** The fooker is so sad. Why is the fooker so sad? The fooker is sad because he doesn't have any poobles to eat and he wanted so many poobles and he can't find any poobles at all, and so he is sad. Poor, poor fooker.

**A2:** *Povero, povero mipo. Pensa che il mipo è così triste perché voleva mangiare i fosi e, invece non ha avuto i fosi. Li ha persi, pensa! Fortunatamente, però, quando lui era così triste, questo mipo, era lì che piangeva, à arrivata la sua amica, la blaba. La facciamo arrivare?* (Poor, poor mipo. Just think: the mipo is so sad because he wanted to eat the fosi and instead he didn't have any fosi. He lost them, just think! But luckily, when he was sad, this mipo, when he was there crying, his friend the blaba arrived. Shall we bring her over?) [Arianna nods her head. A2 takes another puppet out of a bag.]

**A1:** Fooker is very sad, but his friend is coming. You know his friend! He has a very nice friend who's a haytschi. There is haytschi. Hi, haytschi.

**A2:** *Ciao mipo, dice la blaba. Ma mipo, perché sei così triste? dice la blaba. Io son così contenta, son così allegra! E tu, perché sei così triste?* ("Hi, mipo", says the blaba. "But mipo, why are you so sad", says the blaba. "I'm so happy, I'm so pleased! And why are you so sad?")

**A1:** And so she came along and the haytschi said, "Why are you crying? I'm so happy! I ate a lot of poobles. Do you see the poobles? I ate so many poobles and I had some left over. And I brought them with me."

**A2:** *Sì, ha detto la blaba. Io ho mangiato i fosi, questi qua sono i fosi, li vedi? La blaba ha dei fosi sulla spalla. Se li mette qua.* ("Yes", said the blaba. "I ate the fosi; these are the fosi, do you see them?" The blaba has some fosi on her back. She puts them there.)

**A1:** Right on the back. "Hey, listen", said fooker to haytschi, "could you give me one of those delicious poobles to eat? Or are you going to keep them all for yourself?"

**A2:** *Cosa avresti fatto tu? Avresti dato alcune fosi a mipo se tu fossi la blaba?* (What would you have done? Would you have given some fosi to the mipo if you were the blaba?)

**A** says something incomprehensible on the tape recorder.

**A2:** *Tu dici che non si possono mangiare questi fosi?* (You say you can't eat these fosi?) [Arianna nods her head.]

**A2:** *Però il mipo crede che si possano mangiare. Anche il mipo in realtà non può mangiare, ma noi facciamo finta.* (But the mipo thinks you can. The mipo can't really eat, but we're pretending.) [Arianna accepts.]

**A1:** Do you think haytschi is going to give fooker some of the poobles? Is she going to be a nice haytschi? Or is she going to eat all of them herself?

[Arianna takes the poobles from the haytschi and gives them to the fooker.]

After the story, which the child followed with great interest, demonstrating that she was quite capable of good concentration, the adults continued to speak about the objects, and only then did Arianna decide to pronounce their names. She did it with no difficulty, using both languages and repeating them several times, both spontaneously and on request. Some examples:

**A1:** Maybe haytschi wants the other pooble.
**A** [calling it]: Haytschi-i-i-i!
**A1** [pointing to the fooker]: Who is that?
**A:** Fooker.
**A1:** That's right.
**A2:** *Ecco la blaba ... quanto è simpatica.* (Here's the blaba. She's so nice.)
**A:** *Quetto una bla. Una blaba.* (This is a bla. A blaba.)
**A2:** *Come hai detto?* (What did you say?)
**A:** *Una blaba ho detto.* (Una blaba I said.)
**A1:** Can I see haytschi please? [Arianna gives the haytschi to A1.]
**A2:** *Mettiamo anche i fosi qui dentro?* (Shall we put the fosi in here, too?)
**A:** *Anche i fosi.* (The fosi, too.)
**A2:** *Questa qua come si chiama?* (What's this called?) [A2 picks up the blaba.]
**A:** *La blaba.* (The blaba.)
**A1:** *Ecco.* (Right.)
**A1:** Could you put the poobles in the bag? Where are the poobles?
**A** [calling]: Poooobles!
**A2:** Yoo-hoo, *sono qui!* (Here they are!)
**A1:** Could you also put haytschi in the bag?
**A:** Yes. [calling it] Haytschi-i-i-i-!
**A2:** *Non ti piace mipo?* (Don't you like mipo?)
**A:** *Doè mipo? Doè mipo qui?* (Where's mipo? Where mipo here?)
**A1** [showing her a small animal made of black wood]: Do you know what this is?
**A:** This is fooker.
**A1:** Is this fooker? This is fooker's friend. We have two fookers now.
**A:** *Allora andiamo a casa, andiamo a casa di fooker, andiamo.* (Then let's go home, let's go to fooker's home.) [As she speaks to the animal, she acts.]

One last example is perhaps the most interesting, because it shows that the child really seems to have connected the two names to one object:

**A2** [pointing to a green wooden animal]: *Quell' animaletto sembra una blaba.* (That animal looks like a blaba.)
**A:** No-o-o-o.

**A2:** *No, non sembra una blaba.* (No, it doesn't look like a blaba.)

**A1:** It's not haytschi at all.

**A2** [pointing to another stylized wooden animal]: *Questa papera sembra una blaba.* (This duck looks like a blaba.)

**A:** No.

**A2:** *Che cosa sembra una blaba allora?* (What does look like a blaba, then?)

**A:** Haytschi. [A picks up the haytschi.]

If an acquisition experience of this kind occurs when the child is in the second stage, as we have seen with Arianna, [11] the child will learn to name a certain event or object in both languages at the same time, and the two symbols will have only one pragmatic-semantic field. If, on the other hand, the child is still in the first stage and thus has not yet realized that there are two different codes, the equivalent pair can end up being used as a single unit, i.e., as a compound word. One example of this is Giulia's *scotta-heiss*, mentioned in Sect. 2.1. Such examples are also mentioned by many other authors, including Cunze [1980], El-Dash [1978], Imedadze [1967], and Burling [1971].

## 2.3 Does the Bilingual Child Have Twice as Many Words as the Monolingual Child?

If the lexical growth of bilingual children is compared with that recorded for monolingual children in an attempt to determine whether the bilingual child's lexicon is larger, smaller, or the same size as that of the monolingual child, a number of problems arise.

In building up a rich lexicon, the most important requirement is a good memory; as we know, the quality of memory varies from subject to subject. But this skill also depends upon the social and cultural environment in which the child lives, and this variable has any number of facets.

To overcome the problem of the individual differences which make each case unique, statistical studies would have to be carried out on a wide basis among both bilingual and monolingual children. These studies would have to record the children's average monthly or yearly lexical growth and correlate it to the factors of memory and sociocultural environment.

Unfortunately, there have been no such studies conducted to date. Thus, I shall limit myself to a comparison of Lisa's and Giulia's lexical growth with the lexical growth of two monolingual Italian children, Claudia and Francesco (see Benedict [1979], McCarthy [1954], Francescato [1970], Lenneberg [1971] and Nelson [1973] for studies on quantitative lexical development).

My proposal was to ascertain the monthly increase in the number of verbs used by these four children and compare the results. A comparison is justified,

---

11 Arianna was already well into the second stage, and thus used a good number of equivalents.

because the sociocultural class to which these children belong is very similar, and the methods used in collecting data were the same.

Benedict [1979] found that (American) children increase their lexical production by 9.09 units per month. [12] However, Benedict discontinued her count after the first 50 words, and as we have seen, bilingual children are still in the first stage at this point, so it would be wrong to expect that they would show greater lexical growth than monolinguals. In fact, a comparison of the first 50 words of Lisa and Giulia with those of Claudia and Francesco reveals great similarities (see Tables 2.5 – 8). [13]

The comparison which follows was made only for verbs, and not for the entire lexicon. Verbs were chosen because they possess greater communicative power than the other categories of words. As Parisi [1977, p. 43] correctly notes, "the verbs have greater communicative power because for every given verb, there are fewer types of nouns which may be used with it in a sentence than there are types of verbs which may be used with a given noun." A child is more likely to omit nouns, which can be replaced with deixis, than to omit verbs. Furthermore, from a strictly theoretical point of view, as will be seen in the next chapter, the predicate (thus principally the verb) is considered the core of the sentence in this study. As communication takes place mostly by means of the sentence, it is clear that the verb is more important than the other categories.

The verb count was begun while the bilingual children were still in the first stage and was continued on into the second stage. In this way it was possible to measure verb growth in a period which is crucial for bilinguals, i.e., the period covering the end of the first stage and most of the second stage. For each child, the count was begun during the month when he or she had acquired a total of 50 words: for Lisa, at the age of 21 months; for Giulia, at 17 months; for Claudia at 16 months and for Francesco at 19 months. In each case, the count was continued for 11 months.

At the end of this period, Lisa had added 6.6 verbs per month, Giulia 9.2, Claudia 7.9, and Francesco 6.3. This result indicates that there is a difference between the individual levels of each subject, but it does not show any difference between bilinguals and monolinguals. In fact, there was a greater difference between the two monolinguals and between the two bilinguals than between the monolinguals and the bilinguals.

---

12 According to Nelson [1973], the rate of growth is 11.1 words per month.

13 For this initial count, the following criteria were used: a) Sounds such as mhn, nh, mm, and others, not considered to be words in the true sense, were not included. b) Words used by the children exclusively to accompany determined actions, such as *chi è?* or *plonto, plonto* ("who is it?" "hello, hello") when holding the telephone receiver, or "ahm" when opening the mouth to eat, were not included. c) The different meanings a single word might have were not considered. Thus the word *daki* or *tazie*, used by Lisa, Claudia and Giulia both in thanking and in exchanging objects, was included only once, for the meaning of "thanks". I decided to opt for the traditional meaning of the word, because in later recordings Giulia and Claudia replaced their use of *tazie* for exchanges with the verb *dare* ("to give"), and Lisa alone continued to use it actively.

Table 2.5. The first words used by Lisa (1;9, 0). Where necessary, the correct Italian or German follows in brackets; the English translation is in parentheses

| Names of people | Names of objects | Verbs | Other |
|---|---|---|---|
| Mamma (Mommy) | caca cloclolade (chocolate) | nyam nyam [mangiare] (eat) | più (more) |
| Papi (Daddy) | bua (hurt) | laila [lascia] (leave) | ja (yes) |
| Ia [Zia] (Aunt) | Wauwau (dog) | hiudi [chiudere] (close) | daki [danke] (thanks) |
| Dulia (Giulia) | eela [bicicletta] (bicycle) | è (is) | da (there) |
| Tata | cheo (soap) | scotta (burns) | caa [cara] (dear) |
| Lia (Lisa) | nonelnìa [collanina] (necklace) | vai (go!) | tatau [a spasso] (walking) |
| Nonno | matita (pencil) | haia haia [dormire] (sleep) | qui (here) |
| Nonna | tic tac (clock) | ist (is) | là (there) |
| Omi (Nonna) | Baum (tree) | | no |
| Vanna | dito (finger) | | altro (other) |
| | chechea [acqua] (water) | | coa [ancora] (again) |
| | Blle [Blume] (flower) | | nein (no) |
| | Bappo [Trappo] (cork) | | |
| | cane (dog) | | |
| | miao (cat) | | |
| | Käse (cheese) | | |
| | Kita [Kinderwagen] | | |
| | latte (milk) | | |
| | Tasche [Tasche] (pockets) | | |
| | totto [cappotto] (coat) | | |
| | Beine (legs) | | |
| | Schku [Schuh] (shoe) | | |
| | Tuta [Lutscher] succhiotto (sucker) | | |
| | gatta (cat) | | |
| | cotto [biscotto] (cookie) | | |
| | balle [Ball-palla] | | |

**Table 2.6.** The first words used by Giulia (1;6,0). Where necessary, the correct Italian or German follows in brackets; the English translation is in parentheses

| Names of people | Names of objects | Verbs | Other |
|---|---|---|---|
| Mami | popo (bottom) | da sitzi (sit) | no ja |
| Dodo (Rudolfo) | Buch (book) | cade [cadere] (fall) | caa [cara] (dear) |
| Julia (Giulia) | neni (child) | guada [guardare] (look) | da (there) |
| Ia (Lisa) | Bonbon (candy) | kinkinny [trinken] (drink) | nein (no) |
| Papi | caca | scotta (burn) | okay |
| | Iaiatel [Schachtel] (box) | api [aprire] (open) | là (there) |
| | Baum (tree) | aizi [anziehen] (dress) | auch (also) |
| | Haus (house) | fertich (finish) | tatau [a spasso] (walking) |
| | Zahn (tooth) | haiahaia [dormire] (sleep) | tutto tutto (all) |
| | baubau (dog) | baite [arbeiten] (work) | alle alle |
| | auto | | datsie [grazie] (thanks) |
| | bua (hurt) | balla [ballare] (dance) | heiss (hot) |
| | acqua (water) | | wo (where) |
| | chichi [pesce] (fish) | | qua (here) |
| | Bauch (tummy) | | ciao (bye) |
| | tic tac [orologio] (clock) | | |
| | Nase (nose) | | |
| | Beine (legs) | | |
| | balle (ball) | | |
| | uva (grapes) | | |
| | bonnatale (table) | | |

**Table 2.7.** The first words used by Claudia (1;4,0). Where necessary, the correct Italian follows in brackets; the English translation is in parentheses

| Names of people | Names of objects | Verbs | Other |
|---|---|---|---|
| Mamma | a bau [cane] | itto [vedere] | tatti [grazie] |
| Papà | (dog) | (see) | (thanks) |
| Zio | papis [lapis] | oio [volere] | no |
| Miena | (pen) | (want) | |
| (Milena) | totò [botte] | nanna [dormire] | etto [ecco] |
| Luca | (slap) | (sleep) | (here!) |
| me | dicchi [dischi] | è | si |
| (Claudia) | (records) | (is) | (yes) |
| tu | paa [palla] | gia [girare] | ciao |
| (Claudia) | (ball) | (turn) | (bye) |
| mio | bamba [bambola] | dà [dare] | passo [a spasso] |
| (Claudia) | (doll) | (give) | (walking) |
| io | meia [caramella] | api [aprire] | puù [piu] |
| (Caudia) | (candy) | (open) | (more) |
| | tata [carta] | iotta [rompere] | |
| | (paper) | (break) | |
| | jacca [acqua] | tocca [toccare] | |
| | (water) | (touch) | |
| | pappo [tappo] | | |
| | (cork) | | |
| | cacca | | |
| | nanà [altalena] | | |
| | (swing) | | |
| | tai [chiavi] | | |
| | (keys) | | |
| | pitta [pizza] | | |
| | ianne [girandola] | | |
| | (top) | | |
| | mimmi [biscotti] | | |
| | (cookies) | | |
| | pipì | | |
| | pietta [paletta] | | |
| | (racket) | | |
| | pappa | | |
| | (food) | | |
| | pappe [scarpe] | | |
| | (shoes) | | |
| | paia [palla] | | |
| | (ball) | | |
| | cici [uccellino] | | |
| | teta [testa] | | |
| | (head) | | |
| | tai [occhiali] | | |
| | (eyeglasses) | | |
| | baccio [braccio] | | |
| | (arm) | | |
| | micio | | |
| | (cat) | | |
| | ciuccio [cavalluccio] | | |
| | (horse) | | |
| | bozza [borsa] | | |
| | (purse) | | |
| | musica | | |
| | cioi [fiori] | | |
| | (flowers) | | |
| | pupa [bambola] | | |
| | (doll) | | |

**Table 2.8.** The first words used by Francesco (1;7,0). Where necessary, the correct Italian follows in brackets; the English translation is in parentheses

| Names of people | Names of objects | Verbs | Other |
|---|---|---|---|
| Mamma | pappa | nanna [dormire] | grazie |
| Papa | (food) | (sleep) | (thanks) |
| Lalla | pappo [tappo] | uto [seduto] | più |
| Uta | (cork) | (sit) | (more) |
| (Augusta) | acqua | api [aprire] | no |
| Baaba | (water) | (open) | |
| (Barbara) | uci [luci] | c'è | eccole |
| Tete | (lights) | (there is) | (here they are!) |
| Dedi | ciuccio | dà [dare] | là |
| Lilli | (rubber nipple) | (give) | (there) |
| Lullo | cacco [l'uovo] | oio [volvere] | spasso |
| | (egg) | (want) | (walking) |
| | occhi | totto [rompere] | lì |
| | (eyes) | (break) | (there) |
| | popò [auto] | ammo [andare] | eello [bello] |
| | (car) | (go) | (good) |
| | chechi [orecchie] | edi [vedere] | posto [a posto] |
| | (ears) | (see) | (in place) |
| | Bamba | | |
| | (doll) | | |
| | pipì | | |
| | peppi [piedi] | | |
| | (feet) | | |
| | tatti [sassi] | | |
| | (stones) | | |
| | cicci [uccellini] | | |
| | (birds) | | |
| | totò | | |
| | (slap) | | |
| | pecoella [pecorella] | | |
| | (sheep) | | |
| | mimmi [bimbo] | | |
| | (child) | | |
| | taccio [straccio] | | |
| | (rag) | | |
| | bua | | |
| | (hurt) | | |
| | migno [miccio] | | |
| | (cat) | | |
| | babba [cane] | | |
| | (dog) | | |
| | atita [matita] | | |
| | (pencil) | | |
| | bobò [dolci] | | |
| | (sweets) | | |
| | pupo | | |
| | (doll) | | |
| | petti [capelli] | | |
| | (hair) | | |

Between Claudia and Francesco there was a gap of 2.6 words per month, which was greater than the one between Claudia and Giulia (1.3 words per month) and the one between Lisa and Francesco (0.3 words per month).

While it is true that Giulia produced many more verbs than Francesco, there was hardly any difference at all between Lisa and Francesco or between Giulia and Claudia. As there was no great difference between the quantity of verbs produced by the two types of children, must it therefore be said that the bilingual gives lexical form to only half as many concepts?

This is not exactly true, because up to and including the age examined so far, the bilingual child does not command an equal number of new words and equivalent words, as was shown in Sect. 2.2. In fact, although the number of verbs is equally divided between the two languages − 53% of Lisa's verbs were German and 47% Italian, while 54% of Giulia's verbs were German and 46% were Italian − only 27% of Lisa's verbs and only 31% of Giulia's verbs were equivalents. Thus, while the average increase in new words was 6.3 verbs per month for Giulia and 4.8 per month for Lisa, the average increase of equivalents was 2.9 per month for Giulia and 1.8 for Lisa (see also Figs. 2.9, 10, which show the number and distribution of the equivalents in Giulia's and Lisa's total lexicon).

If both languages are taken together, Giulia's total verb production was clearly greater than that of the other children, with Lisa and Francesco at one level and Claudia halfway between them and Giulia. If the languages are taken separately, however, Giulia and Francesco were at one level, while Claudia had given lexical form to a greater number of objects and events and Lisa to fewer.

The bilingual child's maximum individual capacity to produce new words must be divided between the two languages, but the child deals with this by implementing a strategy which gives priority to new words at the expense of equivalents. Thus he is able to speak both languages and to denote the same number of new objects and events as the monolingual child. This process continues through the years, and the list of equivalents becomes longer and longer without impeding the growth of new words.

This process was confirmed by Jarovinsky [1979], who conducted a study on older Hungarian − Russian bilingual children. They were given a test designed to measure their lexical skills. The test sample included 16 children, who were divided into 2 groups. The average age of Group A was 4 years and 2 months, while that of Group B was 6 years and 1 month. One of the tests was the PPVT (Peabody Picture Vocabulary Test), which was given to children in both Russian and Hungarian versions and used to measure their passive lexicon. The children were shown a table with four illustrations and told to point to the picture which corresponded to the adult's utterance. The PPVT was also used differently in a second test aimed at measuring the children's active vocabulary. In the second case, the child had to say what a certain illustration represented.

Of primary interest here is this second test, which gauges the child's active vocabulary or lexical production. Not only did the group of younger children know fewer words than the children in the older group, but they also had fewer equivalents. The test showed that all of the children knew:

a) a large number of equivalent words
   Group A: 49.7% of the active vocabulary
   Group B: 78.8% of the active vocabulary

b) a smaller number of words in Hungarian alone (the dominant language)
   Group A: 24.2% of the active vocabulary
   Group B: 16.8% of the active vocabulary

c) an even smaller number of words in Russian alone
   Group A: 8.0% of the active vocabulary
   Group B: 5.7% of the active vocabulary.

Some of the words were not known by the children in either language:
   Group A: 18.1% of the active vocabulary
   Group B: 3.7% of the active vocabulary.

Jarovinsky's results are very interesting, inasmuch as they are further confirmation of the fact that the bilingual child's lexicon is not made up only of equivalents. In Group A, 32.2% of the active vocabulary had no equivalents; for Group B, this figure was 28.5%.

To return to the bilingual, if he does not have twice the number of words at this age as the monolingual child, he is not handicapped in his ability to communicate, because this factor is not related to a very rich vocabulary. For example, Cunze [1980] found that Dunia's German vocabulary was much richer and more sophisticated than her Italian vocabulary, despite the fact that the language which she spoke more frequently and with greater spontaneity and preferred to use was Italian. Doyle et al. [1979] came to the same conclusions after comparing 22 bilingual children with 22 monolingual children from the ages of $3\frac{1}{2}$ years to 5 years and 7 months. They found that the group of monolinguals had a greater number of words than the group of bilinguals in their dominant language (vocabulary was tested using the PPVT), but that the verbal fluency of the bilinguals, who were tested for their ability to tell stories and, specifically, for the number of concepts expressed by each child per story, was greatly superior to that of the monolingual children. [14]

Furthermore, it must be remembered that towards puberty every person, whether he be bilingual or monolingual, reaches a plateau of words, [15] and at

14 For a brief overview on the subject of linguistic skills in general and the cognitive skills of bilingual as opposed to monolingual elementary and secondary school students, see Titone [1981]. For a more specific and detailed look at the same subjects, see Lamont et al. [1978], Ornstein et al. [1971], Walters and Zatorre [1978] and Durga [1978].

15 "Plateau" is used here to refer to the general lexicon, and not words used for specialized activities. This vocabulary, i.e., the words essential to a certain type of study, hobby, sport or any subject one wishes to learn more about, is usually learned in only one of the two languages.

this point, the bilingual's lexicon is just as rich as that of the monolingual. Moreover, with respect to lexicon size, the relation among bilinguals is the same as the relation among monolinguals, i.e., it moves along a continuum from mediocre to excellent.

## 2.4 Summary

In this chapter we have seen that there are two distinct moments in bilingual lexical acquisition. During the first stage, the child commands a single lexical system composed of words from both languages; there are no equivalents. The ability to relate two different words to a single meaning requires a great effort of generalization and thus depends initially on cognitive as well as interactional factors.

In the second stage, the child begins producing equivalents, which are acquired gradually and never as rapidly as words for new meanings. Pragmatic conditions, i.e., the context in which the child originally learned the words, are of fundamental importance in word choice and use.

If all of the words in the bilingual's two languages are counted during this stage, it is discovered that he possesses a slightly larger lexicon than the monolingual. On the other hand, if his equivalents are eliminated, it is found that the bilingual has slightly fewer words than the monolingual for denoting events and objects.

It is this strategy of giving precedence to the acquisition of new words and relegating the acquisition of equivalents to second priority that explains the merely slight difference between the monthly rate of word growth in the two groups. It is thus, in other words, that the bilingual child easily manages to acquire two lexicons without exhibiting a lexical development greatly differing from that of the monolingual child.

# 3. Development of Basic Sentence Structure

When one has small children, one runs into quite a few people with children of the same age, probably because they spend time at the same places, such as parks, nursery schools, puppet theaters, birthday parties and so on. On such occasions, one usually has the chance to talk, and it is not long before the other adults realize that child X speaks two languages, instead of one, like the other children. At this point, the bilingual child's speech is certain to be subjected to spot checks. If he happens to say two or three well-expressed or intelligent sentences, the adults who hear him may be moved to this sort of admiration: "How do you like that, so little and he already knows things I've never been able to learn!" But if the bilingual child is a bit less brilliant, if he uses the wrong sentence structure or verb tense, the adults who hear him will somehow be relieved, and their faces will betray thoughts which might sound something like, "Well, after all, my child does speak better."

At this point, discussion among the adults usually turns to the benefit or harm of teaching small children to speak two languages. It soon proves that everyone knows someone, or has a distant relative, who is bilingual, and that everyone has an opinion about the linguistic ability of the bilinguals they know. Some think they speak well, others judge their speech to be mediocre, still others think they speak downright poorly, and so on. At any rate, the general impression one receives from such conversations is basically this: there can be no doubt that it is a great advantage to speak two languages, but bilingualism certainly affects the quality of speech.

Such doubts as to the successful outcome of a bilingual upbringing are raised not only by common sense, but also by researchers in the field of bilingualism. For instance, in the thesis, "Bilingualism as a First Language" [1972], Merrill Swain states that some interrogative structures appear at a relatively late age in children who acquire French and English at the same time. However, it is still too early to make such generalizations, because there are as yet no quantitatively meaningful studies on bilingualism or monolingualism. As was pointed out in Chap. 1, there are very great individual differences in lexical development among monolingual children: some learn to speak early, others later; some have a very rich vocabulary and others do not. It is clear that the same individual differences exist among bilingual children. Swain's conclusions about the sequence of interrogative structure acquisition are much more interesting. She writes [1972, p. XVI], "When compared with available data concerning the acquisition of English or of French as a first language, generally speaking, the same developmental sequence was apparent."

It is very probable that an overly idealized opinion of the speech skills of monolinguals is the cause of more doubts about the merits of bilingual acquisition. Firstly, it is easier to pick out the bilingual's errors, whereas those of the monolingual may be more subtle, and often evident only to language teachers, scholars or linguists. Secondly, it is all too easy to compare the language spoken by bilingual children with adult literature. Such comparisons can produce only disastrous results. Furthermore, adults react differently to the errors of bilingual children than to those of monolingual children. Thus, if a 5-year-old monolingual child is still making mistakes in verb form and says "drinked" instead of "drunk", it is very likely that his parents will be moved by tenderness to think, "After all, he's still so little". If, towards the age of 8, he says, "People gets off the bus" instead of "People get off the bus", the adult will come to the conclusion that collective nouns are really quite difficult. But if the bilingual child says such things, the parents' first thought is likely to be, "There you are. It is bilingualism which is causing these mistakes. Poor little thing."

In this and the next chapter, some crucial problems in the study of the simultaneous acquisition of two languages will be examined. Do the different sentence structures develop along parallel lines in the two languages, or are some of these structures, being more difficult in one language than in the other, acquired later? How does the child's speech evolve, taking him gradually from single words to speech which resembles more and more that of adults?[1] Is this evolution of sentence structure the same in monolingual as in bilingual children?

In order to answer these questions, I analyzed two different sides of Lisa's and Giulia's speech: a) the evolution of sentence structure, which is discussed in this chapter, and b) the development of a series of morphological and syntactic aspects, which are discussed in the following chapter.[2]

In this chapter, Lisa's and Giulia's sentences are analyzed from the one-word stage until the point at which complex sentences began to appear. With Lisa this was from the ages of about 19 months to 40 months, and with Giulia

---

1  Brown [1979, p. 87] writes that "the order of development ... is first of all determined by the relative semantic and grammatical complexity of the constructions".

2  Here we are dealing with Brown's distinction between elements with "more" or "less" content. Brown called the elements with more content "fundamental relations", which not only include content words such as nouns, verbs, and adjectives, but also other categories usually considered functors. The elements with less content are the modulations of meaning, i.e., all the categories which do not belong to the fundamental relations and which Brown believes to be the fourteen morphemes described in his book. Brown's fundamental relations have several aspects in common with our structural analysis of the sentence, and his modulations of meaning coincide at times with our syntactic – morphological analysis. At any rate, Brown applied the criteria of fundamental relations only to the first stage in his classification, and not to the other four. From the second stage to the fifth, Brown analyzed the modulations of meaning in the chronological succession in which they were acquired by the children he studied.

from about 14 months to 36 months. The sentences of two monolingual German children, Jana and Oliver, and two monolingual Italian children, Sara and Francesco, were also analyzed during about the same period of linguistic development and age.

The method of data collection used for the monolingual children was the same as that used for bilinguals: recordings were made in the child's natural setting. This made it possible to compare the two groups.

## 3.1 Sentence Structure Analysis

The method of analysis used here belongs among those language analyses in which the predicate, i.e., the verb, is considered the center of sentence structure [see Kalepky, 1928; Regula, 1951; Glinz, 1961]; in more traditional analyses, this role is assigned to the subject, or to the subject and predicate. The works of Helbig and Schenkel [1969] and Parisi and Antinucci [1973] were of great assistance in this study.

Helbig and Schenkel [1969] described, modified and amplified Tesnière's structural analysis of sentences [1953]. In this analysis, Tesnière had introduced to linguistics the fundamental concept of "verb valence," a concept which is used widely in this study. In particular, Helbig and Schenkel analyzed about 500 German verbs, describing the number and nature of the semantic and syntactic valences for each one. (For an interesting look at the development of the concept of verb valence in German, see Helbig and Schenkel [1969, Introduction]).

In Parisi and Antinucci [1973], the predicate does not always coincide with the verb, but is is defined as that element in the sentence which holds all the other elements together; in other words, it determines the number and type of semantic relations in the sentence. Parisi and Antinucci analyzed a small number of sentence structures in adult speech and applied their model to child speech, albeit only partially (see Antinucci and Volterra [1973], Parisi and Gianelli [1974], Bates et al. [1975]). Generally speaking, the different sentence structures which will be described here are those described by Parisi and Antinucci, but this does not mean that the background of generative semantic theory formulated in their work has been adopted here.

This type of sentence analysis was chosen primarily because an instrument was needed which would permit the development of speech to be observed as it progressed from the single word, became more and more complex, and finally resembled adult speech. For this reason it was not possible to use pivot grammar, which does not go beyond the 2- or 3-word stage [Braine, 1963]. For the same reasons, it would not have been sufficient to give even the most careful description of telegraphic speech [Fodor and Bever, 1965; Ervin and Miller, 1964].[3]

---

3 For other studies which analyze all speech of the child for a relatively brief period, see Greenfield and Smith [1976], Camaioni et al. [1976], Wong-Fillmore [1976], Braine [1976], Ochs [1979a].

In addition, it was necessary to conduct an analysis of all of the child's utterances; most studies on child speech have analyzed merely one aspect of speech, such as the development of negatives or relative sentences.[4]

### 3.1.1 The Nuclear Sentence

A sentence is a combination of words which symbolizes events, actions, people, objects, etc.[5] But this combination cannot be entirely random; the words must have a specific relationship to one another. The word which establishes this relationship is called the predicate, and all other elements in the sentence are called arguments. A sentence composed of a predicate and its arguments is called a simple nuclear sentence.

The concept of the argument comes out of the awareness that words belonging to a certain category, i.e., the predicate, open up one or more free spaces near them which are filled by other categories of words [Bühler, 1934]. Thus it is the predicate, or, to be more precise, its meaning, that determines the number and type of relationships between the other elements, and it follows that a predicate may have one or more arguments.

Let us take the predicate "to put" as an example. Its use requires three arguments: who puts, what that person puts, and where that person puts it. In the sentence, "I put the care here", these three arguments are "I", "car", and "here". On the other hand, the predicate "to have" requires two arguments: who has and what is had, i.e., "I" and "pencil" in the sentence, "I have the pencil".

The specific meaning of the predicate determines how many different arguments it requires. Some predicates have not only obligatory arguments, but optional ones as well. For example, in "Mary is reading a book," the predicate "to read" requires only one argument, and that is the person who is reading. What is being read, in this case a book, is an optional argument for the predicate "to read". The decision as to how many arguments are required by each predicate was based upon Helbig and Schenkel's list of verbs and their relative valences, and upon a test by elimination. For example, the sentences, "I put here" and "I put the car" are incomplete because one of the required arguments is missing. Thus, if an element is deleted from the minimal or nuclear sentence, the sentence becomes incomplete. The criteria used in classifying nuclear sentences were as follows:

An incomplete nuclear sentence is one which has no predicate, or lacks one or more arguments (see the columns for complete and incomplete nuclear sentences in Tables 3.1, 2, pp. 64 – 74). The missing elements have been drawn up on the basis of "rich interpretation" [Brown, 1979], in which the researcher uses the context to understand the meaning of the child's utterance.

---

4 For examples, see the studies of Grimm et al. [1975], Cazden [1972], Roeper [1973], Ramge [1975], Antinucci and Volterra [1973], Nelson [1977], Volterra et al. [1979], Karmiloff-Smith [1979a].

5 The definitions used here have been taken from Taeschner et al. [1982].

A complete nuclear sentence is one in which the predicate and all of its required arguments are expressed. If an optional argument is missing, the sentence is still considered complete unless the context specifically requires that argument.

Other studies have shown that during the initial period, the child uses each verb in only one tense and person rather than conjugating it. Examples are: *amo*, a corruption of *andiamo* ("let's go") for "to go", *voio*, a corruption of *voglio* ("I want") for "to want" and *pendi*, i.e., *prendi* ("you take") for "to take". This practice is semantically independent of person or tense. The child is still absorbing the lexical elements of adult speech without analyzing them, and thus produces sentences such as:

**G** (1;8): *Acqua vuoi.* (Water [you] want.)

Here Giulia used the second person singular present indicative of the verb *volere*, even though it was she who wanted the water.

For this reason, sentences with one argument morphologically incorporated into the verb were also considered incomplete. However, in Italian and German it is often correct not to state the pronoun which corresponds to the conjugated verb; such sentences have been marked with a plus sign ( + ). But these elisions do not always correspond in the two languages, and thus the Italian sentence *Voglio bere* ("I want to drink") is marked with ( + ), while the German equivalent, *Will trinken*, is not, because here the German requires explicit mention of the person: *Ich will trinken*. On the other hand, the Italian *Guarda là* ("Look there") and its German equivalent, *Guck dahin*, are both marked with ( + ), because they are both grammatically correct.

It is important to emphasize here that the sentences have not been classified as complete or incomplete on the basis of their communicability, inasmuch as the sentences were completed by the adult and were often more effective for that particular interaction than a complete utterance would have been. Rather, the sentences were classified based on the fact that the child was not yet constructing the entire utterance by himself, as is later the case with complete sentences.

### 3.1.2 The Amplified Nuclear Sentence

Any sentence which contains one or more elements not called for by the meaning of the predicate has been termed amplified. The amplified sentence gives added information with respect to the simple nuclear sentence. These added elements may refer to the predicate and thus to the whole nuclear sentence, or they may refer only to one of the arguments. For example, in

*Mò ti dò uno schiaffo.* (Now I'm going to slap you.)

the word *mò* ("now") is not required by the predicate *dare* ("to give"), which has three arguments: who gives, what is given, and to whom it is given. In the example

*Ho toccato la macchina di zia Teta.* (I touched Aunt Teta's car.)

*di zia Teta* ("Aunt Teta's") is extra information with respect to the argument *macchina* ("car"), and is not required by the predicate *toccare* ("to touch").

Amplified sentences have been classified as complete or incomplete based on the same criteria as those used for nuclear sentences (see Tables 3.3, 4, pp. 74 – 84).[6]

### 3.1.3 The Complex Nuclear Sentence

The complex nuclear sentence includes two types of structures: inserted and relative phrases. In inserted constructions, one predicate argument is a phrase. In relative sentences, an amplified element is a phrase.

The inserted structure can be presented in implicit form:

*Io vado a prendere la torta.* (I'm going to get the cake.)

Here *a prendere la torta* ("to get the cake") is one of the arguments of the predicate *andare* ("to go"). The inserted structure can also appear in explicit form:

*Guarda Alessandra io che faccio co' a macchina bianca.* (Look, Alessandra, what I'm doing with the white car.)

---

6 It is important not to call some nuclear structures amplifield incomplete sentences merely because they contain an adjective or adverb. Sentences such as a) *Più qui.* ("no more here."); b) *Ancora acqua.* ("More water".); c) *Adesso Giulia.* ("Now Giulia".); d) *Altro libro.* ("Other book".); and e) *Solo scarpe.* ("Only shoes".) are all nuclear structures. They do not meet the criteria for amplified structures, which is that of supplying more information than would be supplied in the nuclear structure. Every amplified structure may be dismantled into at least two nuclear sentences. For instance:

|  |  |
|---|---|
| *Io mangio ancora caramelle.*<br>(I eat more candies.) | [*Io mangio caramelle.*<br>[(I eat candies.)<br>[<br>[*Io ancora caramelle.*<br>[(I more candies.) |
| *Vedo un bel fiore.*<br>(I see a beautiful flower.) | [*Vedo un fiore.*<br>[(I see a flower.)<br>[<br>[*Il fiore è bello.*<br>[(The flower is beautiful.) |

Because the predicate is not necessarily considered a verb, but may be any word which establishes a relationship between the elements of the sentence, words such as "more", "no more", "still", "now", and "other" can act as predicates in the sentences above. In fact, underlying the words "more", "also", "other" and "only" is the ability to identify quantity, which Parisi and Antinucci [1973, pp. 212 – 217] call the "add" component. The word "no more" stands for the component of nonexistence, and "now" stands for "it's so-and-so's turn".

*Io che faccio co' a macchina bianca* is the argument of the predicate *guardare* ("to look").

An example of a relative sentence is:

*Questa è la mucca che fa mù.* (This is the cow that says "moo".)

Here *che fa mù* ("that says moo") is added information with respect to the nuclear sentence, *Questa è la mucca.*

As regards completeness or incompleteness, elements either can or cannot be omitted from complex sentences, depending upon whether they are arguments or predicates. Inserted complex sentences are considered incomplete here when one or more arguments are missing. The predicate of inserted and nuclear sentences cannot be omitted, because the sentence would then not be recognized as complex. For example:

*Io voglio la mela.* (I want the apple.)

is a simple nuclear sentence and not an implicit inserted one in which the predicate *mangiare* ("to eat") or *possedere* ("to possess") is missing.

A relative complex sentence is considered incomplete when the predicate or one argument of the nuclear sentence, or both, are missing. However, it is impossible not to have the argument of the nuclear sentence referred to by the amplified element that has become a relative sentence. For instance

*La mela che è rossa.* (The apple which is red.)

is an incomplete relative sentence, while

*Io prendo la mela che è rossa.* (I'm taking the apple which is red.)

is considered complete. Complex sentences which use the connective are marked with the letter 0 (see Tables 3.5 – 10, pp. 84 – 91).

### 3.1.4 Binuclear Sentences

Sentences with two nuclear structures are here termed binuclear. In binuclear sentences, the two sentence structures are not interlocked as in complex nuclear sentences, but rather are found in coordinate or subordinate form. Thus,

*Io porto la macchina dell'omino e passo co' l'aereo.* (I'm taking the little man's car and passing with the plane.)

is a binuclear coordinated sentence, whereas

*Quando un bambino [r]ompe la macchina lo caccio via così.* (When a child breaks the car I throw him out like this.)

is two nuclear sentences joined by a relationship of subordination.

**Table 3.1.** Incomplete (I) and complete (C) nuclear sentences produced by Lisa from the age of 1 year and 7 months to the age of 3 years and 4 months[a]

| Column A Italian | I | C | Column B German | I | C | Column C Mixed | I | C |
|---|---|---|---|---|---|---|---|---|
| 1st stage | | | | | | | | |
| | | | | | | | | |
| 1;7 | | | 1;7 | | | 1;7 | | |
| È tata | × | | Buch eh Lia | × | | Nyam lata | × | |
| Chiu Mamma | × | | Kita Giulia | × | | Lade cacaca | × | |
| Nochiu tata | × | | Giuia upa | × | | Da dita | × | |
| Cheo qui | × | | | | | | | |
| Caa Giulia | × | | | | | | | |
| Giulia è caa | × | | | | | | | |
| Più qui | | × | | | | | | |
| Più iaia eh! | | × | | | | | | |
| Più lata | | × | | | | | | |
| | | | | | | | | |
| 1;8 | | | 1;8 | | | 1;8 | | |
| Caa gatta | × | | Lia Buch | × | | | | |
| E' Giulia | × | | Buch da | × | | | | |
| E' vuu | × | | | | | | | |
| | | | | | | | | |
| 1;9 | | | 1;9 | | | 1;9 | | |
| E' mamma? | × | | Daki Buch | × | | Daki io | × | |
| E' bubu | × | | Da Blume | × | | Tita daki | × | |
| Tita, è tita | × | | Giulia Beine | × | | Nyam lade | × | |
| Non è qua | × | | Nina Buch | × | | Caca Giulia | × | |
| E' miao | × | | Beine Paola | × | | Daki lata | × | |
| E' lalla | × | | O id Giulia? | | × | Balle nyam nyam | × | |
| Qui mamma | × | | | | | Miau nyam nyam | × | |
| Dove è pappa? | | × | | | | Nyam late miao | | × |
| Tata è bum | | × | | | | E' la nyam nyam | | × |
| Balle più | | × | | | | | | |
| Chio io | × | | | | | | | |
| Più latta | | × | | | | | | |
| Bu più | | × | | | | | | |
| Coa chea | × | | | | | | | |
| | | | | | | | | |
| 1;10 | | | 1;10 | | | 1;10 | | |
| Tu mamma | × | | Das ist Giulia | | × | Daki lolo | × | |
| Tu Lisa | × | | Das ist miao | | × | Mamma, Lia miao | × | |
| Qui miao | × | | | | | Qui tutta | × | |
| Caca chea | × | | | | | De la nyam nyam | × | |
| Catta a Giulia | × | | | | | | | |
| La tita Giulia | × | | | | | | | |
| Tota a Giulia | × | | | | | | | |
| Bua tita | × | | | | | | | |
| Miao latte | × | | | | | | | |
| Miao bua | × | | | | | | | |
| Giulia da mamma | × | | | | | | | |

[a] In this and the following tables, a plus sign (+) is used to denote sentences in which the pronoun may correctly be omitted.

**Table 3.1** (continued)

| Column A Italian | I | C | Column B German | I | C | Column C Mixed | I | C |
|---|---|---|---|---|---|---|---|---|
| **1;10** | | | **1;10** | | | **1;10** | | |
| Da mamma | × | | | | | | | |
| Mamma bua popò | | × | | | | | | |
| Chio Giulia | × | | | | | | | |
| **2;0** | | | **2;0** | | | **2;0** | | |
| Tata è bum | | × | Da Ball | × | | Nyam nyam la pappa | × | |
| Giulia bua | × | | Mama Hals | × | | Daki Giulia atita | × | |
| Da Giulia la mamma | × | | Giulia Popo | × | | Daki eh Giulia tita | × | |
| Tatta latte chechea | × | | Ting Milch | × | | | | |
| Giulia fa | × | | Guck Ida (+) | × | | | | |
| Ti(ra) palle (+) | × | | Haia Mama | × | | | | |
| **2;3** | | | **2;3** | | | **2;3** | | |
| | | | Heuch mu (+) | × | | Gatto miao la Boot | × | |
| | | | Giulia sehn ja? | × | | Pastasciutta hier | | |
| | | | Guck Giulia | × | | pastasciutta | × | |
| | | | Giulia Gabel | × | | | | |
| | | | Pupi iatel | × | | | | |
| | | | Guck Buch | × | | | | |
| | | | Duck badi badi | × | | | | |
| | | | Anda Buch | × | | | | |

**2nd stage**

| Column A Italian | I | C | Column B German | I | C | Column C Mixed | I | C |
|---|---|---|---|---|---|---|---|---|
| **2;4** | | | **2;4** | | | **2;4** | | |
| Lisa cade no | | × | Lisa komm ida | | × | Lisa lo fa pesch | | × |
| Cosa c'è mamma? | | × | No no Giulia komm | | | Lisa haben la penna | | × |
| Giulia dillo: cocona | | × | ida | | × | Lisa sagt specchio | | × |
| La mamma c'è | | | Mama ist hier | | × | Giulia bua gemacht | | × |
| schitto | | × | Lisa macht ò | | × | Fa pili pilli no | × | |
| La panna è là su | | × | Komm her Giulia | | × | Sehen olologio | × | |
| Nan Nan Giulia fa | | × | Mami pilli pilli | | × | | | |
| Lisa va da la no | | × | Mami sitzi sitzi | | × | | | |
| Ada mammi ada | × | | Lisa mutsi macht | | × | | | |
| Lisa fatto | × | | Lisa sehen | × | | | | |
| Mette lì | × | | Lisa gemacht | × | | | | |
| Sono Lisa (+) | × | | Giulia sehen ja? | × | | | | |
| Itto Mammi? | × | | Mami nimm | × | | | | |
| Guarda Giulia | × | | Mami mach | × | | | | |
| Lascia penna li (+) | × | | | | | | | |
| **2;6** | | | **2;6** | | | **2;6** | | |
| Guarda Giulia (+) | × | | Lisa gemacht | × | | Fertig la mamma | × | |
| Fallo hophop (+) | × | | Fertig arbeit | × | | Mikrofon lascia | | |
| Visto Giulia? (+) | × | | Lisa macht Giulia | | × | lì (+) | × | |
| Guarda pipì (+) | × | | A Mami gemacht a | | | Papier, dovè Papier? | | × |
| Ho paura (+) | × | | Buch | | × | Dove è Mikofon? | | × |
| Paura Lisa | × | | Nein, Lisa arbeit | | × | | | |

**Table 3.1** (continued)

| Column A Italian | I | C | Column B German | I | C | Column C Mixed | I | C |
|---|---|---|---|---|---|---|---|---|
| 2;6 | | | 2;6 | | | 2;6 | | |
| Senti la musa? (+) | × | | Lisa arbeit ja? | | × | | | |
| Da bacetto | × | | Lisa hat Angst | | × | | | |
| Guarda bottone (+) | × | | Lisa sitzi | | × | | | |
| Bicicletta lascia lì | × | | | | | | | |
| Fale l'acqua | × | | | | | | | |
| Tieni la mano (+) | × | | | | | | | |
| Tieni Lisa (+) | × | | | | | | | |
| Dove è Papi? | | × | | | | | | |
| Dov'è la carta? | | × | | | | | | |
| Lisa legge | | × | | | | | | |
| Lisa tocca Miao | | × | | | | | | |
| Cosa fa la musa? | | × | | | | | | |
| Come fa la musa? | | × | | | | | | |
| Lisa fa batti | | × | | | | | | |
| Quello è la donna | | × | | | | | | |
| Quetto è Mammili | | × | | | | | | |
| Quetto è Papi | | × | | | | | | |
| Quetto è un uomo | | × | | | | | | |
| Itto Papi Giulia? | | × | | | | | | |
| 2;8 | | | 2;8 | | | 2;8 | | |
| Quetto fa fatina | | × | Giulia sagt Taute | × | | Quella à kaputt | | × |
| Quetto è bambola | | × | Lisa sagt Musaka | × | | Fa badi badi Boot | | × |
| Quetto è mio | | × | Mama komm | × | | Lisa fa sitzi sitzi | | × |
| Quetto è tuo no | | × | Lisa kommt | × | | Quello è Vogel | | × |
| Cosa è quello? | | × | Lisa spicht, OK? | × | | Quetto non è Telling | | × |
| Cosa è rosso? | | × | Was macht Schwein? | × | | Quetto fa pilli pilli | | × |
| Mamma, Lisa vado di là sì? | | × | Lisa arbeit | × | | Cosa fa Schwein? | | × |
| Lisa clive? | | × | | | | Dov'è Garten? | | × |
| Barchetta fatto Lisa | | × | | | | Quella è Berlin | | × |
| Pallone gioca Lisa | | × | | | | Cosè tantanzi? | | × |
| Quella è la casetta | | × | | | | Quello fa tantanzi | | × |
| Quella piange | | × | | | | Quello fa badi badi | | × |
| Mamma guarda il vento | | × | | | | Quello è Baum | | × |
| Lisa vuole pantaloni | | × | | | | Ein Boot, la barca fa badi badi | | × |
| Quella è autobus | | × | | | | Fa badi badi la barca | | × |
| Taute è tonata | | × | | | | Landkarte sagt: Natale a Roma | | × |
| Quella è la musica | | × | | | | Kein giogioletto kaputt nein | × | |
| Quello non è la bottiglia | | × | | | | Cecae Heft si? | × | |
| Quella è bichele | | × | | | | | | |
| Quello mangia pane | | × | | | | | | |
| E' bichele quello | | × | | | | | | |
| Quella è Mamma | | × | | | | | | |
| Lisa penda gionale | | × | | | | | | |
| Quella è blutto | | × | | | | | | |

**Table 3.1** (continued)

| Column A<br>Italian | I | C | Column B<br>German | I | C | Column C<br>Mixed | I | C |
|---|---|---|---|---|---|---|---|---|
| 2;8 | | | 2;8 | | | 2;8 | | |
| Quello è museo | | × | | | | | | |
| Quello è la bimba | | × | | | | | | |
| Quello è un nonno? | | × | | | | | | |
| Pende la medicina Taute | | × | | | | | | |
| Lisa ha feddo | | × | | | | | | |
| Dove sono le gambe? | | × | | | | | | |
| E' teno | × | | | | | | | |
| E' fafalla | × | | | | | | | |
| Lisa dà bacetto | × | | | | | | | |
| Fa la barchetta si? | × | | | | | | | |
| Non fa totò no | × | | | | | | | |
| Mammi andiamo di là (+) | × | | | | | | | |
| La bua ce l'ha (+) | × | | | | | | | |
| Guada aeoplano (+) | × | | | | | | | |
| | | | | | | | | |
| 2;10 | | | 2;10 | | | 2;10 | | |
| Chiudi capuccio (+) | × | | Lisa gegeben | × | | Dovè Jacke? | | × |
| Fa la nina | × | | Lisa gesuchen | × | | Lisa fa sitzi sitzi | | × |
| Ricordi il nonno? (+) | × | | Lisa spricht Mama | | × | Quello è Teller | | × |
| Mamma guarda | × | | Was macht das Schwein? | | × | Teller casca | | × |
| Guarda mamma | × | | Lisa macht die Sonne | | × | Quetta è Schwein | | × |
| Lascia là | × | | | | | Quetto gemacht Lisa | | × |
| Ha fatto la bua | × | | | | | Lisa fa die Sonne | | × |
| Gioca la palla | × | | | | | Fa badi badi | | |
| Lisa cercato | × | | | | | Mädchen | | × |
| Lisa dormito | | × | | | | Il Wolf non c'è | | × |
| Giulia gioca con la scarpa | | × | | | | Quella son Schwein | | × |
| Quetto è sporco | | × | | | | Questa è Baum | | × |
| Ha fatto mamma la medicina | | × | | | | Schwein prende la mela | | × |
| Tutto s'era rotto | | × | | | | | | |
| Lisa fa sole | | × | | | | | | |
| La donna fa bum | | × | | | | | | |
| Dove è la donna? | | × | | | | | | |
| Cosa ha fatto Mammi, eh? | | × | | | | | | |
| La butto io | | × | | | | | | |
| Quetto ha fatto bua Lisa | | × | | | | | | |
| Mammi ape la porta | | × | | | | | | |
| Parla con Lisa Giulia | | × | | | | | | |
| Cosa è questa? | | × | | | | | | |
| Questa è di Giulia | | × | | | | | | |
| E' bella la casetta | | × | | | | | | |
| Lisa andare la casetta | | × | | | | | | |

**Table 3.1** (continued)

| Column A<br>Italian | I | C | Column B<br>German | I | C | Column C<br>Mixed | I | C |
|---|---|---|---|---|---|---|---|---|
| 2;10 | | | 2;10 | | | 2;10 | | |
| Questo è una porta | | × | | | | | | |
| Quetta è la porta | | × | | | | | | |
| Quetto suona | | × | | | | | | |
| Dove è măe? | | × | | | | | | |
| | | | | | | | | |
| 3;0 | | | 3;0 | | | 3;0 | | |
| Non c'è Giulia | | × | Wo ist der Sand? | | × | Giulia is uscire | | × |
| Chi è quello? | | × | Wo ist das Meer? | | × | Cosa è geschrieben? | | × |
| Quetto chi è? | | × | Lisa spielt | | × | Lisa fa pilli pilli | | × |
| Qui è sette? | | × | Der weint | | × | Cosa schreibt Mami? | | × |
| Papà prende pallone | | × | Lisa hat Hunger | | × | Giulia hat ausbevuto | | × |
| Cosa fatto tu? | | × | Lisa friert | | × | | | |
| Lisa fa chiude | | × | Lisa Spielsachen | | | | | |
| Papi si arrabbia si? | | × | bring | | × | | | |
| Lisa fa un bagno | | × | Das ist Piegel | | × | | | |
| Lisa vuoi bene a | | | Die Strümpfe ist im | | | | | |
| Mamma? | | × | Schrank ja Mami? | | × | | | |
| Giulia se l'ha togliata | | × | Lisa zumachen | × | | | | |
| Cosa scrive Mammi? | | × | | | | | | |
| Si dice vieni | | × | | | | | | |
| Lisa ha tolto | × | | | | | | | |
| Piange | × | | | | | | | |
| Di Lisa sono | × | | | | | | | |
| Cià chiaciato piede | × | | | | | | | |

3rd stage

| 3;2 | | | 3;2 | | | 3;2 | | |
|---|---|---|---|---|---|---|---|---|
| Un buco è | × | | Lisa gibt | × | | Lisa hat eine Fritate | | |
| Andiamo da Paola | | | Lisa macht | × | | gemacht | | × |
| sì? (+) | × | | Lisa gemacht | × | | Io lo dà für Mami | | × |
| Mi fai una | | | Nich Brot gegessen | × | | | | |
| casetta? (+) | × | | Hintun hier | × | | | | |
| Mettilo lì (+) | × | | Mami guck da | | × | | | |
| La telline si chia- | | | Wo ist Kitty? | | × | | | |
| mano le conchiglie | | × | Lisa is klein | | × | | | |
| Dovè Kitty? | | × | Lisa is munter | | × | | | |
| Me lo dai questo? | | × | Ist Papi gekommen | | × | | | |
| Nonna andata in | | | Nein, Papi ist nicht | | | | | |
| Verona | | × | hier drinne | | × | | | |
| Giulia ha rotto il | | | | | | | | |
| cavallo | | × | | | | | | |
| Papi comprare malo- | | | | | | | | |
| lino | | × | | | | | | |
| Questi sono grandi | | × | | | | | | |
| E' Giulia così | | × | | | | | | |

**Table 3.1** (continued)

| Column A Italian | I | C | Column B German | I | C | Column C Mixed | I | C |
|---|---|---|---|---|---|---|---|---|
| 3;4 | | | 3;4 | | | 3;4 | | |
| Che fai tu Mammi? | | × | Das Schwein weint | | × | Lisa hat kein Topo- | | |
| Questi sono i botini | | × | Im Haiabettchen ist | | | lino | | × |
| Mammi conta una fa | | | das Buch | | × | Lisa hat botini | | × |
| vola dai Mammi | | × | Das ist der Himmel | | × | Grembiulino hat | | |
| Mami, cosa sono io? | | × | Lisa zeigt dich | | × | Knöpfe | | × |
| Guarda là in fondo | | | Lisa hat nich Haare | | × | Teddybear und Lisa | | |
| Mammi | | × | Lisa hat nicht ge- | | | fa ninaò | | × |
| Guarda nell'angolo | | | sehen Frau Rieti | | × | Quella è Strasse | | × |
| Giulia | | × | Ich nicht bin müde | | × | Die Boote macht così | | × |
| Io lo do a Sara | | × | Ist nicht da ein Pinzel | | × | | | |
| Sono duri questi | | × | Teddybear hat ge- | | | | | |
| Dove sono i gelati? | | × | spuken | | × | | | |
| Cosa è successo? | | × | Ich hab ein Spuk | | | | | |
| Giulia gioca con Sara | | × | gemacht | | × | | | |
| Cosa state facendo? | | × | Wer macht uhu? | | × | | | |
| La maestra ha preso | | | Mami erzählt eine | | | | | |
| una bambola | | × | Geschichte ja? | | × | | | |
| Lisa è più grande di | | | Lisa hat die Tür | | | | | |
| Sara | | × | zugemacht | | × | | | |
| Hai visto il diri- | | | Das ist grün | | × | | | |
| gibile? | × | | Der Mann gibt Briefe | | | | | |
| Fa la nanna | × | | für Lotte | | × | | | |
| Lisa ha mettato lì | × | | Ein Zicklein hat der | | | | | |
| Cuocere le pere | | × | Bat | | × | | | |
| | | | Die sind bei Janko | | × | | | |
| | | | Was macht der Janko | | | | | |
| | | | und Zicklein? | | × | | | |
| | | | Da geht Mami | | × | | | |
| | | | Kommt Micki Maus | | × | | | |
| | | | Tuh da auf | | | | | |
| | | | Decke (+) | × | | | | |
| | | | Guck rot (+) | × | | | | |
| | | | Lisa zeigt dich ja? | × | | | | |
| | | | Ja war gestern | × | | | | |
| | | | So Mami Lisa macht | | × | | | |
| | | | Mami hat so gemacht | | × | | | |
| | | | Taute macht so | | × | | | |

**Table 3.2.** Incomplete (I) and complete (C) nuclear sentences produced by Giulia from the age of 1 year and 2 months to the age of 3 years

| Column A Italian | I | C | Column B German | I | C | Column C Mixed | I | C |
|---|---|---|---|---|---|---|---|---|
| **1st stage** | | | | | | | | |
| 1;2 | | | 1;2 | | | 1;2 | | |
| Iaia cade | | × | Da sitzi | × | | | | |
| Cade Giulia | | × | | | | | | |
| 1;3 | | | 1;3 | | | 1;3 | | |
| | | | Julia Haus | × | | Datsie Bonbon | × | |
| | | | | | | Da Bonbon | × | |
| 1;5 | | | 1;5 | | | 1;5 | | |
| Fa bibi | × | | Da sitze | × | | | | |
| | | | A Bu (ch) fertig | × | | | | |
| | | | Aizi wo? | × | | | | |
| | | | Buch Mami | × | | | | |
| 1;6 | | | 1;6 | | | 1;6 | | |
| La cucu Mamma | × | | Mama wo? | × | | | | |
| A bata mu | | × | | | | | | |
| 1;7 | | | 1;7 | | | 1;7 | | |
| Ese zitta | × | | Wauwau böse | × | | Badi badi la | × | |
| Mamma tita | × | | Mami arbeit | × | | | | |
| | | | Giulia Eis | × | | | | |
| | | | Plina arbeit | × | | | | |
| | | | Wo auch? | × | | | | |
| **2nd stage** | | | | | | | | |
| 1;8 | | | 1;8 | | | 1;8 | | |
| Galato a Nonna | × | | Gos Fisch | × | | Via Haale | × | |
| E' tuo bambola | × | | Klein Babau | × | | Gos la pappa | × | |
| Acqua vuoi | × | | N Giulia Boot | × | | Mamma guck: la | | |
| Baubau via | × | | Gos Teller | × | |  mamma | | × |
| Baubau pappa | × | | Julia Buch | × | | Ancora bonbon | × | |
| Glande plano | × | | Buch Giulia | × | | | | |
| Via Baubau | × | | Guch Teller (+) | × | | | | |
| A pedi Giulia | × | | Noch mehr a Teller | × | | | | |
| Butta a tita | × | | Ander Teller | × | | | | |
| Mae qui | × | | Auch Giulia Daumen | | × | | | |
| Pende a tita | × | | | | | | | |
| A mano Antonio | × | | | | | | | |
| Pentola vedi | × | | | | | | | |
| Auto a Vanna | × | | | | | | | |
| mbaca a Giulia | × | | | | | | | |
| Io sono Lisa | | × | | | | | | |
| Cade Giulia | | × | | | | | | |
| Antonio è blutto | | × | | | | | | |
| Ancoa acqua | × | | | | | | | |

**Table 3.2** (continued)

| Column A Italian | I | C | Column B German | I | C | Column C Mixed | I | C |
|---|---|---|---|---|---|---|---|---|
| 1;8 | | | 1;8 | | | 1;8 | | |
| E due alanci | × | | | | | | | |
| Solo afante | × | | | | | | | |
| Mucca anche popò | | × | | | | | | |
| | | | | | | | | |
| 1;9 | | | 1;9 | | | 1;9 | | |
| Julia a butta hm? | × | | Giulia böse | × | | Quetta Augen | × | |
| Giulia alabbia booo | × | | Das hier Hund | × | | Hose quetta | × | |
| Tatoa quetta | × | | Klein klein Babau | × | | Quetta Schwein | × | |
| Mammi mette? | × | | Schuhe anziehen | × | | Badibadi quetta | × | |
| Julia cerca | × | | Giulia macht | × | | Hut chiama | × | |
| Capse chiama | × | | Mama macht | × | | Quetta Stuhl | × | |
| Damelo (+) | × | | Giulia Küche | × | | Sono Birne | × | |
| Vuoi mela | × | | Mama anziehen | × | | Macht guida, fährt | × | |
| E' dulo | × | | Gos a Mama | × | | Sagt tutto tutto | × | |
| Mo(r)to Chichi | × | | Stümpfe aus | × | | Haiabette chiama | × | |
| Momò fa | × | | Weg Haare | | × | Löwe allà Leche | | × |
| E' sopla | × | | Mama Giulia schleibi | | × | Schweine allà | | |
| Tocca no pipì no | × | | Alli Alli sagt Nonna | | × | Schwanz | | × |
| Attua chiama | × | | Mama sitzi | | × | Haiabett c'è | | × |
| Quetto popò | × | | Sitzi da | × | | C'è Schukuchuku- | | |
| Popò chiama | × | | Sitzi Haiabettchen | × | | giam | | × |
| Julia a penda | × | | Kinder auch | × | | E' la Blume, è là | | × |
| Quetto libo | × | | Auch Clistina | × | | A Schuhe a nè | | × |
| Quetta è mamma | | × | Auch Lisa popò | | × | Anche Schuku- | | |
| Julia a penda hm? | | | | | | schukugiam | × | |
| Afante a penda | | × | | | | Solo Schuhe | × | |
| Allà a nenni a Giulia | | × | | | | Tutte e due Fisch | × | |
| Attona Papi attona | | × | | | | Afante a nanna | | |
| C'è a gonna | | × | | | | Haiabettchen | | × |
| Flanca è mucca | × | | | | | Anch'io Giulia Kopf | | × |
| Ancoa piedini | × | | | | | | | |
| Solo babau | × | | | | | | | |
| | | | | | | | | |
| 1;11 | | | 1;11 | | | 1;11 | | |
| Cocò bello | × | | Mama pilli pilli? | × | | Giulia sagt subito | | × |
| Capello a Giulia | × | | Cocò hässlich | × | | Dove è Null | | × |
| Giulia fa | × | | Schleife binden | × | | Quetta è Null | | × |
| Mamma tieni | × | | Mama nimm | × | | Anche quetta Zähne | | × |
| Buttala a mamma | | × | Lisa gibt a Buch a | | | Anche quetta Schuhe | | × |
| Giulia fa anza | | × | Mama | | × | | | |
| Dov'è Giulia? | | × | Mami hol a Stuhl | | × | | | |
| | | | | | | | | |
| 2;2 | | | 2;2 | | | 2;2 | | |
| Giulia non se passa | | × | Giulia erzählen | × | | E' eine Klammer | × | |
| Giulia ha dormito | | × | Kaki machen | × | | Mettela die | | |
| Pala dentlo? | × | | Guck die | | | Tasche (+) | × | |
| Mammi aple? | × | | Tasche (+) | × | | Giulia mettela li | | |
| Giulia fa una capiola | | × | Guck Teppich (+) | × | | getan | | × |

**Table 3.2** (continued)

| Column A<br>Italian | I | C | Column B<br>German | I | C | Column C<br>Mixed | I | C |
|---|---|---|---|---|---|---|---|---|
| 2;2 | | | 2;2 | | | 2;2 | | |
| Giulia fa la po(r)ta | | × | Mami macht nyam | | | Dove è ein Kissen? | | × |
| Io ce(r)co | × | | nyam? | | × | Giulia fa Teppich | | × |
| No, Giulia conta una | | | Mami macht kully | | | Mami fa badi badi | | × |
| favola | | × | kully | | × | Dovè Tasche? | | × |
| Uno fa signora! | | × | Mami und Giulia lest | | | Lein pala | × | |
| Fa dindon | × | | ja? | | × | | | |
| | | | Das hier ist kaputt | | × | | | |
| | | | Giulia nicht spuken | | × | | | |
| | | | Mami guck a böse | | | | | |
| | | | Wolf | | × | | | |
| | | | Mami geht zuhause? | | × | | | |
| | | | Ein Babyli tinki tinki | | × | | | |
| | | | Giulia Paola bleiben | | × | | | |
| | | | Giulia bleibt mit | | | | | |
| | | | Paola | | × | | | |
| | | | Giulia nicht Blot | | | | | |
| | | | essen | | × | | | |

3rd stage

| Column A<br>Italian | I | C | Column B<br>German | I | C | Column C<br>Mixed | I | C |
|---|---|---|---|---|---|---|---|---|
| 2;4 | | | 2;4 | | | 2;4 | | |
| Hai visto Mammi? | × | | Guck Babau (+) | × | | Dove è soviele? | | × |
| Mangia una pecorella | × | | Babau guck (+) | × | | Mi dai de Blei- | | |
| Non si mangia | × | | Ich nimm de Babau | | × | stift? (+) | × | |
| Mammi aple | × | | Will die Mami | × | | Mi dai de Blatt? (+) | × | |
| E' la bilancia | × | | Ich will de Bleistift? | | × | Chiude Mund | × | |
| E' il bambolotto | × | | Ich schleib | | × | Tute e due hat de | | |
| Giocava con la porta | × | | Auch Giulia | × | | Stlenfe | | × |
| Si chiama per Lisa | × | | Ich hat Zunge | | × | Die Schleife fo (+) | × | |
| E' il lupo | × | | Babau anfassen die | | | | | |
| E' l'orso | × | | Zunge | | × | | | |
| E' bambi | × | | Guck de Locken (+) | × | | | | |
| Giocarala si chiama | × | | Ist gros Giulia | | × | | | |
| Quetto è buono | | × | Giulia ist klein | | × | | | |
| Quetto parla no | | × | Ich hat die Stlenfe | | × | | | |
| Hai visto mammi? | | | | | | | | |
| Hai visto una pupi? | | × | | | | | | |
| Giulia ha fatto ble | | × | | | | | | |
| Quello fa prrr prrr | | × | | | | | | |
| Lisa ha dato totò al | | | | | | | | |
| lupo | | × | | | | | | |
| Cosa è quello? | | × | | | | | | |
| Quello fa un cavallo | | × | | | | | | |
| Quello non è la coda | | × | | | | | | |
| Quello cià una barca | | × | | | | | | |
| Io faccio una pupi | | × | | | | | | |
| Papi l'aggiusta | | × | | | | | | |
| Io sono Luca | | × | | | | | | |

**Table 3.2** (continued)

| Column A Italian | I | C | Column B German | I | C | Column C Mixed | I | C |
|---|---|---|---|---|---|---|---|---|
| 2;4 | | | 2;4 | | | 2;4 | | |
| Quetta è di Lisa | | × | | | | | | |
| Quello è Bambi | | × | | | | | | |
| Quello è una donna | | × | | | | | | |
| Io sono Monica | | × | | | | | | |
| Io sono caduta | | × | | | | | | |
| Guarda Lisa la scatola | | × | | | | | | |
| Cosa ha fatto Luca? | | × | | | | | | |
| 2;6 | | | 2;6 | | | 2;6 | | |
| Io sono piccola | | × | Ja ist hübsch | × | | Hat guance | × | |
| Ecco! Giulia c'era | | × | Macht nyam nyam | × | | Guarda das Männlein (+) | × | |
| Quello cià baffi | | × | Macht plipli | × | | Vuoi ein petenino (+) | × | |
| Cosa c'era lì? | | × | Hab Spukerei gemacht | × | | Hast du getolto mami? | × | |
| Quello mangia | | × | Mami ich bin Giulia | | × | Questo is ein pallone | | × |
| Donald Duck cià un pesce | | × | Ich bin klein | | × | | | |
| Quello cià una spatola | | × | Ich sprich auf deutsch | | × | | | |
| Cosa c'era lì? | | × | Was ist diese? | | × | | | |
| Questo è un pallone | | × | Ich bin Monica | | × | | | |
| Papi è andata and'asilo | | × | Ich schreib | | × | | | |
| On cià le gambe | × | | Was machst du? | | × | | | |
| Guarda lì (+) | × | | Das ist kakaka | | × | | | |
| Guardami (+) | × | | Der ist kaputt | | × | | | |
| | | | Des is für Mami | | × | | | |
| | | | Mami noch mehr ein Blatt? | | × | | | |
| 2;8 | | | 2;8 | | | 2;8 | | |
| Mi accompagni? | × | | Guch die Sonne (+) | × | | Macht eine Madonnina | × | |
| Andava allo scivolo | × | | Papi guck | × | | Io ho gevinto | | × |
| Ho mangiato rotondo (+) | × | | Hat ein anderes (+) | × | | Das is fine | | × |
| Soni bagnati | × | | Spieln mitn Besen | × | | Giulia hat gescappa in Bett | | × |
| Sono qua (+) | × | | Giulia hat gesagt | × | | | | |
| Io tuo è marrone | | × | Hast verstanden? | × | | | | |
| Fiorellino gioca con te | | × | Diese ich will | | × | | | |
| Mammi s'arrabia con tu eh! | | × | De Lisa ist da | | × | | | |
| Io non li conosco | | × | Die sind klein klein | | × | | | |
| Io questa la voglio | | × | Das ist Giulia | | × | | | |
| Anche l'ucello | × | | Mami wie ist Giulia? | | × | | | |
| | | | Wo ist de mein? | | × | | | |
| | | | Dieses ist Nonna | | × | | | |
| | | | Das Fahrrad ist das | | × | | | |
| | | | Nicht macht Spuk Mami nein | | × | | | |
| | | | Papi hat geweint | | × | | | |
| | | | Ich hab gewonnen | | × | | | |

**Table 3.2** (continued)

| Column A Italian | I | C | Column B German | I | C | Column C Mixed | I | C |
|---|---|---|---|---|---|---|---|---|
| 2;8 | | | 2;8 | | | 2;8 | | |
| | | | Hast du Brot ge- kaufen? | | × | | | |
| | | | Giulia sagt das | | × | | | |
| | | | Giulia nicht versteht nicht | | × | | | |
| | | | Giulia spricht auf deutsch | | × | | | |
| | | | Diese sind Buntstifte | | × | | | |
| | | | Das ist meins Mami | | × | | | |
| | | | Giulia macht eine Uhr | | × | | | |
| | | | Giulia will ein Blatt | | × | | | |
| | | | Und dieses ein Strick | × | | | | |
| 3;0 | | | 3;0 | | | 3;0 | | |
| Le zampe sono le mani | | × | Wie macht man? | × | | Ich hat die Füsse in ruota getreten | | × |
| Questo è a letto | | × | Das ist eine Hose | | × | | | |
| Questa è una casa | | × | Nonna Tina kommt? | | × | | | |
| Lisa sei pasticiona? | | × | Ich will ein Roten | | × | | | |
| Chi ha vinto? | | × | Ich zank nicht | × | | | | |
| Tu sei caca | | × | Ich wein nicht | | × | | | |
| Io sono Simona | | × | Mami singt bum bum bum | | × | | | |
| Io vado da Paola | | × | Ich will Plinze | | × | | | |
| Io te la porto | | × | Papi hat Kraft, Mami | | × | | | |
| Silvia stai qua | | × | Ich nicht bin ein Jungel | | × | | | |
| | | | Hier ist die Küche | | × | | | |
| | | | Das ist der Hund | | × | | | |
| | | | Erst ich | | × | | | |
| | | | Auch den Zucker | × | | | | |

**Table 3.3.** Incomplete (I) and complete (C) amplified sentences produced by Lisa from the age of 1 year and 9 months to the age of 3 years and 4 months

| Column A Italian | I | C | Column B German | I | C | Column C Mixed | I | C |
|---|---|---|---|---|---|---|---|---|
| 1st stage | | | | | | | | |
| 1;9 | | | 1;9 | | | 1;9 | | |
| No no più e cotta | × | | | | | | | |
| 1;10 | | | 1;10 | | | 1;10 | | |
| Anch'io Lisa la | | × | Mama ah! Buch | | | Daki eh! Giulia tita | × | |
| | | | Giulia daki daki | × | | | | |

**Table 3.3** (continued)

| Column A Italian | I | C | Column B German | I | C | Column C Mixed | I | C |
|---|---|---|---|---|---|---|---|---|
| 2;0 | | | 2;0 | | | 2;0 | | |
| | | | | | | Là anda Balle | × | |
| 2;3 | | | 2;3 | | | 2;3 | | |
| | | | Da badi badi | × | | Più Giulia Buch | × | |
| | | | Auch badi badi | × | | Da gatto miao nyam nyam | | × |
| | | | | | | Anda Papi sein | × | |
| | | | | | | Cocò alles nyam nyam la pappa | | × |

2nd stage

| Column A Italian | I | C | Column B German | I | C | Column C Mixed | I | C |
|---|---|---|---|---|---|---|---|---|
| 2;4 | | | 2;4 | | | 2;4 | | |
| Mamma fatto là | × | | Taute Hanny macht Lisa Hose | | × | Fa pilli pilli li | × | |
| E lei è mamma | | × | | | | Lisa la Schuhe guarda rein | | × |
| E lei è Giulia | | × | | | | Quetto pantalone Lisa anzi Giulia | | × |
| Codi Codi Mamma Giulia cocona | | × | | | | Edi Baum, Lisa Baum, edi Mami? | | × |
| Un'altra pizza lompe eh! | × | | | | | | | |
| Guarda Giulia bua (+) | × | | | | | | | |
| Guarda Lisa bua (+) | × | | | | | | | |
| 2;5 | | | 2;5 | | | 2;5 | | |
| Mammi fatto la | × | | | | | | | |
| Lascia penna li (+) | × | | | | | | | |
| Edi la penna là? (+) | × | | | | | | | |
| E lei è Lisa | | × | | | | | | |
| 2;6 | | | 2;6 | | | 2;6 | | |
| Lisa adesso paura Mammi | | × | Lisa auch arbeit? | × | | Anche Mami li Buch scheibi scheibi | | × |
| Anche Lisa lascia lì | × | | Mama Lisa arbeit | × | | Anche la nonna arbeit | | × |
| | | | Lisa arbeit Mama | × | | Adesso Lisa sucht Mama | | × |
| | | | Lisa fertig Lisa arbeit | × | | Lisa arbeit da Mamma | | × |
| | | | | | | Tieni Giulia quetto Traktoa Lisa | | × |
| | | | | | | Anche Giulia cami-cina blau | | × |
| | | | | | | Giulia canòssina bunt | × | |
| | | | | | | Sono Giulia Geld | × | |

**Table 3.3** (continued)

| Column A Italian | I | C | Column B German | I | C | Column C Mixed | I | C |
|---|---|---|---|---|---|---|---|---|
| **2;8** | | | **2;8** | | | **2;8** | | |
| Anche Mami fa (+) | × | | Giulia komm mit Lisa | | × | Mami, anche Lisa schleibi schleibi | | × |
| Senti poco poco complano? | × | | Aleoplano in deutsch Flugheusch | × | | Flugheusch vola come aeroplano | | × |
| Come Lisa gioca la pallone | × | | Auch Lisa blaune Haare | | × | Lisa specht di la | | × |
| Adesso leggi un po' mammi? | | × | | | | Nur Lisa stanca qua | | × |
| Lisa stanca adesso | | × | | | | Mami anche Lisa scheibi | | × |
| E zio Nando dove è? | | × | | | | Badi badi con le mani | × | |
| Lisa giocato di là | | × | | | | Quello è l'ander la barca | | × |
| Quella è ladio Lisa | | × | | | | Quetto è Lisa Stuhl | | × |
| Quello è bichele vino | | × | | | | Dovè Bleistift Lisa | | × |
| Quello è bichele Lisa, O.K.? | | × | | | | Dove sono la mia Schappen? | | × |
| Quella è medicina mammi | | × | | | | Quello è anda palla | | × |
| Dovè la matita di Lisa? | | × | | | | La penna là scheibi scheibi | | × |
| Grande pesciolino fa pipì | | × | | | | | | |
| Papi, dove sono la mia pantofole? | | × | | | | | | |
| Quello elicotto è come plano | | × | | | | | | |
| Quello è bichele, tutto bichele | | × | | | | | | |
| Quello è bichele vino qua | | × | | | | | | |
| Dovè chiavi di qua? | | × | | | | | | |
| La vedi la bua di Lisa Mammi? | | × | | | | | | |
| Guarda Giulia stanca (+) | × | | | | | | | |
| Andiamo l'antro ah? (+) | × | | | | | | | |
| Lisa bicicletta quello | × | | | | | | | |
| Giulia va solo Lisa | × | | | | | | | |
| **2;10** | | | **2;10** | | | **2;10** | | |
| Adesso basta | × | | Auch Mami hat keine Strümpfe no | | × | Fa sitzi sitzi nur qua | × | |
| Totò a Mammi forte forte | × | | Taute sagt und Lisa und Giulia | | × | Il Wolf non c'è più | | × |
| Va solo Lisa | × | | Der Wolf des nicht mehr da | | × | Sale su nur Lisa | | × |
| Lisa mangiato tutto un pancino | | × | Denn Taute sagt: Giulia und Lisa | | × | Nur Lisa sale qua | | × |
| Adesso è passata? | × | | | | | Pende Schwein con le mani | × | |
| Anche Lisa è mae | | × | | | | Jetzt faccio ein Fisch (+) | × | |
| La toia da sola | × | | | | | | | |

**Table 3.3** (continued)

| Column A Italian | I | C | Column B German | I | C | Column C Mixed | I | C |
|---|---|---|---|---|---|---|---|---|
| 2;10 | | | 2;10 | | | 2;10 | | |
| Lisa apre la porta | | | | | | Adesso badi badi | | |
| adesso | | × | | | | quello | | × |
| Giocando qua Lisa | | × | | | | Mami böse per Lisa? | × | |
| Ha fatto mamma la | | | | | | Anche Schwein | | |
| medicina come | | | | | | Apfel essen | | × |
| questa | | × | | | | Fa sitzi nur qua | × | |
| Giulia dorme ancora | | × | | | | Son nur Boote | × | |
| Mammi vuoi tanto | | | | | | Guarda Halzkette | | |
| bene a Lisa | | × | | | | della Pupi (+) | × | |
| La donna fa bum | | | | | | Dovè l'anda la | | |
| bum come quello | | × | | | | tasca? (+) | | × |
| Non c'è più la | | | | | | Dovè Papier di Lisa | | × |
| casetta no | | × | | | | Guarda Halzkette | | |
| Dove è chiavi di | | | | | | della Puppi (+) | × | |
| qua? | | × | | | | | | |
| Dovè la chiavi di | | | | | | | | |
| qua? | | × | | | | | | |
| Quetto è di Giulia | | | | | | | | |
| libo | | × | | | | | | |
| Sono i capelli di | | | | | | | | |
| Lisa | × | | | | | | | |
| Fa niente pora bam- | | | | | | | | |
| bola Giulia | | × | | | | | | |
| Bella scala per | | | | | | | | |
| Lisa fatto papi | | × | | | | | | |
| Mamma guarda | | | | | | | | |
| Lisa la nave | | × | | | | | | |
| Lisa ce l'ha mani | | | | | | | | |
| porche | | × | | | | | | |
| Dovè la collana di | | | | | | | | |
| Lisa? | | × | | | | | | |
| Quetta è la tua | | | | | | | | |
| mamma | | × | | | | | | |
| C'è una sola pancia | | × | | | | | | |
| Giulia gioca con la | | | | | | | | |
| scarpa Lisa | | × | | | | | | |
| La vedi la bua di | | | | | | | | |
| Lisa? (+) | × | | | | | | | |
| 3;0 | | | 3;0 | | | 3;0 | | |
| Adesso è buio | | × | Jetzt ist dunkel | | × | Mami hat gekauft | | |
| Cosa c'è scritto | | | Spielen da | × | | für Lisa ein fazz- | | |
| lì? | | × | Sn' mehr da der | | × | zoletto | | × |
| Cosa fatto di qua | | | Wolf | | | Lisa badt qui | | × |
| mamma? | | × | Lisa käuft für | × | | Come lisa ausziehen | × | |
| Mammi ha comprato | | | Giulia | | | Quetto fa arbeit così | | × |
| per Lisa un fazzo- | | | Was ist das | | | | | |
| letto | | × | da? | | × | | | |

**Table 3.3** (continued)

| Column A Italian | I | C | Column B German | I | C | Column C Mixed | I | C |
|---|---|---|---|---|---|---|---|---|
| 3;0 | | | 3;0 | | | 3;0 | | |
| Va dentro bambino quello lì | | | Und Lisa macht arbeitet | | × | | | |
| Quello l'auto è cattivo | | × | Lisa ist böse mit Mami | | × | | | |
| | | | Das hier eine Schleife von Lisa | | × | | | |

3rd stage

| Column A Italian | I | C | Column B German | I | C | Column C Mixed | I | C |
|---|---|---|---|---|---|---|---|---|
| 3;2 | | | 3;2 | | | 3;2 | | |
| Si chiamano Michele e anche Lisa | | × | Noch nicht ge-kommen | × | | Dov'è Kaugummi auch? | | × |
| Dò le totò così (+) | × | | Warum ist Sonne | | × | | | |
| La vedi Giulia in braccio alla nonna? (+) | × | | Ganz alleine Lisa geht | | × | | | |
| E anche stata brava | | × | Weil Lisa ist satt | | × | | | |
| Adesso io sputo | | × | Wem sein ist das alles Haus? | | × | | | |
| Perché è di Giulia la bicicletta | | × | Giulia hat Feige Lisa ihren gegessen | | × | | | |
| E tu vai in piscina | | × | Lisa hat kurze Haare ja Mami? | | × | | | |
| Adesso io scendo | | × | Mami mach ein Haus, ein kleines Haus | | × | | | |
| Poi quello è di Lisa | | × | Lisa ihren Schlappen sind groß | | × | | | |
| Questa è la mia casetta | | × | Wo ist Lisa ihren Regenschirm? | | × | | | |
| Lisa piccolina cià pigiama | | × | Nicht meine Schlappen anziehen Giulia | | × | | | |
| Questa è Lisa piccolina | | × | Das Flugzeug Papi ihren bleibt so | | × | | | |
| La mia piscina è bella | | × | | | | | | |
| Di chi è tutta questa cosa? | | × | | | | | | |
| Che arriva quei bambini | | × | | | | | | |
| 3;4 | | | 3;4 | | | 3;4 | | |
| Lisa pende in braccio | × | | Hier spucken | × | | Und kommt der böse Wolf a Lisa | | × |
| Ti ricordi ieri, Mammi Papi Lisa e Giulia? | | × | Jetzt guck (+) | × | | Ja, und Lisa la chiude | | × |
| Lisa fa cuoce così | | × | Und das hier kein Baum | | × | Ti ricordi gestern, il nonno (+) | × | |
| Ha buttata così | × | | Und auch den Apfel gegessen nein? | × | | L'ander mano dovè? | | × |
| Lisa ha finito prima | × | | Des hier ist auch Wasser | | × | Io mangio Reis di Giulia | | × |
| Non c'è Camilla oggi | | × | Und das im Dorf sind der Janko | | × | | | |
| Dopo non ci sono le nuvole | | × | | | | | | |

**Table 3.3** (continued)

| Column A Italian | I | C | Column B German | I | C | Column C Mixed | I | C |
|---|---|---|---|---|---|---|---|---|
| 3;4 | | | 3;4 | | | 3;4 | | |
| Adesso tiene le | | | Und das hier sind | | | | | |
| nuvole | | × | die Hörner da | | × | | | |
| Io l'ho tagliato | | | Aber nachher komm | | | | | |
| invece | | × | die Autos | | × | | | |
| Questo è due invece | | × | Und auch Joghurt | | | | | |
| Poi nonna dice | | | hat Lisa gegessen | | × | | | |
| subita | | × | Und da geht Janko | | | | | |
| Questa ha un po' di | | | mit Zicklein | | × | | | |
| tosse | | × | Auch ich friere | | × | | | |
| E' il naso mio | | | Lisa spricht auf | | | | | |
| questo | | × | deutsch wie Marco | | × | | | |
| Cosa si chiama | | | Auch das ist rot | | × | | | |
| questi bambini? | | × | Der Hund macht ciao | | | | | |
| Io adesso mangio il | | | mit das Schwanz | | × | | | |
| suo riso | | × | Was macht der | | | | | |
| Una scopa come | | | Janko da? | | × | | | |
| questa lì io prendo | | × | Mami, nachher | | | | | |
| Riccordi tutti e due | | | kommt Crista | | × | | | |
| letto (+) | × | | Jetzt Lisa geht tot | | × | | | |
| | | | Einmal die Taute | | | | | |
| | | | sagt: die Tasse | | × | | | |
| | | | Und das sind die | | | | | |
| | | | Bäume | | × | | | |
| | | | Mami ihr Strickzeug | | | | | |
| | | | nicht anfassen | × | | | | |
| | | | Guck das Händchen | | | | | |
| | | | sein Paola (+) | × | | | | |
| | | | Lisa ihren Brett hat | | | | | |
| | | | Pierina wegge- | | | | | |
| | | | nommen | | × | | | |
| | | | Ist liebe Sonne da | | × | | | |
| | | | Giulia esst nicht | | | | | |
| | | | Giulia ihren Reis | | × | | | |
| | | | Die drei Schweine | | | | | |
| | | | reisseaus | | × | | | |
| | | | Das ist alles Strand | | × | | | |
| | | | Wo sind diese | | | | | |
| | | | Besen? | | × | | | |
| | | | Zwei Schweine | | | | | |
| | | | spielen | | × | | | |
| | | | Und das hier sind | | | | | |
| | | | die klein Hörner | | × | | | |
| | | | Die drei Schwein | | | | | |
| | | | riest aus von den | | | | | |
| | | | bösen Wolf | | × | | | |
| | | | Das hier ist ein | | | | | |
| | | | groß Zicklein | | × | | | |
| | | | Das hier ist ein klein | | | | | |
| | | | Zicklein | | × | | | |

**Table 3.4.** Incomplete (I) and complete (C) amplified sentences produced by Giulia from the age of 1 year and 8 months to the age of 3 years

| Column A Italian | I | C | Column B German | I | C | Column C Mixed | I | C |
|---|---|---|---|---|---|---|---|---|
| **2nd stage** | | | | | | | | |
| 1;8 | | | 1;8 | | | 1;8 | | |
| Andiamo cade | | | Noch ein esach Giulia | | × | Giulia upa tanto | | |
| più (+) | | × | | | | tanto | | × |
| Giulia ha detto | | | | | | Mama schnell api | × | |
| Cristine | | × | | | | Auch Giulia sedia | | |
| A vava Giulia tutto | | | | | | sitzi sitzi | | × |
| finito | | × | | | | | | |
| | | | | | | | | |
| 1;9 | | | 1;9 | | | 1;9 | | |
| Anche Giulia lide | | × | Ioia ganz müde | × | | Ann Giulia qui | × | |
| La buco Giulia là | × | | Auch Mami haia haia | | × | A Puppi ha le pù | | × |
| Ha bua ha dine ha | | | Kaputt Lisa e Puppi | × | | Anche Lisa klein | | |
| bua come Giulia | | | No Giulia a Bea | | | klein Zeh | | × |
| ha | × | | Hiabettchen | × | | Eccolo Giulia Mund | | × |
| Giulia ha bua | | × | Gos Haiabettchen a | | | Chiama Haiabett- | | |
| | | | Lisa | × | | chen Lisa | × | |
| | | | Auch Giulia gos | | | Bella Lock Giulia | | |
| | | | haia haia | | × | Lock | × | |
| | | | Schue a na Giulia | | | Anche Jatel suo a | | |
| | | | Schuhe | | × | mamma | | × |
| | | | | | | Non è Mami Haale, | | |
| | | | | | | non è | × | |
| | | | | | | Dovè Stuhl mia? | | × |
| | | | | | | Mama adesso kaputt | | |
| | | | | | | Schlappen von | | |
| | | | | | | Papi | | × |
| | | | | | | Buch letto Mamma | × | |
| | | | | | | | | |
| 1;11 | | | 1;11 | | | 1;11 | | |
| Adesso toia | × | | Das von Giulia | | | Adesso kaputt | | |
| Qui dento dito | × | | Schuhe | × | | gemacht | × | |
| Adesso basta | × | | A Giulia klein | | | Adesso mamma | | |
| Mammi siede qui un | | | klein cleme | × | | macht Hut | × | |
| cuscino | | × | No Giulia klein | | | Mamma Babili | | |
| Quetto a Giulia atito | × | | Kinda | × | | quetta | × | |
| Giulia piccolo | | | | | | Quetta a Giulia | | |
| cleme si? | × | | | | | Schuhe | × | |
| Quette dine ha | | | | | | Anche questa klein | | |
| bucco | | × | | | | klein Zeh | × | |
| Dovè la bambola | | | | | | Guarda Giulia ihre | | |
| mia? | | × | | | | Zähne | × | |
| | | | | | | Non è Mami Haale, | | |
| | | | | | | non è | × | |
| | | | | | | Dovè Stuhl mia? | | × |
| | | | | | | Das hier bianco | × | |

**Table 3.4**  (continued)

| Column A Italian | I | C | Column B German | I | C | Column C Mixed | I | C |
|---|---|---|---|---|---|---|---|---|
| 2;2 | | | 2;2 | | | 2;2 | | |
| | | | Ein bißchen gemacht Teddybear | × | | Adesso offen | × | |
| | | | Jetzt ein anderen Blatte | × | | Teddybear spukt piano | | × |
| | | | Giulia nicht spukt da | | × | Come Mami malt | × | |
| | | | Giulia hat gemacht das hier | | × | Giulia gemacht a casetta per a böse Wolf | | × |
| | | | Das hier macht badi badi? | | × | Giulia spukt lettino di Giulia | | × |
| | | | Das hier ist kaputt | | × | Mami macht tua Haus | | × |
| | | | Mami, Birne sein Lisa das hier? | × | | Mami das hier per sclibele | | × |
| | | | Auch das hier sitzt | | × | | | |
| | | | Auch das hier macht badi | | × | | | |
| | | | Mami nicht zum schreiben das hier | | × | | | |

3rd stage

| Column A Italian | I | C | Column B German | I | C | Column C Mixed | I | C |
|---|---|---|---|---|---|---|---|---|
| 2;4 | | | 2;4 | | | 2;4 | | |
| Ha fatto pipi nelle mutande come Luca | × | | | | | Macht così | × | |
| Oggi giocava così | × | | | | | Una volta die pecore fa bumpete | | × |
| E ho fatto con sedere | × | | | | | Giulia ha preso Papi ihren Haarekem | | × |
| Dove è per questo, per questo? | × | | | | | Questa luce non fare Licht an | | × |
| Anche quelli vedi? (+) | × | | | | | | | |
| Mangia da sola | × | | | | | | | |
| Fanno così | × | | | | | | | |
| Caduta dal bidet | × | | | | | | | |
| Si fa così | × | | | | | | | |
| E fa chichichirini | × | | | | | | | |
| Quella è una per Monica | × | | | | | | | |
| Io oggi io andata alla nevia | | × | | | | | | |
| Sono di Giulia gambine | × | | | | | | | |
| E' un libro di Luca | × | | | | | | | |
| Non fare alla bocca di Giulia i capelli di Mammi | × | | | | | | | |

**Table 3.4** (continued)

| Column A Italian | I | C | Column B German | I | C | Column C Mixed | I | C |
|---|---|---|---|---|---|---|---|---|
| 2;4 | | | 2;4 | | | 2;4 | | |
| Dovè la matita quanti? | | × | | | | | | |
| Due pecore fanno pumpete | | × | | | | | | |
| Mammi, quella è la coperta mia | | × | | | | | | |
| Io sono il pulcino di Nonna | | × | | | | | | |
| Giulia cià le mani porche perché | | × | | | | | | |
| 2;6 | | | 2;6 | | | 2;6 | | |
| Tanti bimbi piccoli | × | | Giulia gemacht so | × | | Und jetzt di la | × | |
| E io sono l'amichetta di Luca | | × | Auch das hier | × | | Lisa ich hat auch cucchiaino | | × |
| E io voglio questo coltello | | × | Das is für Mami Revolver | | × | Quello è wie ein Teller | | × |
| | | | Das ist wie Bonnatale | | × | Mein costume ist gros | | × |
| | | | Mami auch das ist ein Jungel | | × | Bambino ihren Haare macht so | × | |
| | | | Ich sprich auf italianisch mit Mami | | × | Auch das hier ist orso | × | |
| | | | Ich auf italienisch spricht mit Luca | | × | | | |
| | | | Jetzt kommt Virginia? | | × | | | |
| | | | Und ich wein | | × | | | |
| | | | Ich sag immer kaki | | × | | | |
| | | | Ich schreib wie Mami | | × | | | |
| | | | Das ist wie Luca | | × | | | |
| | | | Weil da ist ein Buch wie Mama | | × | | | |
| | | | Mami, und Giulia weint denn | | × | | | |
| | | | Guck soviele Regen (+) | × | | | | |
| | | | Mach ein gos Haus, mach | × | | | | |
| | | | Mami das hier ist Schmetterling wie diese | | × | | | |
| | | | Ich spreche nur Italienisch wie Papi | | × | | | |
| | | | Das hier ist ein Buch | | × | | | |
| | | | Giulia macht soviele Ball | | × | | | |

Table 3.4 (continued)

| Column A Italian | I | C | Column B German | I | C | Column C Mixed | I | C |
|---|---|---|---|---|---|---|---|---|
| 2;6 | | | 2;6 | | | 2;6 | | |
| | | | Mami, diese ist mein | | | | | |
| | | | Tisch | | × | | | |
| | | | Ich nicht mach | | | | | |
| | | | kaputt diese | | | | | |
| | | | Flasche | | × | | | |
| 2;8 | | | 2;8 | | | 2;8 | | |
| Lascia così | × | | Schreiben so | × | | Warum is de | | |
| Cosa hai agli orec- | | | Erst malen | × | | Bicicletta | × | |
| chi? (+) | × | | Und dieses ein Strich | × | | Guck ein Baum für | | |
| Ti do anche | | | Jetzt eine andere | | | dich von ieri | × | |
| questa (+) | × | | Sonne | × | | Prima diesen da | × | |
| Va giù alla strada | × | | Und dieses ist dein | | × | Auch an die Zunge | | |
| Giulia scrive da fuoi | | × | Da die Kinder spielen | | × | la bua | × | |
| Anch'io lo prendo | | × | Auch Suor Antonia | | | Io malt pasticiona | × | |
| Anche il pulcino non | | | ist in Klasse | | × | Ecco soviele pallon- | | |
| fa il bagno | | × | Binden hat der da | | × | cini | | × |
| Anche questa è rotta | | × | Und hast du ge- | | | Guck da ein klein | | |
| Anche le signore han- | | | weint? | | × | palloncino von die | | |
| no la mantella | | × | Giulia nicht will | | | eine riga von filo | × | |
| Ha tanti denti | × | | dieses da | | × | Eccolo mein Blei- | | |
| Mio scotsch era | × | | Guck mami guck | | | stift | | × |
| Il mio ha due occhi | | × | diese Junge | | × | Mami wo ist der | | |
| E' uno sola la gabbia | | × | Diese Valentina ist | | | amico von Babau? | | × |
| Questo è la gonna | | | diese | | × | Capelli wie die | | |
| lunga | | × | Das beide is Nonna | | | Sonne mach ich | | × |
| Il leone solo nella | | | Tina ihren | | ,× | Mami hat schon drei | | |
| gabbia | × | | Auch Giulia will ein | | | bottoni | | × |
| L'altro orsacchiotto | | | Blatt von dein | | | | | |
| anche | × | | Buch | | × | | | |
| Questa è la nostra | | | | | | | | |
| casinha | | × | | | | | | |
| Dove è il mio rin- | | | | | | | | |
| ghenghino? | | × | | | | | | |
| Non ce l'ho il leone | | | | | | | | |
| un altro | | × | | | | | | |
| Io ce l'ho un altro | | × | | | | | | |
| Non ce nè un altro | | | | | | | | |
| elefante | | × | | | | | | |
| Dovè la mia giraffa? | | × | | | | | | |
| Sta per terra quella | | | | | | | | |
| palla | | × | | | | | | |
| Io cià bambino solo | | | | | | | | |
| mio | | × | | | | | | |
| Anch'io ce l'ho lo | | | | | | | | |
| specchio rotto | | × | | | | | | |

**Table 3.4** (continued)

| Column A Italian | I | C | Column B German | I | C | Column C Mixed | I | C |
|---|---|---|---|---|---|---|---|---|
| 3;0 | | | 3;0 | | | 3;0 | | |
| Adesso mettiamo | | | Ist weiter weg | × | | E anch'io non sono | | |
| nella barca | × | | Ich will aber nicht | × | | più böse | | × |
| Così non si romperà | × | | Mami hast du ge- | | | Ich habe das per | | |
| Il quadro guarda qua | | | macht mit das | × | | finta gemacht | | × |
| sotto | | × | Bitte so machen Lisa | × | | Schnell kaufen zwei | | |
| E io dove siedo? | × | | So, jetzt Haare ab- | | | kleine Fahrrad | | |
| E io anche vado in | | | schneiden | × | | nuovi | × | |
| piscina | | × | Und wie macht | | | | | |
| E poi qua c'è la | | | Mami noch? | | × | | | |
| tenda | | × | Dann ich bin böse | | × | | | |
| E dopo come ti | | | Das ist mal schön | | × | | | |
| chiami? | | × | Mama auch das ist | | | | | |
| Voglio un grande | | | meine | | × | | | |
| posto (+) | × | | Papi hat ganz Kraft | | × | | | |
| Guarda tutta la | | | Ich will auch das | | × | | | |
| casa (+) | × | | Ich hat nicht weh- | | | | | |
| E il piccolo lupo | | | getan hier | | × | | | |
| guarda | | × | Guck eine Hose | | | | | |
| Povera Lisa come | | | so (+) | | × | | | |
| ti chiami? | | × | Ist nicht ganz egal | | × | | | |
| | | | Lisa hat mein Kissen | | × | | | |
| | | | Ich nicht will mein | | | | | |
| | | | Eierschlag | | × | | | |
| | | | Ich will soviel | | | | | |
| | | | Fahrräder | | × | | | |
| | | | Mein Name ist | | | | | |
| | | | Kikida | | × | | | |
| | | | Mein Haus ist unter | | | | | |
| | | | hier | | × | | | |
| | | | Ja, warum das ist | | | | | |
| | | | mein Bett | | × | | | |

**Table 3.5.** Incomplete (I) and complete (C) implicit complex sentences produced by Lisa from the age of 2 years and 4 months to the age of 3 years and 4 months

| Column A Italian | I | C | Column B German | I | C | Column C Mixed | I | C |
|---|---|---|---|---|---|---|---|---|
| 2nd stage | | | | | | | | |
| 2;4 | | | 2;4 | | | 2;4 | | |
| Mammi? Vuoi toglia | × | | Mami scheibi scheibi | | | | | |
| | | | macht | | × | | | |
| | | | Scheibi scheibi Lisa | | | | | |
| | | | macht | | × | | | |
| | | | Lisa heia heia | | | | | |
| | | | machen no | | × | | | |

**Table 3.5** (continued)

| Column A<br>Italian | I | C | Column B<br>German | I | C | Column C<br>Mixed | I | C |
|---|---|---|---|---|---|---|---|---|
| 2;6 | | | 2;6<br>Lisa pumsi gemacht | | × | 2;6<br>Andare letto haia<br>  haia<br>Giulia vuole haia<br>  haia no | ×<br> <br> <br> | <br> <br> <br>× |
| 2;8<br>Giocare vuole bimbo<br>Legge un pò vuoi? | | ×<br>× | 2;8<br>Lisa geht arbeiten | | × | 2;8<br>Lisa vuole schaun<br>Io, adesso Lisa geht<br>  arbeit | ×<br> <br> | <br> <br>× |
| 2;10<br>Andare a dormire<br>  adesso dopo sì?<br>Andiamo lavare<br>Lisa vuole scendere,<br>  Giulia<br>La sedia fa cadê,<br>  cadê Lisa<br>Mamma vai a pren-<br>  dere la farfalla | <br>×<br>×<br> <br>×<br> <br> <br> | <br> <br> <br> <br> <br> <br>×<br> <br>× | 2;10 | | | 2;10<br>Andare haia haia<br>  adesso dopo sì?<br>Lisa vuole schreiben | <br>×<br> | <br> <br>× |
| 3;0 | | | 3;0 | | | 3;0<br>Adesso Lisa will<br>  prende | <br>× | |

**3rd stage**

| 3;2<br>Andiamo a cercare?<br>La suora ha detto:<br>  stare brava | ×<br> <br>× | | 3;2<br>Jetzt will Lisa um-<br>  rühren<br>Wollen wir Hände<br>  waschen Mami?<br>Lisa will das alles<br>  aufräum<br>Gehen wir suchen<br>  Lisa Schlappen?<br>Giulia will nicht<br>  weiter schlafen<br>Armer Federiko will<br>  trinki trinki<br>  machen | ×<br> <br>×<br> <br>×<br> <br>×<br> <br>×<br> <br>× | | 3;2 | | |
| 3;4<br>Mamma, posso la<br>  banana pren-<br>  dere? (+) | <br> <br>× | | 3;4<br>Ich will Kaki<br>  machen<br>Lisa will eine Pupi<br>  machen mit die<br>  Kreide | ×<br> <br> <br>× | | 3;4 | | |

**Table 3.6.** Incomplete (I) and complete (C) implicit complex sentences produced by Giulia from the age of 2 years and 2 months to the age of 3 years

| Column A Italian | I | C | Column B German | I | C | Column C Mixed | I | C |
|---|---|---|---|---|---|---|---|---|
| **2nd stage** | | | | | | | | |
| 2;2 | | | 2;2 Giulia will sehen | × | | 2;2 | | |
| | | | Giulia will caki machen | | × | | | |
| **3rd stage** | | | | | | | | |
| 2;4 Si fa aggiustare | × | | 2;4 | | | 2;4 | | |
| Voglio dare totò alla pupi | | × | | | | | | |
| 2;6 | | | 2;6 Ich will genen | × | | 2;6 Ich will prendere ja | × | |
| | | | Mami ich will studiern | | × | Ich will pettinare | × | |
| | | | Musse Kraft machen Lisa | | × | Ich macht piove | | × |
| | | | Ich will sehen Mami | × | | Mami ich will eine matita zum Schreiben | | 0 |
| | | | Giulia kann nicht machen Mami | × | | | | |
| 2;8 Lisa mi fai fare pipì? | | × | 2;8 Ich will schreiben | | × | 2;8 | | |
| Come si fa a farle stare in piedi? | | 0 | Ich will die Haare waschen | | × | | | |
| Io ti faccio vedere io il vestitino blu | | × | Gehn wa studiern | | × | | | |
| Perché io voglio fa re una barchetta | | × | Giulia will dieses malen | | × | | | |
| Io vado via con la donna senza mangiare | | × | Giulia kann nicht anfassen | × | | | | |
| 3;0 Adesso andiamo a fare un passeg- gio (+) | | 0 | 3;0 Ich will anziehen. Eine Spielhose will anziehen | | × | 3;0 Ich will drei Biciclet kaufen | | × |
| Vuoi mangiare? (+) | | × | Will Kraft machen | × | | Schnell kommen die peli hier ange- flogen | | × |
| | | | Du möchst du sehen? In die Stube das sehen? | | × | | | |
| | | | Ich will schlafen in dein Bett | | × | | | |

**Table 3.6** (continued)

| Column A Italian | I | C | Column B German | I | C | Column C Mixed | I | C |
|---|---|---|---|---|---|---|---|---|
| 3;0 | | | 3;0 Ich will dich kämmen | | × | 3;0 | | |
| | | | So, ich will dich hübsch machen, ganz hübsch | | × | | | |
| | | | Ich will nicht studiern | | × | | | |
| | | | Mami, Lisa muß gehen | | × | | | |
| | | | Lisa hat nicht gehelfen zum daraus gehen | | 0 | | | |

**Table 3.7.** Incomplete (I) and complete (C) explicit complex sentences produced by Lisa from the age of 2 years and 4 months to the age of 3 years and 6 months

| Column A Italian | I | C | Column B German | I | C | Column C Mixed | I | C |
|---|---|---|---|---|---|---|---|---|
| 2nd stage | | | | | | | | |
| 2;4 Giulia attenta bua Lisa letto | | × | 2;4 | | | 2;4 Mama ada Lisa macht | × | |
| Ada mammi Lisa fatto | × | | | | | Ada Mami Lisa mutzi macht | × | |
| | | | | | | Edi Lisa sitzi ganz gos Buch? (+) | × | |
| | | | | | | Edi Baum zu klein quetto da Giulia (+) | × | |
| 2;6 | | | 2;6 | | | 2;6 Mami guarda Lisa pumsi gemacht | | × |
| | | | | | | Guarda Lisa gemacht (+) | × | |
| 2;8 Giulia non ce l'ha, guarda (+) | × | | 2;8 | | | 2;8 Guarda Lisa fa badi badi (+) | × | |
| Quello là è lotto vedi? (+) | × | | | | | Guarda Lisa fa sitzi sitzi (+) | × | |
| Guarda non c'è sole (+) | × | | | | | Guarda questo fa nyam nyam (+) | × | |

**Table 3.7** (continued)

| Column A Italian | I | C | Column B German | I | C | Column C Mixed | I | C |
|---|---|---|---|---|---|---|---|---|
| **2;8** | | | **2;8** | | | **2;8** | | |
| Mammi guarda quello fa pipì (+) | × | | | | | | | |
| Lisa vedele va bene? | × | | | | | | | |
| | | | | | | | | |
| **2;10** | | | **2;10** | | | **2;10** | | |
| Hai visto ha la bua la bambola? (+) | × | | | | | Ada il Wolf non c'è più (+) | × | |
| Ti ricordi il nonno, la nonna è venuta (+) | × | | | | | Schwein penda la mela vedi? (+) | × | |
| Mammi aeroplano vedi con la gente se va via | | × | | | | | | |
| Lisa si è fatta male sai? (+) | × | | | | | | | |
| Guarda andiamo a lavare i panni | × | | | | | | | |
| C'è ancora Chichi vedi? (+) | × | | | | | | | |
| Lisa cercato vedi? | × | | | | | | | |
| Mammi guarda di Lisa la nave che bella è | | 0 | | | | | | |
| Sono quanti guarda | × | | | | | | | |
| È come qui hai visto? | × | | | | | | | |
| Guarda io toia da sola hai visto? | × | | | | | | | |
| Sai quella è la stellina di nonna | × | | | | | | | |
| | | | | | | | | |
| **3;0** | | | **3;0** | | | **3;0** | | |
| Guarda chi è? | × | | | | | Vedi Lisa hat müde? (+) | × | |
| Aspetta Lisa porta giocattoli (+) | × | | | | | | | |
| Vedi Lisa cià sonno? (+) | × | | | | | | | |

**3rd stage**

| Column A Italian | I | C | Column B German | I | C | Column C Mixed | I | C |
|---|---|---|---|---|---|---|---|---|
| **3;2** | | | **3;2** | | | **3;2** | | |
| La vedi Giulia in braccio alla nonna? (+) | × | | Guck Mami da is eine Schachtel | | × | Nein Lisa hat eine Fritate gemacht guck Mami | | × |
| | | | Mami komm mach den Schrank auf (+) | × | | | | |

**Table 3.7** (continued)

| Column A Italian | I | C | Column B German | I | C | Column C Mixed | I | C |
|---|---|---|---|---|---|---|---|---|
| 3;4 Ti ricordi ieri dove siamo ieri? (+) Vedi le nuvole come i pedali fanno così? (+) | × × | | 3;4 Lisa hat nicht Haare guck (+) | × | | 3;4 | | |
| 3;6 E vedi che gira tutto intorno? (+) | 0 | | 3;6 Mami guck da Lisa was hat gemacht | | × | 3;6 | | |

**Table 3.8.** Incomplete (I) and complete (C) explicit complex sentences produces by Giulia from the age of 1 year and 9 months to the age of 3 years

| Column A Italian | I | C | Column B German | I | C | Column C Mixed | I | C |
|---|---|---|---|---|---|---|---|---|
| 2nd stage | | | | | | | | |
| 1;9 A sopla gada a sopla c'è (+) Son sporchi vedi? | × × | | 1;9 | | | 1;9 | | |
| 1;11 Vedi è sporco Vedi c'è il sole, vedi (+) | × × | | 1;11 | | | 1;11 | | |
| 2;2 | | | 2;2 Guck Mami Giulia geholt ein Kissen | | × | 2;2 | | |
| 3rd stage | | | | | | | | |
| 2;4 Hai visto Giulia cosa ha fatto? (+) Vedi non cià foide? | × × | | 2;4 | | | 2;4 | | |
| 2;6 Mammi guarda cosa c'è (+) Guarda lì cosa c'è (+) Guarda cosa c'era guarda | × × × | | 2;6 Mami guck ich hat | × | | 2;6 Vedi ist wie Roma ihren Mami guck das ist bambino ihren Bettchen (+) | × × | |

**Table 3.8** (continued)

| Column A Italian | I | C | Column B German | I | C | Column C Mixed | I | C |
|---|---|---|---|---|---|---|---|---|
| 2;6 Guarda cosa c'è scritto: banana (+) | × | | 2;6 | | | 2;6 Mami guck bambino legt sich hin an die Erde (+) | × | |
| 2;8 Vuoi vedere che piango forte? (+) | 0 | | 2;8 Guck Mami Giulia macht ein Baum (+) | × | | 2;8 Ricordi mami ge- macht diese da fiori (+) Ecco Lisa fatto una puppi | × | × |
| 2;10 Io lo dico alla mam- ma che io non sono un bimbo | | 0 | 2;10 | | | 2;10 | | |
| 3;0 Guarda come io so fare (+) Aspetta che devo fare un bel le- gato (+) Aspetta facciamo un bel legato Guarda io faccio una scarpa bella (+) Vedi che sono? | × 0 × × 0 | | 3;0 Guck das ist eine Hose (+) Ich wein nicht, hast verstanden! (+) | × × | | 3;0 Guck così hat Kraft | × | |

**Table 3.9.** Incomplete (I) and complete (C) relative sentences produced by Lisa from the age of 2 years and 8 months to the age of 3 years and 6 months

| Column A Italian | I | C | Column B German | I | C | Column C Mixed | I | C |
|---|---|---|---|---|---|---|---|---|
| 2nd stage | | | | | | | | |
| 2;8 Ti ricordi un cicio- lino si chiamava Federico | | × | 2;8 | | | 2;8 | | |
| 2;10 | | | 2;10 Mami wo is Hals- kette Lisa is? | | × | 2;10 | | |

**Table 3.9** (continued)

| Column A Italian | I | C | Column B German | I | C | Column C Mixed | I | C |
|---|---|---|---|---|---|---|---|---|
| 3;2 | | | 3;2 | | | 3;2 | | |
| Mi dai una potofia dove c'è Lisa piccola? (+) | 0 | | | | | | | |
| Una cartolina c'è Lisa | 0 | | | | | | | |
| E' la casa che aveva lei | | 0 | | | | | | |
| 3;6 | | | 3;6 | | | 3;6 | | |
| | | | Wo ist die Puppe wo sagt Mama? | | 0 | | | |

**Table 3.10.** Incomplete (I) and complete (C) relative sentences produced by Giulia from the age of 2 years and 2 months to the age of 3 years

| Column A Italian | I | C | Column B German | I | C | Column C Mixed | I | C |
|---|---|---|---|---|---|---|---|---|
| 2nd stage | | | | | | | | |
| 2;2 | | | 2;2 | | | 2;2 | | |
| | | | Giulia will Bonbon haben gekauft mami, Giulia will | | × | | | |
| 3rd stage | | | | | | | | |
| 2;4 | | | 2;4 | | | 2;4 | | |
| Mamma tieni quello peso che è pesante | | 0 | | | | | | |
| 2;8 | | | 2;8 | | | 2;8 | | |
| Dove è il lupo che cammina in bosco? | | 0 | Das is eine Puppe die is wie Nonna Tina is | | 0 | Wo ist eine Luna wie de große Bild is? | | × |
| Lupo è in mia stanza che cammina | | 0 | | | | | | |
| Io ho piccolo coso che sta in piedi | | 0 | | | | | | |
| 3;0 | | | 3;0 | | | 3;0 | | |
| Dovè questo che vede? | | 0 | | | | | | |
| Òòò un pinguin brut-to che mangia | | 0 | | | | | | |

**Table 3.11.** Incomplete (I) and complete (C) binuclear sentences produced by Lisa from the age of 2 years and 6 months to the age of 3 years and 4 months

| Column A Italian | I | C | Column B German | I | C | Column C Mixed | I | C |
|---|---|---|---|---|---|---|---|---|
| **2nd stage** | | | | | | | | |
| 2;6 È di Mammi auto to-ta, Lisa aggiusta | × | | 2;6 | | | 2;6 Vitto Mami? Più auto kaputt. Vava Lisa. | × | |
| 2;10 Mamma, la bambola fa la nina nanna, adesso è andata a letto dormiva. | | × | 2;10 | | | 2;10 Mami, andiamo eine Geschichte Lisa vuole schreiben. | × | |
| Giulia zitta che dorme la bambola. | | 0 | | | | | | |
| Scappa scappa topo-lino, adesso vene pezzo di legno, testa di Giulia, adesso scappata. | | × | | | | | | |
| C'è ancora Chichi vedi, non è morto Chichi no. (+) | × | | | | | | | |
| Giulia gioca con la canossina. | | × | | | | | | |
| 3;0 Non toccare è di Papi. (+) | × | | 3;0 | | | 3;0 Mami prende Was-ser, io fa cin cin. | | × |
| Non toccare, si sporca si? (+) | × | | | | | | | |
| Questa è Lisa, Giu-lia è dentro. | | × | | | | | | |
| **3rd stage** | | | | | | | | |
| 3;2 Papi, dove sono Mamma e Giulia perché non le ho viste. | | 0 | 3;2 Guck Mami, da eine Schaukel und da soviele Kinder und Lisa will in Auto. | | 0 | 3;2 | | |
| Quando andiamo nella spiaggia fa così. | × | | Tante Hanny, Onkel Carlos nicht versteht Italie-nisch, T.H. O.C. spricht Portu-giesisch. | | | | | |
| Ho fame, voglio una minestrina. | | × | | | × | | | |

**Table 3.11** (continued)

| Column A<br>Italian | I | C | Column B<br>German | I | C | Column C<br>Mixed | I | C |
|---|---|---|---|---|---|---|---|---|
| 3;2 | | | 3;2<br>Armer Federico will tinki tinki machen, schon tot.<br>Lisa will Topolino nehmen und Papi gehen. | | ×<br><br>0 | 3;2 | | |
| 3;4<br>Questo è un secchiello per andare al mare?<br>Non si fa sennò si rompe.<br>Non si fa non cià sue gambe.<br>Adesso Lisa prende leone e fa prr prr. | | 0<br>0<br>×<br>0 | 3;4<br>Pierina geht jetzt weg und Lisa ist lieb nachher kommt Nadia<br>Guck Mami Giulia hat Schuhe und Lisa nur Strümpfe.<br>Sonst Lisa in Terasse gehen, sonst Lisa Strümpfe mutzich, will Schuhe.<br>Wenn Mami geht da da und Lisa spukt da wenn Mami geht da.<br>Andere spielt Flöte und andere spielt Violin.<br>Lisa hat weiss und rot ist nicht da.<br>Und auch Lisa hat nicht ein Buch genommen und nicht die Bananen gegessen.<br>Wenn Lisa hat kaputt gemacht dann ist Tasche wie Papi.<br>Das hier ist nicht lieb, das hier ist böse.<br>Und das Baum ist grün und das Zicklein ist bei Janko. | 0 | 0<br><br>0<br><br>0<br><br>0<br><br>0<br>0<br><br>0<br><br>0<br><br>0 | 3;4<br>Wenn Lisa ist schön brav mit Haarewaschen, denn Lisa kriegt auch codini vero?<br>Und das Mädchen hat soviele Äpfel und mangiano<br>Das hier sind le ruote und cammina. | | 0<br><br>0<br><br>0 |

**Table 3.12.** Incomplete (I) and complete (C) binuclear sentences produced by Giulia from the age of 1 year and 9 months to the age of 3 years

| Column A Italian | I | C | Column B German | I | C | Column C Mixed | I | C |
|---|---|---|---|---|---|---|---|---|
| **1st stage** | | | | | | | | |
| 1;9 A toia quetto, aiato | × | | 1;9 | | | 1;9 | | |
| **2nd stage** | | | | | | | | |
| | | | | | | Io voglio a Giulia vestita a sitzi no. | | × |
| 1;11 | | | 1;11 | | | 1;11 Papi näht, non è cipcip näht no. Papi näht. | | × |
| 2;2 | | | 2;2 Ein Blatt das hier kaputt, das hier schreiben, das hier nicht kaputt. | × | | 2;2 | | |
| | | | | | | Das hier Bleistift per Schreiben ja? Cià la punta. | | × |
| | | | | | | Mami das hier kaputt, non può schreiben così, nein Mami. | | × |
| **3rd stage** | | | | | | | | |
| 2;4 Giulia non può capace. Giulia è piccola vedi. | | × | 2;4 Mami und Giulia lest ja? Ein Blatt will. | | × | 2;4 | | |
| Giulia fa mal al dito, Lisa è glande. | | × | Giulia macht die Augen nein, Giulia macht die Füße. | | × | | | |
| Io cià due patate, tu ciai tanti. | | × | | | | | | |
| Quella è piccola e quella è grande. | | 0 | | | | | | |
| 2;6 Quello è mio perché è mio. | | 0 | 2;6 Mami diese ist kaputt, ist ein Loch diese. | | × | 2;6 Ich hat male agli occhi, ich muß nach Frascati. | | × |
| E' di Fabio quello, è di Fabio e di Luca. | | 0 | Jetzt ist fertig, ich mach eine andere. | | × | | | |

**Table 3.12** (continued)

| Column A Italian | I | C | Column B German | I | C | Column C Mixed | I | C |
|---|---|---|---|---|---|---|---|---|
| **2;6**<br>C'è posto. Quella<br>  seg giola è per te,<br>  quello è per me. | | ×| **2;6**<br>Ist nicht zum Lachen<br>  ist zum Weinen.<br>Und das hier ist<br>  Stella, ich bin<br>  Monica.<br>Das ist für Mami<br>  Revolver, und<br>  das ist für mich.<br>So ist ein Flugzeug<br>  so macht ù ù ù.<br>Mami ich hat ausge-<br>  trunken ich hat<br>  nich kaputt ge-<br>  macht.<br>Giulia nicht schläft<br>  aber Giulia trinkt<br>  aber.<br>Giulia hat so ge-<br>  macht und Mami<br>  hat so gemacht. | ×| 0<br><br>0<br><br><br>×<br><br><br>×<br><br>0<br><br>0 | | | |
| **2;8**<br>Io voglio quella che<br>  piange e tu quella<br>  dura e poi un'al-<br>  tra palla.<br>Lavare la bocca<br>  perché io voglio<br>  mangiare.<br>No! E' dura, c'è<br>  l'osso.<br>Due orsi metto fuori<br>  e animali no, non<br>  metto. (+)<br>Sta in piedi, sta<br>  sveglio.<br>Non piange Gigi,<br>  sta così. (+) | | 0<br><br><br>0<br><br>×<br><br>0<br><br>×<br><br>× | **2;8**<br>Ich will der Hocker,<br>  Giulia will auch<br>  studiern Mami.<br>Diese is mein und<br>  diese is Mami ihrs. | | ×<br><br>0 | **2;8**<br>Mami Giulia will<br>  lavara die Hände<br>  klebono warum.<br>Da spiel und guck<br>  cavallo.<br>Mami guck ein Filen,<br>  bitte in der Müll<br>  tun. | 0<br><br>0 | ×|
| **3;0**<br>Io non mi tieno che<br>  sono grande va<br>  bene? (+)<br>Io non voglio dor-<br>  mire perché io<br>  non sono stanca.<br>Allora tu sei la suora<br>  e io sono la bimba. | | 0<br><br>0<br><br>0 | **3;0**<br>Ich will rot warum<br>  ich bin gros.<br>Guck so machen<br>  wenn ich schnell<br>  fahre.<br>Ich will so warum<br>  ich bin groß. | | 0<br><br>0<br><br>0 | **3;0**<br>Die Gomma kostet<br>  teuer Geld muß<br>  man essen, ja.<br>Guck ich geb immer<br>  mein Bleistift für<br>  dich, ich bin schön<br>  allora. | | ×<br><br>0 |

**Table 3.12** (continued)

| Column A<br>Italian | I | C | Column B<br>German | I | C | Column C<br>Mixed | I | C |
|---|---|---|---|---|---|---|---|---|
| 3;0<br>La mia casa è vicina<br>e basta e io vado<br>adesso in piscina.<br>E io ho ancora un<br>brutto e poi non<br>ciavevo paura. | | 0<br><br>0 | 3;0<br>Wenn ist Sonne,<br>jetzt ist dunkel<br>Nicht abschneiden<br>die Nase sonst<br>geht kaputt.<br>Schnell laufen und<br>so machen.<br>Das ist dein Bett,<br>das ist mein Bett.<br>Ich bin die Mami<br>und du bist das<br>Kind. | | 0<br><br>0<br><br>0<br><br><br>×<br><br>0 | 3;0<br>Ich hat male Nase<br>warum Giulia<br>kann nicht<br>laufen.<br>Das ist das Mare<br>das ist das Boot. | | 0<br><br><br>×  |

A binuclear sentence is considered incomplete when one or more arguments are missing in one or both of the nuclear sentences comprising it. As is the case for complex sentences, binuclear sentences using the connective are also marked with the letter 0 (see Tables 3.11, 12, pp. 92 – 96).

## 3.2 Results

We may distinguish three steps in basic sentence structure development:
– During the first stage, the children's sentences include only complete and incomplete nuclear structures.
– During the second stage, the children acquire the other basic structures, i.e., amplified, complex and binuclear structures. However, these last two structures are only juxtaposed; in other words, they do not yet contain connectives.
– During the third stage, the children learn to form complex and binuclear sentences using the connective.

As will be seen, bilingual children pass through these three stages simultaneously in their two languages.

### 3.2.1 The First Stage

The first examples of nuclear structure may be found in "vertical constructions."[7] According to Scollon [1978a], a vertical construction occurs when

---

7 With respect to the ability of children to combine single words, Greenfield and Smith [1976] have given the term "two-interlocutor sentences" to such sentences as:
Mother [pointing to the sun]: Sun.
Lauren (1;3): Hot.

two or more utterances of a word are linked by meaning or temporal vicinity but not by intonation. Scollon shows that a single word pronounced by a child is part of a more complex utterance whose components are at times verbalized by the child with the help of the person to whom he is speaking, and at times verbalized after a pause, either with or without repetitions. [8]

The first predicate + argument structures used by Lisa and Giulia in German and Italian were:

| Child's utterance | Interlocutor | Structure |
|---|---|---|
| 1) **L** (1;7):<br>*Buah* (Book)<br><br>*Daki* (Thanks [for exchange]) | The child looks at her father. When he does not answer, she says: | Argument<br>+<br>Predicate |
| 2) **L** (1;7):<br>*Ghia!* (Giulia!)<br><br>*Daki, daki* | She gives her sister a necklace. | Argument<br>+<br>Predicate |
| 3) **L** (1;7):<br>*Nyam nyam?* (Eat?)<br>*Nyam nyam?*<br>*Nyam nyam?*<br>*Iolata* (Chocolate) | She gives her mother an interrogative look. | Predicate<br>+<br>Argument |
| 4) **G** (1;2):<br>*Daa, daa* (Give)<br>*Buch, Bu* (Book)<br><br>Okay | She pauses and then says:<br><br>Lisa says: *Giulia Buch, ja?* And her sister answers: | Predicate<br>+<br>Argument |
| 5) **G** (1;2):<br>*Daa!* (Here!)<br><br>*Neni* (Doll) | *Ah, Giulia hat die Puppe gefunden!* (Ah, Giulia found the doll!) | Predicate<br>+<br>Argument |

---

8 Leopold [1956/57] gave some examples of this: H (1;8) says, *"Dada, Wäscht!"* ("Daddy, washes!"). Oksaar [1977, p. 189] also speaks of this habit of pairing single words, in which the single words are uttered one after the other with a pause in between. She calls them Wortsatz-blöcke ("word-sentence blocks"). For instance, S (1;6) says, *"Auto. Fahren."* The child says these words as he watches a car pass. But Ramge [1975, p. 77] comes to the reverse conclusion on this subject. He maintains that "three consecutive linguistic acts such as *da! / . / Ball! / . / haben* ("there!" / . / "ball!" / . / "have") are autonomous linguistic acts which only superficially give the impression that they are a single connected utterance. Ramge supports this idea, by pointing to the fact that the three linguistic acts do not have intonational continuity but are instead separated by pauses.

These examples show that Lisa and Giulia produced two-word utterances in which a predicate and one or two arguments can clearly be distinguished. They produced these utterances with pauses or repetition of the same word, and often they needed the adult's help to continue their utterance. In these cases, the girls did not yet make any distinction between the two languages, and used all of the words which were part of their lexical production.

Later, the child begins to express himself using a structure in which there are not as many pauses, repetitions of one-word utterances, or cases of adult intervention between the different elements of the utterance. These are true nuclear sentences.

At first, Lisa's and Giulia's nuclear sentences were for the most part incomplete, and exhibited structures in which the predicate or one argument was missing. These incomplete nuclear sentences gradually increased, passing through a stage in which they were quite numerous, and then they gradually decreased again while the complete nuclear sentences increased (see Figs. 3.1, 2). The incomplete nuclear sentences with no predicate completely disappeared, while those with a missing argument continued to show up here and there (see Tables 3.1 – 4, pp. 64 – 84). In the final examples, only arguments are missing, and never predicates. [9]

It was considered best to distinguish between cases in which a structure merely appeared or was used only sporadically, and cases in which the child actually used such a structure frequently and systematically. This distinction allows us to understand whether a structure represents an isolated, random event, or whether it represents the way in which the child expresses himself. The different ways in which the child uses a certain structure, first sporadically and then more and more frequently, were clearly demonstrated by the recordings. For example, in Giulia's third recording (1;3), she made 55 utterances, of which only 3 were nuclear sentences. The rest were either one-word utterances or vertical constructions. But in the eighth recording (1;8), 16 of her 50 utterances were nuclear sentences. Thus, even if a few examples of the complete nuclear structure do appear at the same time as the incomplete nuclear structure, it is only at a later age that this structure appears more frequently, with the incomplete structures gradually beginning to decrease until only a few examples show up. [10] This process can be understood more clearly

---

9 This study does not aim at supplying one pragmatic or semantic hypothesis to explain this phenomenon, but such a goal would be worthy of treatment elsewhere. This part of the study is meant to clarify the question of whether the acquisition of sentence structures in the bilingual's two languages occurs simultaneously or at different stages, and whether bilingual acquisition differs from or is the same as monolingual acquisition.

10 Stern and Stern [1928, p. 199] observed the simultaneous appearance of complete and incomplete nuclear structures which they suggested should be called *primitive Satzketten* (primitive sentence chains). Leopold [1956/57, p. 123] observed that these structures appear successively, the incomplete structures first and then the complete structures. Keeping our concept of sporadic and actual use in mind, we may agree with both of these points of view. In fact, our data show a great tendency toward quantitative succession, despite the fact that both structures appeared at the same time.

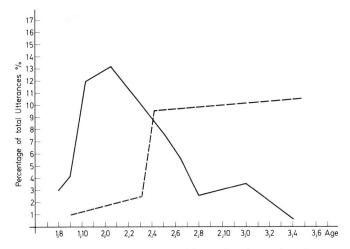

**Fig. 3.1.** Lisa's complete (– – –) and incomplete (———) nuclear sentences

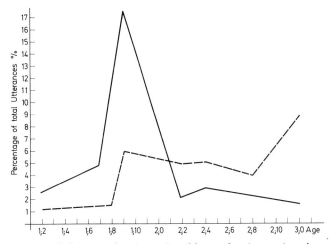

**Fig. 3.2.** Giulia's complete (– – –) and incomplete (———) nuclear sentences

with the help of Figs. 3.1, 2. [11] Although the two girls began using these sentences at different ages, a comparison of their graphs reveals that Lisa's curve for incomplete nuclear sentences developed in much the same way as Giulia's; the same is true of the curves for complete nuclear sentences. As the examples in Tables 3.1, 2 (pp. 64 – 74) clearly demonstrate, this development was also analogous in the two languages. In fact, simultaneously and during the whole

---

11  The percentage of utterances exhibiting each structure was calculated over the total utterances produced during a certain period. Every figure was associated with a coefficient of uncertainty on the basis of sample size.

process observed, there were several examples in Italian (column A) and in German (column B) and of mixed sentences (column C).

Scollon's vertical construction concept [1978] is also applicable during a period which postdates the one-word stage. The period referred to is the one in which the child uses numerous incomplete nuclear sentences. The incomplete nuclear sentences are linked by meaning and temporal vicinity, but not by intonation, so that they form a complete nuclear structure or even an amplified structure; the parts are usually verbalized by the child with the adult's help.

In her work on the speech development of her bilingual Italian – German daughter, Cunze [1980] gave one example which perfectly illustrates this mechanism:

[Dunia's father has often drawn her hands.]

**D** (1;11): *Papi mala.* (Papa, draw.) [She points to the piece of paper, where other figures have already been drawn.]

**F**     [trying not to draw any more]: *Papi?*

**D:**    *Male Kia.* (Draw Dunia.) [So far, we have seen a complete nuclear sentence, "Papi draw Dunia". But then Dunia continues:]

**D:**    *Dunia mano.* (Dunia hand.) [This is interpreted by her father to mean, "Draw Dunia's hand".]

**F:**    *Prendi il telefono, Dunia!* (Take the phone, Dunia.)

**D:**    *Mano si.* [She whines and points to the paper.]

**F:**    *Vieni, vieni. Andiamo. Vieni qua, vieni, vieni.* (Come, come. Let's go. Come here. Come.)

**D**     [whining]: *Mano, mana, mojo, mano. Mano Papi. Paapi!*

**F:**    Eh!

**D:**    *Kia mano. Kia, kia, kia.*

**F:**    *Allora facciamo un'altra volta la mano di Dunia.* (Okay, let's draw Dunia's hand again.)

Monolingual children also use the same type of vertical nuclear constructions. The following examples were recorded by Miller [1976, p. 378] in his study on the speech development of two monolingual German girls:

**Simone:** *Mone Arm.* (Simona arm.)

**M:**    *Willste Maxe auf'n Arm?* (Do you want Maxe to hold you?)

**Simone:** *Mone Arm.*

**M:**    *Ach, mußt doch nicht auf meinen Arm. Bist doch kein kleines Wickelkind mehr.* (Oh, you don't need to be held. You aren't a little baby any more.)

**Simone:** *Armi komm.* (Arm come.)

Another example from Miller [1976, p. 363]: Meike is given a handkerchief.

**Meike:** *Nase putzen.* (Clean nose.)

**M:**    *Nase putzen, ja.* (Clean nose, yes.)

**Meike:** *Meike putz.* (Meike clean.)

Or, again from Miller [1976, p. 337]:

**M:** *Jack au.* (Sweater off, or sweater open.)
**MU:** *Die hab ich mir gerade angezogen.* (I just put this on.)
**M:** *Aufmachen.* (Open.) [laughs]
**MU** [laughs]
**M** [looks at T]: *Mama ausziech.* (Mamma take off.)

During the first stage, we can see that the sentence proceeds from vertical constructions to incomplete nuclear sentences and then to complete nuclear sentences. [12] This process implies that the language is slowly detaching itself from the context and becoming more and more self-sufficient. While a series of utterances made up of incomplete nuclear sentences is only comprehensible if it is closely tied to the context, a series of complete sentences can be understood even if it is not uttered in the actual context.

An example of the first case: Lisa (1;10) came home from a walk one day and said to her mother, *"Miao bua"*, accompanying her words with numerous gestures and repeated coughing. Then she said, *"Miao caa"*, and bent over, pretending to pet an animal. Her mother could not understand her story, but her father, who had been with her on the walk, was enthusiastic about the "perfect" way she told the story. What had happened was that they had seen a cat coughing and Lisa's father had told her that the poor thing was sick. Then they went up to the cat and it let them pet it.

An example of the second case: Lisa (2;8) looked out the window and said, *"Guarda, non c'è sole. E' andata via. Vene notte, va letto."* ("Look, there's no sun. "She" went away. Night come, go bed.")

---

12  The sentences described by Ervin and Miller [1964] and called telegraphic speech, or by Braine [1976] and called pivot grammar partially correspond to our incomplete nuclear sentences. Examples are:

| back on | fix on | all gone shoe | big plane |
| back off | fix off | all gone hot | my plane. |

Although Brown calls them modifiers and Ervin calls them operators, these authors nonetheless include such sentences as:  that may coat
                          want my coat
in the telegraphic speech category, thus grouping them with the others. But I consider the last two examples to be part of a later stage of development, namely, the second stage.

On the other hand, when Grimm [1977, p. 27] considers the quantitative aspects of the elements of an utterance (two- and three-word sentences), she includes within the category of modifiers such sentences as:

*das ein Haus* ("this a house")
*das ein Bibilein* ("this a hurt").

In my opinion, such sentences do not contain modifiers but should be placed within the previous category of nuclear sentences, because it is unlikely that *ein* is used to distinguish singular from plural. In other words, I doubt that the child is saying *ein Haus* as opposed to *zwei Häuser*.

Thus, this analysis shows with respect to nuclear sentence development that the question of completeness or incompleteness is linked to the growing capacity to communicate using a structure of speech which expresses a complete meaning and not merely a part of the child's thoughts. In the child who is learning to speak two languages, these structures develop identically in the two languages, and are not dependent upon one or the other language or on the fact that the child is learning two languages instead of one. Furthermore, the process of speech organization is the same for bilinguals as it is for monolinguals.

### 3.2.2 The Second Stage

At the same time that Lisa and Giulia started using complete nuclear sentences more frequently, they also began to produce the other basic structures. The second stage is one in which the child moves from one type of speech, formed of simple nuclear sentences, to another, in which such sentences are accompanied by amplified, complex and binuclear sentences.

There were only a few examples of amplified sentences at the beginning of the second stage. More and more complete amplified sentences appeared, while incomplete amplified sentences continued to appear now and then. Figs. 3.3, 4 show that the curve for incomplete sentences is constant at fairly low levels, while the curve for complete sentences rises sharply.

Tables 3.3, 4 (pp. 74 – 84) show that the German and Italian amplified structures developed simultaneously. During the period of speech acquisition observed, the girls produced German, Italian and mixed examples. But while Giulia produced roughly the same amount of German examples as Italian examples, the same cannot be said for Lisa, who produced few amplified sentences in either language until the age of 2;4, at which time she began to use numerous Italian examples. The German examples began to increase only at the age of 3;0. In Lisa's case, this greater use of one of the two languages for a certain period of time can be attributed to the greater contact she had with Italian. As will be seen in Chap. 6, Lisa had less contact with German than with Italian between the ages of 2;6 and 3;0.

In both girls, the implicit complex structure appeared [13] first in German and then in Italian (see Tables 3.5, 6, pp. 84 – 87) and Tables 3.13 – 3.18, pp. 104 – 105). At this point, the explicit structure was appearing only in Italian, although Lisa did use it in mixed sentences (see Tables 3.7, 8, pp. 87 – 90). This is the first sign the girls gave of differences between German and Italian. If we compare these results with those for monolingual children, we see that Lisa and Giulia exhibited the same development in German as monolingual German children and the same development in Italian as monolingual Italian children. In fact, Jana and Oliver, the two German monolinguals analyzed

---

13  For this study, a structure was considered to have "appeared" only when it had been used at least twice.

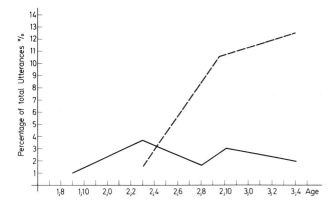

**Fig. 3.3.** Lisa's complete (– – –) and incomplete (————) amplified sentences

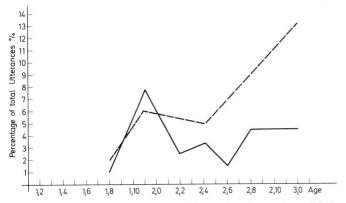

**Fig. 3.4.** Giulia's complete (– – –) and incomplete (————) amplified sentences

using the same procedure, began to use the implicit structure very early, at the beginning of the second stage, at the same time that adverbials and modifiers appeared. But their explicit sentences did not appear until the beginning of the third stage. Sara and Francesco, the Italian monolinguals, began to use the implicit and explicit structures simultaneously, but this was only towards the end of the second stage (see Tables 3.19 – 22, p. 106).

The fact that the implicit sentences were learned first in German was probably due to the use that each adult made of structures in his own language, this use being different in German and Italian. As Chap. 4 will show more explicitly, to express communicative intentions (see Volterra et al. [1979]) such as interrogatives and imperatives, German adults usually address their children with constructions containing modal verbs, which were considered implicit structures in this study. On the other hand, the Italian adult uses nuclear sentences to express the same communicative intentions.

**Table 3.13.** Sentence structure development in Lisa's German [a]

| Age | Nuclear | Amplified | | Complex | | | Binuclear | |
|---|---|---|---|---|---|---|---|---|
| | A | B | C | D | E | F | G | H |
| 1;7 | × | | | | | | | |
| 2;3 | | × | | | | | | |
| 2;4 | | | × | × | | | | |
| 3;2 | | | | | × | | 0 | |
| 3;4 | | | | | | | | 0 |
| 3;6 | | | | | | 0 | | |

[a] Key to Tables 3.13 – 22.

A – Nuclear sentences  F – Relative sentences
B – Adverbials  G – Coordinated sentences
C – Modifiers  H – Subordinate sentences
D – Implicit sentences  × – Structures without connective
E – Explicit sentences  0 – Structures with connective

**Table 3.14.** Sentence structure development in Lisa's Italian [a]

| Age | Nuclear | Amplified | | Complex | | | Binuclear | |
|---|---|---|---|---|---|---|---|---|
| | A | B | C | D | E | F | G | H |
| 1;7 | × | | | | | | | |
| 1;10 | | × | | | | | | |
| 2;4 | | | × | | × | | | |
| 2;8 | | | | × | | | | |
| 2;10 | | | | 0 | | | × | |
| 3;0 | | | | | | | | × |
| 3;2 | | | | | | 0 | | 0 |
| 3;4 | | | | | | | 0 | |
| 3;6 | | | | 0 | | | | |

[a] For key, see Table 3.13.

**Table 3.15.** Sentence structure development in Lisa's mixed sentences [a]

| Age | Nuclear | Amplified | | Complex | | | Binuclear | |
|---|---|---|---|---|---|---|---|---|
| | A | B | C | D | E | F | G | H |
| 1;7 | × | | | | | | | |
| 2;3 | | × | × | | | | | |
| 2;4 | | | | | × | | | |
| 2;6 | | | | × | | | | |
| 2;10 | | | | | | | | × |
| 3;0 | | | | | | | × | |
| 3;4 | | | | | | | 0 | 0 |

[a] For key, see Table 3.13.

**Table 3.16.** Sentence structure development in Giulia's German [a]

| Age | Nuclear | Amplified | | Complex | | | Binuclear | |
|---|---|---|---|---|---|---|---|---|
| | A | B | C | D | E | F | G | H |
| 1;3 | × | | | | | | | |
| 1;9 | | × | × | | | | | |
| 2;2 | | | | × | | | | |
| 2;4 | | | | | | | × | × |
| 2;6 | | | | | × | | 0 | |
| 2;8 | | | | | | 0 | | |
| 3;0 | | | | | | | | 0 |

[a] For key, see Table 3.13.

**Table 3.17.** Sentence structure development in Giulia's Italian [a]

| Age | Nuclear | Amplified | | Complex | | | Binuclear | |
|---|---|---|---|---|---|---|---|---|
| | A | B | C | D | E | F | G | H |
| 1;3 | × | | | | | | | |
| 1;8 | | × | × | | | | | |
| 1;9 | | | | | × | | | × |
| 2;4 | | | | × | | | × | |
| 2;6 | | | | | | | 0 | 0 |
| 2;8 | | | | 0 | | 0 | | |
| 2;10 | | | | | 0 | | | |

[a] For key, see Table 3.13.

**Table 3.18.** Sentence structure development in Giulia's mixed sentences [a]

| Age | Nuclear | Amplified | | Complex | | | Binuclear | |
|---|---|---|---|---|---|---|---|---|
| | A | B | C | D | E | F | G | H |
| 1;3 | × | | | | | | | |
| 1;8 | | × | | | | | | |
| 1;9 | | | × | | | | | |
| 1;11 | | | | | | | × | |
| 2;2 | | | | | | | | × |
| 2;6 | | | | × | | | | |
| 2;8 | | | | | × | | | |
| 3;0 | | | | | | | 0 | 0 |

[a] For key, see Table 3.13.

**Table 3.19.** Sentence structure development in the Italian of Sara, a monolingual [a]

|  | Nuclear | Amplified | | Complex | | | Binuclear | |
|---|---|---|---|---|---|---|---|---|
| Age | A | B | C | D | E | F | G | H |
| 1;11 | × | | | | | | | |
| 2;1 | | × | × | | | | | |
| 2;3 | | | | × | × | | × | × |
| 2;4 | | | | | | | 0 | |
| 2;7 | | | | | 0 | | | 0 |

[a] For key, see Table 3.13.

**Table 3.20.** Sentence structure development in the Italian of Francesco, a monolingual [a]

|  | Nuclear | Amplified | | Complex | | | Binuclear | |
|---|---|---|---|---|---|---|---|---|
| Age | A | B | C | D | E | F | G | H |
| 1;5 | × | | | | | | | |
| 2;0 | | | × | | | | | |
| 2;2 | | × | | | | | | |
| 2;4 | | | | × | × | | × | × |
| 2;6 | | | | 0 | | | 0 | 0 |
| 2;9 | | | | | | 0 | | |
| 3;0 | | | | | 0 | | | |

[a] For key, see Table 3.13.

**Table 3.21.** Sentence structure development in the German of Jana, a monolingual [a]

|  | Nuclear | Amplified | | Complex | | | Binuclear | |
|---|---|---|---|---|---|---|---|---|
| Age | A | B | C | D | E | F | G | H |
| 2;1 [b] | × | × | | × | | | × | |
| 2;5 | | | × | | | | | |
| 2;9 | | | | | × | | 0 | × |
| 3;1 | | | | | | | | 0 |

[a] For key, see Table 3.13.    [b] Jana was first observed when she was already in the second stage.

**Table 3.22.** Sentence structure development in German of Oliver, a monolingual [a]

|  | Nuclear | Amplified | | Complex | | | Binuclear | |
|---|---|---|---|---|---|---|---|---|
| Age | A | B | C | D | E | F | G | H |
| 2;4 [b] | × | × | × | × | | | | × |
| 2;8 | | | | | × | | 0 | |
| 3;0 | | | | | | | | 0 |
| 3;4 | | | | | | 0 | | |

[a] For key, see Table 3.13.    [b] Oliver was first observed when he was already in the second stage.

It is no coincidence that in their first implicit structures in German, Jana, Oliver, Lisa, and Giulia all used the modal verbs, while these same structures appeared only later in the Italian of Sara, Francesco, Lisa, and Giulia. At this point, we are confronted with the still unresolved problem of whether it is correct to consider modal constructions implicit structures rather than nuclear structures, or, to be more precise, of where modal verbs stop and auxiliary verbs begin.

In Lisa's case, it should be observed that Italian dominated during the first 6 to 8 months of the second stage, thus causing an increase in mixed sentences and an absence of German. Thus, even implicit and nuclear structures were exhibited less in Lisa's German than in her Italian during this period.

The same can be said of Lisa's binuclear structures, which appeared in the second stage. There were Italian and mixed examples, but no German ones. On the other hand, Giulia's binuclear sentences were largely mixed, with almost none in either German or Italian; these appeared later and then simultaneously (see Tables 3.11, 12, pp. 92 – 96).

As was the case for amplified sentences, the curve for incomplete complex and binuclear structures was also constant and fairly low, while the complete curve for these structures rose sharply (see Figs. 3.5, 6).

If all of the curves are compared with one another, it can be seen that the curves for the structures which appear during the second stage do not repeat the pattern traced by the nuclear sentences in the first stage. In other words, while the child's process of nuclear acquisition goes through a process whereby incomplete structures first prevail and then give way to complete structures, which steadily increase, the same does not occur in the acquisition of complex, amplified and binuclear sentences.

If the ability to develop structures were dependent upon the number of words the child is able to produce when making a sentence, it would be reasonable to suppose that when a new structure appeared, the process would be the same as the one observed during the first stage. Thus, for example, the first inserted sentences would be incomplete inserted. But the data show that the degree of completion in all of the structures proceeds at the same rate as the development of completion in nuclear sentences. Thus, the child does not stop producing a part of the nuclear structure in order to produce an amplified sentence, but will, for example, produce incomplete amplified structures as long as he is producing incomplete nuclear structures, beginning to produce complete amplified structures only when he starts producing complete nuclear ones.

Thus, the increase in the number of words in a sentence should not be considered from a merely quantitative point of view, but rather from the most important aspect, which is the structural one. When the child has learned the complete nuclear structure, he will be able to produce complete sentences in all of the other structures as well.

There were no periods in which the children used more incomplete sentences in one of the two languages, and for this reason we may say that in both

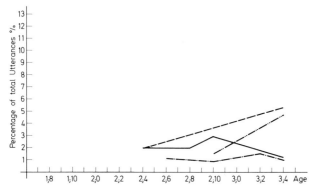

**Fig. 3.5.** Lisa's complete (– – –) and incomplete (————) complex sentences and complete (– ·· – ·· –) and incomplete (– · – · – · –) binuclear sentences

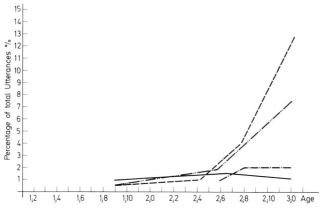

**Fig. 3.6.** Giulia's complete (– – –) and incomplete (————) complex sentences and complete (– ·· – ·· –) and incomplete (– · – · – · –) binuclear sentences

of the girls the aspect of completeness or incompleteness in sentence structure developed in German and Italian at the same time. However, the explicit and binuclear complex sentences that the girls were able to produce at this stage were still juxtaposed and unconnected. The term "connected" describes a sentence which contains a word, the connective, which has the specific duty of establishing or reinforcing the semantic relationship between the phrases. In "juxtaposed" sentences, the child does not yet use the connective and thus says, for example, "I want to eat, I'm hungry", which is a juxtaposed binuclear sentence, instead of "I want to eat because I'm hungry", which is a connected binuclear sentence. Naturally, not all complex or binuclear sentences call for a connective. As a matter of fact, many such sentences are correct only without the connective. But in this second stage, even the sentences which do call for the connective lack it (see Tables 3.7 – 12, pp. 87 – 96). These sentences are much less ambiguous if they are formulated with the connective, because the connective is the explicit expression of the nature of the relationship existing between two or more nuclear sentences. In fact, some connections between two nuclear sentences are very hard to understand without the connective; conditional sentences are an example.

The child acquires the ability to use the connective in sentence structure only later, during the third stage.

### 3.2.3 The Third Stage

During the third stage of sentence structure development, the child learns to say words which stand for meanings such as CAUSE, CONDITION, EMPHASIS, and TIME to relate phrases within a sentence. It was during this stage that complex and binuclear sentences containing the connective began to appear in Lisa's and Giulia's speech. The girls began to use binuclear coordinated and subordinate sentences with connectives at the same time, but only in Italian. In this, their development was the same as the development of Francesco, but it differed from that of Jana and Oliver (see Tables 3.13 – 22, pp. 104 – 106). The German monolinguals acquired the connected coordinates first and then the connected subordinates. It should be borne in mind that in most German subordinate structures, as in the explicit and relative structures, the conjugated and finite verb is placed at the end of the sentence. Thus, in cases such as

*Ich gehe nach Hause. Es ist spät.* (I'm going home, it's late.),

if the cause – effect relationship between the two sentences is expressed using the connective, the word order in the second sentence is changed and becomes:

*Ich gehe nach Hause, weil es spät ist.* (I'm going home because it late is.)

This sort of change does not take place in Italian, and so a purely syntactic change in word order such as this could become an additional hardship for children who are learning German, with the result that subordinates appear after coordinates. This does not mean, however, that the later appearance is characteristic only of children learning German. Sara, an Italian monolingual, also used connected coordinates first and connected subordinates later.

The connected explicit sentences did not appear at the same time in both languages. Thus, while Giulia began using numerous examples of connected explicit sentences in Italian at the beginning of the third stage, she began using examples in German only after the period treated in this study. Lisa used only a few examples of connected explicit sentences in Italian, but like her sister, she did not begin using this structure in German until after the period studied.

This is the second instance in which a difference was discerned between Lisa's and Giulia's German and Italian, but again the development was the same in the respective monolingual children. Tables 3.21, 22 (p. 106) show that neither Jana nor Oliver had begun using connected explicit sentences at this stage, and the available data on older German monolinguals, analyzed using the same procedure, show that even they develop connected explicit structures late and use the connective rarely. It should also be remembered that the connective in explicit sentences is not always used in the same way in Italian and German. Sentences which correspond perfectly require the connective in one language but not in the other. For instance:

a) *Guarda che lavo il vestito.*                    *Guck, ich wasche das Kleid.*
                                                    (Look, I'm washing the dress.)
b) *Vedi, che lavo il vestito?*                     *Siehst du, daß ich das Kleid*
   (Do you see that I'm washing                     *wasche?*
   the dress?)

As Tables 3.7, 8 (pp. 87 – 90) show, Lisa's and Giulia's explicit German sentences were always constructed like example a.

My explanation for the fact that the subordinates appeared at different periods in Italian and German also applies to the explicit structures, which pose the same syntactic difficulty as the subordinates in German: the finite and conjugated verb is moved to the end of the sentence when the connective is used.

In all of our recordings, there were only a few examples of relative phrases (see Tables 3.9, 10, pp. 90 – 92). The first example of this structure was juxtaposed, and it appeared in German in Giulia's speech at the end of the second stage:

**G** (2;2): *Giulia will Bonbon haben gekauft Mami.* (Giulia wants candy have bought Mommy.)

The second example appeared two months later in Italian, at the beginning of the third stage, and the connective was used:

**G** (2;4): *Mamma tieni quello peso che è pesante.* (Mommy, hold that weight which is heavy.)

It was only four months later that Giulia began to use the relative structure more frequently, but at that time she began to use it in both Italian and German:

**G** (2;8): *Das ist eine Puppe die ist wie Nonna Tina.* (This is a doll that is like Grandma Tina.)
**G** (2;8): *Dov'è il lupo che cammina?* (Where is the wolf that's walking?)

Conversely, with the exception of one relative juxtaposed sentence uttered at the age of 2 years and 10 months (*Mammi, wo is Halskette Lisa is?* [Mommy, where is necklace Lisa is?]), Lisa probably learned to use the relative construction in Italian first. This assumption is supported by an example of simultaneous translation: at the beginning of the third stage, when Lisa produced her first example of relative sentence structure in Italian, she translated the sentence into German for her mother using not a relative sentence, but an amplified structure:

**L** (3;2): *Mi dai una fotofia dove c'è Lisa piccola?* (Will you give me a picture where Lisa is little?)

**L** (3;2): *Gib mir ja? Bildchen für Lisa von Lisa klein klein.* (Give me, yes? Picture for Lisa of Lisa little.)

The next example of the relative structure appeared when Lisa was 3 years and 6 months old, this time in German:

**L:** *Wo ist die Puppe wo sagt Mama?* (Where is the doll that says Mommy?)

It was only two months later that Lisa began to use relative sentences more frequently. These examples appeared in both German and Italian at that point.

## 3.3 Summary

This chapter began with three questions: a) how do sentence structures evolve? b) do these structures evolve at the same time in the two languages? and c) are the structures which are considered more complex in one language learned later than their equivalent structures in the other?

In answer to the first question, it has been seen that there are three stages of sentence structure acquisition. In the first stage, the child acquires the ability to speak using nuclear structures; in the second, this ability is extended to the other structures as well; in the third, the child begins to use the connective, which marks the interphrasal relationship. Furthermore, these structures evolve towards completion hand in hand with the nuclear structure.

As for the other two questions, the data studied have shown that all structures save the explicit inserted structure (and perhaps the relative structure, but the available data are not sufficient to warrant such a conclusion) appear at the same time and develop together in both languages. The fact that the explicit form does not appear simultaneously can be understood by means of a comparison of sentence structure development in monolingual German and Italian children: the Italians began to use the relative and explicit structures last, as did Lisa and Giulia in Italian. On the other hand, the Germans developed the explicit inserted structures much later than they did the relative structures, just as Lisa and Giulia did in their German.

Thus, the blame for the late development of the German explicit sentence in bilingual children cannot be placed upon bilingualism; rather, this development must be due to the fact that bilinguals acquire typical sentence structure in the same sequence as the monolinguals of each language.

# 4. Several Aspects in the Acquisition of Morphology and Syntax

Such well-known researchers in the fields of monolingual and bilingual language acquisition as Stern [1928], Leopold [1939], Gvozdev [1949], Imedadze [1967], Tabouret-Keller [1969], Oksaar [1977], Brown [1979], and Klima and Bellugi [1966] have observed that a child's speech follows no morphological or syntactic rules during the first period. And in fact, my analysis of the German, Italian, and mixed sentences of bilingual children also confirmed that there is a period when morphology and syntax are not in evidence. The girls made their statements less ambiguous through emphasis, gestures, eye or facial expressions, body position, previous discussions, background, and knowledge shared by their listeners. They also referred repeatedly to the situational context and showed a tendency to speak of present events (see also Swain and Wesche [1975], Berko [1958], and Oksaar [1977]).

Thus during this first period, they used no articles, prepositions, or conjunctions, nor did gender, number, or case appear. Adjectives, nouns, and verbs appeared in one form alone. For instance, Giulia always said *gos Fisch, gos Teller*, and *gos pappa* ("big fish, big plate, big meal"), never changing the ending of *gos*, though it should be declined in accordance with case, gender and number, taking the forms *grosser, grosse, grosses, grossen, gross*.

Verbs were used in one tense and one person, some of them appearing only in the imperative mood and others in the indicative, either as a participle or in the present tense. If a verb was used in the present, it appeared either in the second or third person singular or in the first person plural. For instance, Giulia used:

| German | Italian |
| --- | --- |
| *Guck Teller* (look plate) | *Cade Giulia* (falls Giulia) |
| *Fährt* (drives) | *Guarda Giulia* (look at Giulia) |
| *Gibt Mamma a Buch* (give Mamma book) | *Andiamo* (let's go) |
| | *Acqua vuoi* (water want) |
| | *Giulia vuoi* (Giulia want) |

In the second period, progress is made towards speech that is coordinated by morphological and syntactic rules as it becomes more and more decontextualized.

The arduous task of learning to use the morphological and syntactic rules of adult speech calls for a drawn-out process of organization, analysis and arrangement, continued input, corrections, and, if one wants to excel, adequate schooling. As morphemes and syntactic rules begin to appear here and there in child speech, they begin to grow like ivy within and above the principal elements of the sentence, and their development is sometimes prolonged for years [Brown, 1979]. In fact, the use of certain morphological rules does not mean that the child has completely mastered them. As Mussen et al. [1976, p. 208] point out, "a great deal of time may elapse between the appearance of a certain morpheme and the moment when it begins to be used correctly at all times".

It has often been observed that the first forms are used correctly by children and then replaced or joined by incorrect forms [Clark, 1977; Karmiloff-Smith, 1978]. In this vein, Bever [1970] points to the example of passive English sentences which the child starts out saying correctly but then begins to misuse as he generalizes the form. According to Leopold [1956, p. 124], the incorrect forms are the best evidence of the child's ability to make rules (*Konstruktionsleistung*), while the initial correct forms are merely mechanical repetition. In the bilingual child, this ability to make rules appears in both languages, and instead of remaining fixed in one, it may pass back and forth, sometimes producing forms which are nonexistent in conventional usage. But as the people around the child correct these forms and continually propose the conventional ones to him, he ends up using only the latter. Once the rules have been crystallized in the right channels, they are transferred from one language to the other only in certain circumstances.

The "mistakes", i.e., the results of the child's ability to make rules, which unfortunately scholars of bilingualism all too often see in a negative light as linguistic imperfections and corruptions, can give us the information we need to achieve a greater understanding of the processes involved in bilingual acquisition and, in more general terms, in all language acquisition.

My systematic observations of Lisa's and Giulia's speech gradually led me to conclude that the simultaneous acquisition of two languages is not an automatic juxtaposition of two processes of language acquisition; it is instead the formation of two linguistic systems under conditions of complex interaction which are both based or depend upon the same process of cognitive, linguistic, social, and emotional maturation.

The child gradually evolves, and as he reaches each new level of development, both languages benefit, because there is only one level of speech organization, which in the case of bilingual children unfolds along two lines. Chapters 2 and 3 of this work have amply confirmed this hypothesis. Bilinguals start from one lexical system formed of words from both languages, in which they give priority to new words over equivalents. Not even at the point when the child realizes he is learning two different languages does he begin to learn through equivalents. Furthermore, we have seen that sentence structures appear at the same time in both of the languages and/or in mixed sentences, as soon as the child is able to construct them. Similarly, the ability to speak using more and more complete sentences also develops simultaneously in the two languages. But if the child has less contact with one of the two languages for a time, some structures of that language may not be used at all. When the contact is resumed and the child goes back to speaking the language, he does not regress to the previous level, but starts out from the level he has since attained in the other language.

Raffler-Engel [1965, p. 177] notes that "the transition from baby talk to adult speech occurs simultaneously in both languages." This surprised her, because the child observed used Italian much more than English, in which his vocabulary was extremely poor. She continues, "The transition took place shortly after his third birthday; from then on, the child preferred to deal with his ignorance of an English word by using Italian words and endings in a sentence he meant to say in English, rather than limiting himself to his old system of the holophrastic sentence".

Within the sentence itself, a distinction may be made between semantic elements and the rules which must be respected if the sentence is to be grammatically correct. According to Slobin [1975], languages have identical semantic structures which, however, are expressed using different grammatical rules. The child who is learning to speak must come to understand which specific set of rules is formally marked in his language. Thus the bilingual child must learn not only two different lexical systems made up of words having basically the same meanings, but also all the different ways of combining these words by grouping them according to two wide-ranging sets of rules: those belonging to language A and those belonging to language B.

Certain aspects of morphology and syntax are equivalent in German and Italian, while others are different.[1] Studies on lexical-phonological interferences [Zydatiss, 1976] have shown that languages with similar phonological systems are harder to distinguish from one another. But as the types of sounds used in German are completely distinct from those used in Italian, German-Italian bilingual children have less trouble distinguishing and keeping the two languages separate, and can thus elaborate precise phonological rules for each language. These rules are supported by sound, a concrete factor which is easily perceived and is full of contrasts between one language and the other.

But there is no such distinction between the morphological aspects of the two languages. Certain aspects are equivalent, while others are only partially similar. Furthermore, within the rules of each language there are numerous exceptions which make it even harder to learn morphology.[2]

In learning the morphological rules of Italian and German, the bilingual child also has to learn that:

---

1 "Equivalent" is used here to mean aspects which exist in the grammar of both languages and serve the same function.

2 For example, German verbs of motion "always" call for the accusative, except when used with the prepositions *mit, von, aus,* and so forth, which always call for the dative.

— Certain aspects exist in both languages. For instance, both languages use single and plural definite and indefinite articles, and form the present perfect with an auxiliary verb and participle.
— Other aspects only exist in one of the two languages. For instance, the neutral article exists only in German, as does the rule requiring the auxiliary to be placed last in secondary clauses.
— The aspects which do exist in both languages and are the same from a functional point of view may still be partially different. For instance, equivalent nouns may have different genders, e.g., *der Stuhl* (m.) ("chair") and *la sedia* (f.), while others have the same gender, e.g., *der Baum* (m.) ("tree") and *l'albero* (m.).
— Equivalent aspects may be used differently in the two languages. For instance, adult Italians often speak to their child in first person plural: *andiamo, giochiamo, facciamo,* etc. ("let's go", "let's play", "let's do"), while adult Germans use the modal *wir wollen spielen, wir wollen singen,* etc. ("we want to play", "we want to sing", etc.).

It must also be remembered that every morphological rule goes through a long process from its first appearance to the stage of correct adult usage. Based on the literature on this subject and my own observations, this process can be represented as follows:

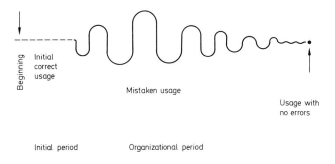

Beginning · Initial correct usage

Mistaken usage

Usage with no errors

Initial period        Organizational period

Naturally, the line in the diagram will vary in length and amplitude depending on the rule under consideration, the child, the environment he lives in, and the language itself.

This chapter investigates the question of how the bilingual child manages to learn such a complex system. Does the bilingual child take the same steps as the monolingual child in acquiring speech, or does he follow a uniquely bilingual process? Do the equivalent aspects appear at the same time in the two languages? Do the aspects which are not equivalent appear in the same sequence as they do for monolinguals?

Unfortunately, there are no exhaustive studies on the development of early morphology and syntax in monolingual Italian or German children, and even less research has been done with Italian-German bilingual children; a complete model for the acquisition of these aspects is still lacking. However, several studies which treat various aspects of morphology and syntax will be referred to in this chapter.

There are numerous morphological-syntactic rules, and they influence a wide range of spheres. In the following, a series of illustrations is given for those aspects that are of interest in the field of bilingual acquisition, beginning with the ones which exhibit the greatest number of analogies and then going on to those that are distinct in each of the two languages.

## 4.1 Verb Tenses and Conjugations

It has already been pointed out that the child commands only one person and tense for each verb at first, and begins to conjugate only later. In bilinguals, this process occurs simultaneously in the two languages. The first verbs used by Lisa and Giulia in more than one person and tense were:

**Giulia** (1;9)
German: *sag, sagt* (I say, he says)
            *macht, machen* (he does, to do)
Italian: *vuoi, voglio* (you want, I want)
            *cade, caduta* (she falls, she fell)
**Lisa** (2;4)
German: *nehm, nimmt* (I take, he takes)
            *macht, machen* (he does, to do)
Italian: *vuole, vuoi* (he wants, you want)
            *edi, visto* (you see, seen)

Lisa and Giulia first used the present and the participle in Italian and the present and the infinitive in German, and continued to do so for a while. Then they also began to use the infinitive in Italian and the participle in German (see Sect. 4.7).

## 4.2 Past Perfect

The past perfect also appears simultaneously in both languages. For example:

**G** (3;5) [telling about something that had happened a week earlier]: *Io ero andata qui e tu eri andata qui.* (I had gone here and you had gone here.)

**G** (3;5) [telling about the previous summer, when she had gone to see her aunt in the country]: *Guck Mami, ich hatte für zia Angela gesagt, die Schweine machen so: ho, ho.* (Look, Mommy, I had told Aunt Angela, pigs say this: ho, ho.)

## 4.3 Intralanguage Hypercorrection

One classic example of morphological "error" is hypercorrection of irregular forms based upon the rules the child is learning, e.g., the conjugation of verbs. Lisa and Giulia began to make errors of this sort at the same time in both languages. Giulia (2;2) used *vieno* instead of the irregular *vengo* ("I come") and *geschneid* instead of the irregular *geschnitten* ("cut"). Lisa (2;10) said *togliata* instead of *tolta* ("taken away"), and *gesuchen* instead of *gesucht* ("searched").[3] The examples of this type of superextension produced by monolingual children are very similar.

*German:*
Oliver (2;4)
*aufgehengt* instead of *aufgehangen* ("hung")
*reingegeht* instead of *reingegangen* ("entered")
*Italian:*
Marta (2;6)
*beveto* instead of *bevuto* ("drunk")
*vedeto* instead of *veduto* ("seen")

## 4.4 "Mistakes" of Agreement

"Mistakes" of agreement also occur at the same time in both Italian and German. For example:

**L** (3;9):  *Lisa ist hübsch und hübsch und hat ein hübsches Knoten.* [pause] *Ein Knodes.* (Lisa is beautiful and beautiful and has a beautiful bow [+ accusative or nominative ending *en*].) (A bow [+ *es*, in accordance with the *es* ending of *hübsches*].) [She says this while tying her bow and looking at herself in the mirror. Then]:
**L:**  *Mami!* [pointing to the bow so that her mother will look at it]
**M:**  *Uh! Einen hübschen Knoten hast du!* (Ah! A beautiful bow you've got.) [Her mother uses the accusative ending and Lisa corrects her]:
**L:**  *Ein hübsches!*

---

3  There are many similar examples in the literature:

Ervin [1964, p. 179] did – doed, broke – broked
Oksaar [1977, p. 198] *gesessen – gesitzt* and *gelesen – gelest*
Stern and Stern [1928, p. 249] *umgekippt – umkoppen* and *geklebt – kloben.*

Simões and Stoel-Gammon [1979] distinguish no less than five stages in their subject's acquisition of the first person singular present of the irregular Portuguese verb *fazer* ("to do"): *fez, fazeu, fazer, fazi,* and, finally, *fiz.* See also Leopold [1949b] and Mikés [1967], who are all of the same opinion.

Obviously, Lisa is convinced that it should be *hübsches* (nominative neuter), and thus she matches *Knoten* with *hübsches*, so that the result is the word *Knodes*, which does not exist and which the child surely could never have heard.

At the same age, Lisa used Italian sentences such as:

L:          *Questi sono troppi grandi.* (These are too big.) Here she makes the adverb *troppo* plural.

Or:

L:          *Questi soni troppi grandi.* She makes the adverb plural and gives the verb an ending which to her seems to be plural: *i*.

At the same age:

L:          *Mami, guck, eine Margherite.* (Mommy, look, a daisy.)
L           [to herself]: *Una margherita, eine margherite.*

Similarly, Giulia:

G (2;10):   *Und die vielen Rosinen wein so dollen?* (And all the *Rosinen* cry so much?) She gives to the word *dolle* ("much") a plural ending: *en*.

Or:

G (2;9):    *Un dento rotto* instead of *dente rotto*.
G (2;8):    *Soni bagnati* instead of *sono bagnati*.
G (2;9):    *Anche i tuoi piedini soni freddi.* (Your feet are cold, too.)

G (2;9):    *Ho lo persa.* (I it lost.) "Lost" has been made feminine because "ball" is feminine.
L (3;10):   *No. Ho lo perso.* Lisa accentuates the *o* to correct her sister, but Giulia misunderstands her:
G:          *Lisa, io ha la persa!* Giulia accentuates the word *io* ("I") and puts the entire sentence in the feminine.

G (3;2):    *Guarda che bel fungo ho trovato. Ho trovato uno buono. Uno russolo.* (Look at the nice mushroom I found! I found a good one. A *russola*). The feminine proper noun *russola* has been made masculine, like *fungo*.

## 4.5 Diminutive and Augmentative

The ability to form the diminutive and the augmentative also appears at the same time in both languages. Giulia (2;6) had been using the words *Knopf* ("button") and *latte* ("milk") for quite a while. In the following, Giulia compares differently sized buttons:

**G:**    *Knöpfchen von Giulia das. Knopf gross, ganz gross von Mami.* (That is Giulia's small button. Mommy's button is big, really big.)

**G** (2;7) [looking in the refrigerator and seeing one half-liter carton of milk and one two-liter carton]: *Piccolo piccolo lattino, Grande grande lattone.* [She has used the diminuitive *ino* and the augmentative *one* for the milk cartons.]

It is interesting to note that when Giulia pronounced the diminutives her voice was quite high, while she used a low voice in pronouncing the augmentatives.

Lisa and Giulia had no trouble learning that apart from such specific words as *grande, molto grande* ("big", "very big"), etc., Italian has suffixes which increase or decrease the size of the objects (see Bates and Rankin [1979] for a study on the acquisition of diminutives and augmentatives in monolingual Italian children). They also learned that German only has such suffixes for the diminutive. For example:

**L** (3;9):    *Die Fische sind hässlich. Und die kleinen und die grossen.* (Fish are ugly. And the small ones and the big ones.)

**M:**    *Die grossen?* (The big ones?)

**L:**    *Das hier pesciolini, das hier pesciolone.* (These are little fish, this is a big one.)

**M:**    *Was ist das?* (What is this?)

**L:**    *Pesciolone, Fescione* [ = *Fisch* + *pesciolone*]

**M:**    *Fescione?*

**L:**    *Ja, ein Fisch ganz gross. Pesciolone. Fescione!* (Yes, a really big fish ...)

**M**    [laughing]: *Ah! Und das ist ein kleiner Fisch, wie sagt man auf italienisch dazu?* (Oh! And this is a small fish, what's the Italian for that?)

**L:**    *Un piccolo pesciolino.* (A small fishy.)

**M:**    *Und auf deutsch?* (And in German?)

**L:**    *Ein klein Fischlein.* (A small fishy.)

## 4.6 Articles

German and Italian articles are only partly equivalent, and the former are more complex than the latter.[4] German has three genders: feminine, masculine and neuter, while Italian has only the first two. The German article is modified in the plural and the singular and in four cases: nominative, accusative, dative, and genitive. In Italian, the article is not declined. The use of the article in German is complicated even further by the fact that different

---

4 The greater difficulty of the German article causes errors among German monolingual children, and it was a great obstacle for Lisa and Giulia as well.

genders and cases are phonetically identical. Thus, *der* is the masculine nominative definite article, but it is also the feminine dative definite article. For example: *die Frau ist nach Hause gegangen* ("the woman went home") and *der Mann ist nach Hause gegangen* ("the man went home"), but *ich habe es der Frau gesagt* ("I told it to the woman"). Here the child is likely to protest that it should be *die Frau* and not *der Frau*, and one of the reasons for this is that he learns the gender before the case.[5] In German, articles which are identical in appearance but different in meaning can be found in virtually all cases and genders, as is shown by the following list of definite (D) and indefinite (I) articles.

|  | Feminine D/I | Neuter D/I | Masculine D/I | Plural D/I |
|---|---|---|---|---|
| Nominative | die/eine | das/ein | der/ein | die |
| Accusative | die/eine | das/ein | den/einen | die |
| Dative | der/einer | dem/einem | dem/einem | den |
| Genitive | der/einer | des/eines | des/eines | der |

On the other hand, the use of Italian articles is simplified by very precise rules: both the definite and the indefinite singular feminine articles always end with *a*, masculine definite and indefinite articles usually end with *o*, and the respective plurals with *e* and *i*. This rule applies not only to articles but also to nouns and adjectives, and thus it is reinforced. The ending of the article is almost always the same as that of the noun and the adjective, as in *la bella bambola*, or *lo zio allegro*, whereas in German there are no clear rules at all [Roeper, 1973]. The simple and easily discernible Italian rules have two exceptions:

1) The masculine definite article is *il*, rather than *lo*, if the word directly following it begins with certain letters: *lo zio*, but *il gatto*.

2) Both masculine and feminine definite articles must be apostrophized before vowels, as in *l'uomo, l'anima, l'elefante*.

It is obvious that the errors made by Italian children stem from these two aspects. It is easy to say *il zio* instead of *lo zio*, or to think, for example, that *l'elefante* is one word, and thus be led to say *lelefante* or *lo lelefante*, even while using *un elefante* at the same time.

Another aspect of usage which is not always the same in German and Italian relates to the omission of articles [see Manzotti, 1978, p. 147]. In Example 1 below, the Italian sentence requires the article. In Example 2, the German equivalent of Example 1, the article is not necessary. In Examples 3 and 4, neither the Italian nor the German sentence requires an article.

---

5 The use of the declined article begins at about 2;6 – 3;0, while the protests come much later, at about 6 or 7, probably when the child realizes the different meanings of the article in the accusative and the dative. Karmiloff-Smith [1978] convincingly proves that the child only gradually discovers the manifold functions of the article.

1) *Il ferro ha molti usi.* (Iron has many uses.)
2) *Eisen wird vielfältig benutzt.* (Iron has many uses.)
3) *Ho comprato vino, pane e marmellata.* (I bought wine, bread and jam.)
4) *Ich habe Wein, Brot und Marmelade gekauft.* (I bought wine, bread and jam.)

Although German articles are more complex than Italian ones, they nevertheless appear at the same time. Lisa and Giulia began placing sounds in front of Italian and German words very early. For example:

Lisa (1;9)                        Giulia (1;8)
*m pappa* (food)                  *a Teller* (plate)
*a nonna* (grandma)               *a piedi* (feet)
*e pupa* (baby)
*e Bauch* (tummy)
*n Buch* (book)

Italian children also use a proto-article of this sort:

Francesco (1;10)                  Claudia (1;8)
*a palla* (ball)                  *a bambola* (doll)
*a vite* (screw)

as do German children:

Peter (2;1) [Ramge, 1975, pp. 89, 90]
*n Haus* (house)
*n Stuhl* (chair)
*n Fahrrad* (bicycle)

English and French children also have an initial proto-article, which according to Karmiloff-Smith's hypothesis [1979, p. 216] serves at least two important functions: "It enables the child to make a distinction between proper names (absence of article-like element) and common names (presence of article-like element [see Katz et al., 1974]) and ... it enables the child to separate 'thing-like' words from 'action-like' words."

However, these proto-articles were also sometimes used by Lisa and Giulia in front of verbs. It is excessively optimistic to attribute to these sounds such distinct functions as those theorized by Karmiloff-Smith; there is as yet no data which convincingly supports the idea that children are able in this early period to make distinctions (and thus true linguistic analyses) such as: this is a man (common noun) and not Daddy (proper noun), and consequently use a sound for the first and not for the second. Nor is it feasible that they are able to realize that "table" is not an "action-like" word and that they can therefore use a sound before it. Probably the child's first step is to recognize that certain words are preceded by a sound, without exactly identifying the sound itself or the words that are preceded by it. However, it is interesting to note that the use of these proto-articles appeared at the same time in the two languages.

The first true articles, which appear a bit later, serve to distinguish between the definite and indefinite aspects [Brown, 1979; Karmiloff-Smith, 1979a], and the masculine, feminine and neuter genders. Lisa and Giulia mainly used the masculine and/or neuter indefinite articles in German, and the feminine definite article in Italian. For Lisa, this period extended from 1;10 to 2;10, while in Giulia it was shorter, lasting from 1;8 to 2;0.

The examples in recordings 20 and 21 of Lisa's speech are typical of the way the girls were using the articles during that period.

| Lisa (2;10) Italian | | German | |
|---|---|---|---|
| Feminine Definite | Other | Masculine/Neuter/ Indefinite | Other |
| la porta (the door) | un pane (a bread) | ein Glas (a glass) | der Ball (the ball) |
| la bua (the hurt) | una ruota (a wheel) | ein Tisch (a table) | der Wolf (the wolf) |
| la casetta (the little house) | una barca (a boat) | ein Buch (a book) | die Sonne (the sun) |
| la sedia (the chair) | gli occhi (the eyes) | ein Pferd (a horse) | |
| la bicicletta (the bicycle) | | ein Märchen (a fable) | |
| la fenessa (the window) | | ein Fahrrad (a bike) | |
| la coda (the tail) | | ein Fisch (a fish) | |
| la mano (the hand) | | ein Stuhl (a chair) | |
| le mani (the hands) | | ein Kissen (a cushion) | |
| la barca (the boat) | | ein Boot (a boat) | |
| la pallina (the little ball) | | ein Vogel (a bird) | |
| la palla (the ball) | | | |
| la mela (the apple) | | | |
| la scarpa (the shoe) | | | |
| la bambola (the doll) | | | |

Like Lisa and Giulia, Italian monolingual children also use the article *la* most at first. The examples for Francesco were similar to those for Claudia.

| Claudia (1;8) Feminine | Italian Other |
|---|---|
| a bambola (the doll) | i peccioncini (the little pigeons) |
| a bossa (the purse) | i pallone (the big ball) |
| a pipi (the birdy) | i bittoto (the cookie) |
| a palla (the ball) | i occhiai (the eyeglasses) |
| a mano (the hand) | una pallina (a little ball) |
| a pallina (the little ball) | |
| a poltrona (the armchair) | |
| a macchina (the car) | |

Table (continued)

| *Claudia* (1;8) Feminine | Italian | Other |
|---|---|---|

a mamma (the mommy)
a bottotto (the biscuit)
la toletta (the toilet)
la piccoletta (the little girl)
la luce (the light)

(1;9)

la luce (the light)
la poltrona (the armchair)
la pastasciutta (the pasta)
la macchina (the car)
la pentola (the pan)
la pizza (the pizza)
la bambola (the doll)
la nonna (the grandmother)
la barchetta (the little boat)
a manina (the little hand)
a teta (the head)
a sambuca (the Sombuca)
a scatola (the box)
a povere (the dust)
a papa (the food)
a (l)uce (the light)

il lupo (the wolf)
il vino (the wine)
il disco (the record)
il tavaiolo (the tablecloth)
i occhiai (the eyeglasses)
il telefono (the telephone)

(1;10)

la papiella (the ducky)
la giacca (the jacket)
la molletta (the hairclip)
la pentoa (the pan)
a macchina (the car)
la zia (the aunt)
la caramella (the candy)
la palla (the ball)
a tazzina (the cup)
a Befana (the Christmas witch)

il fiore (the flower)
il vitellino (the calf)

(1;11)

a pottona (the armchair)
una radio
la mucca (the cow)
la cioccolata (the chocolate)
una caramellina (a candy)
la carta (the paper)
a adio (the radio)
a musica (the music)
la capiola (the somersault)
la pipi (the birdy)

i braccialetti (the bracelets)
il cappotto (the coat)

This preference for the article *la* may be due to the fact that it is more clearly heard than the others. The masculine definite article is often apostrophized when *lo* precedes a vowel. But this does not explain why the indefinite article is almost never used.

No thorough studies have been reported on the acquisition of the article in German, and the observations that several authors have made are not in agreement. Park [1974] maintains that *eine* is more generalized, while Mills [in press] thinks that *die* is more generalized among subjects from 4 to 6 years of age. Mills pinpoints the reason for this generalization in the greater frequency of *die* in German; it is not only the feminine article in the nominative and accusative singular, but also the plural article in all cases. However, such reasoning could also be applied to *ein*, which is used for both masculine and neuter, and is the same for all declensions, because the endings are often slurred in speech. Most of Miller's examples [6] are of definite articles. Wintermantel's two subjects, Jana and Oliver, used *ein, die, der,* and *das* with equal frequency.

*Jana* (2;1)

| | |
|---|---|
| die Puppe (the doll) | ein Tiergarten (a zoo) |
| der Papi (the father) | ein Wasser (a water) |
| das Schwein (the pig) | ein Bub (a boy) |
| der Engel (the angel) | ein Uhu (an owl) |
| die Omama (the grandma) | ein Mädchen (a girl) |
| die Hose (the pants) | ein Löwe (a lion) |
| die Mama (the mother) | ein Fedling (a bird) |
| | ein Garten (a garden) |

According to Grimm's data [1973] the article *ein* is used most often.

More thorough studies need to be conducted on the acquisition of articles in German and Italian children. Not only child speech, but also the speech of the adults who interact with the children should be analyzed. It is possible that these adults use certain articles more often than others with children.

The fact that the bilingual child uses definite, indefinite, singular, and plural articles does not necessarily mean that he has understood their function. In the beginning, certain words are used only with the definite or only with the indefinite article, and only in the singular or only in the plural. For instance, the child may consistently say *la casa* ("the house") and not *le case*

---

6 It is interesting that Miller's subject (Simone) used a series of sentences containing the article *de*, which is clearly not *die, der,* or *das*, but rather a sort of universal article good for all three genders:

| *Simone* (1;10): | de Mofa (Moped) | de Finger (finger) |
|---|---|---|
| | de Lala | de Brille (glasses) |
| | de Baby | de Balla (ball) |
| | de Mami | die Gummibärche (candy) |

Giulia also used this compromise for a while.

("the houses"), and so forth. These constructions may only be said to have been learned when the child begins to use all of them for each noun, i.e., the house, the houses, a house, etc.

Furthermore, there are examples of misuse of the definite and indefinite articles, such as:

**L (2;4)** [playing with a cardboard farm complex, and holding half a tree]: *Ein Baum?*
[Her mother thinks she wants confirmation of her statement.]
**M:**  *Ja, das ist ein Baum, mein Schatz.* (Yes, that's a tree, dear.)
**L:**  *Das da ein Baum wo?* (This there is a tree where?)
[Now her mother understands that she is looking for the missing half of the tree.]
**M:**  *Ja, wo ist denn der Baum, du hast nur das Unterteil vom Baum, nicht wahr?* (Yes, but where is the tree? You only have the lower half of the tree, don't you?)
[Then her mother finds the other half of the tree and gives it to the girl, who is thrilled and puts the two halves together.]

During this period, the girls were still not using the articles consistently, nor did they understand that the article functions as a distinction between definite and indefinite objects. Karmiloff-Smith [1979b] observed the ability to make this distinction beginning at the age of 2;10, when the children observed used both articles consistently. Clark [1977] strongly emphasizes the importance of the imitative strategy in the process by which morphology and syntax are acquired. Lisa and Giulia frequently used articles imitatively before they began to use them spontaneously. In addition, the words which later appeared most often, if not always, with articles in spontaneous speech were the ones which were first imitated with the article. The process of article acquisition might be said to be based upon recognition and imitation in this stage. But imitation alone cannot explain why Lisa imitated some articles and not others in the examples which follow.

**L (1;9)** is looking at a magazine with her mother. They see a picture of a child sitting on the grass and her mother points to its nose.
**M:**  *Das ist die Nase.* (This is the nose.)
**L:**  *Nade.*
**M**  [pointing to the eyes]: *Das sind die Augen.* (These are the eyes.)
**L:**  *Auge.*
**M**  [pointing to the flowers]: *Das sind Blumen. Die Blumen sind schön.* (These are flowers. The flowers are beautiful.)
**L:**  *Blua.*
[Later, M looks at the same picture.]
**M:**  *Das ist ein Bock, ein Bock und der macht bäh-bäh.* (This is a goat, a goat and it says baa, baa.)
**L:**  *Ein Bock.*

**M**          [pointing to the ball]: *Guck, da ist ein Ball.* (Look, there's a ball.)
**L:**          *Ein Ball.*
**L** (1;10) [playing ball with her parents, looks for the ball]:
**L:**          *Non è qua.* (It's not here.)
**F**          [pointing to it]: *Guarda, guarda, la palla, Lisa!* (Look, look, the ball, Lisa!)
**L:**          *Oh! La palla!*
              [Later, the child loses the ball again and M points to it]:
**M:**          *Da Lisa, da ist der Ball.* (Lisa, the ball is there.)
**L:**          *Da Balle!* (There ball!)

As we saw in Chap. 1, the bilingual child does not develop his lexicon through equivalents, but instead gives priority to new words. When he begins to use articles he is just starting the second lexical stage (i.e., he has just begun to use equivalents), and he has not yet acquired the feminine/masculine, definite/indefinite distinctions. Thus, Lisa's and Giulia's "specialized" or "split" use of the Italian feminine definite and the German masculine indefinite articles would seem to be a logical consequence of the preference for new words.

According to Brown [1979], English-speaking children, who have fewer hardships with articles because the only distinction made is between definite and indefinite, complete their acquisition of the article at about 3;0 or 3;6. By this Brown means that articles are not missing from sentences which should have them. This point is also reached by bilingual children. Giulia omitted some articles until the age of 2;2, and Lisa until 2;10, but after this they did it only rarely. The transition occurred in both languages at the same time. It is interesting to note that in both the girls this age corresponded to the period when they were beginning to use articles other than *la* and *ein* frequently, and to produce the first examples of plural and declined articles. Like the bilinguals, both Italian and German monolingual children acquire the plural articles after the singular ones. In the German of both monolingual and bilingual children, the case was acquired after the definite and indefinite singular articles. Some examples given by Miller [1976] and in Wintermantel's data show that even when articles are frequently used in the nominative, there are still none in the dative or accusative. Thus, with respect to the appearance and incorporation of the first acquisitions, the bilingual child develops the article in much the same way as the monolingual. [7]

---

7 Keller's results [1976, p. 163] in a test inspired by Bever [1970] and Maratsos [1974a] on the development of passive and active sentences give further support to the hypothesis that identical morphological and syntactical aspects are learned in the two languages at the same time and in the same manner as by monolingual children. Keller tested 70 bilingual English-and-Spanish-speaking subjects between 3;0 and 5;0. The test consisted in giving children dolls and asking them to do as they were told in sentences such as:

The bull pushes the lion (active)
The lion is pushed by the bull (passive)

The peculiarities of each language are respected in this process; for instance, even though the neutral article and case declension do not exist in Italian, they are nevertheless learned and used in German.

## 4.7 Participle and Infinitive

The participle and the infinitive do not appear at the same time in the two languages. The participle appears first in Italian, while the infinitive appears first in German. The first examples of the participle were:

| Giulia German | Age | Italian | Lisa German | Age | Italian |
|---|---|---|---|---|---|
| | 1;6 | fatto (done) | | 2;4 | schitto (written) |
| | 1;8 | detto (said) | | 2;4 | itto (seen) |
| gemacht (done) | 1;8 | rotto (broken) | | 2;4 | fatto (done) |
| | 1;9 | finito (finished) | gemacht (done) | 2;6 | tonata (returned) |
| | 1;9 | aiato (wet) | gegeben (given) | 2;8 | |
| gekauft (bought) | 2;3 | | geschrieben (written) | 3;0 | |
| geholt (brought) | 2;3 | | gekauft (bought) | 3;0 | |
| geschrieben (wrote) | 2;3 | | gegessen (eaten) | 3;2 | |

The first examples of the infinitive were:

| Giulia German | Age | Italian | Lisa German | Age | Italian |
|---|---|---|---|---|---|
| schauen (to look) | 1;7 | | sehen (to see) | 2;3 | |
| sehen (to see) | 1;9 | | schauen (to look) | 2;3 | |
| anschauen (to look at) | 1;9 | | haben (to have) | 2;4 | |
| ausziehen (to undress) | 1;9 | | machen (to do) | 2;4 | |
| zumachen (to close) | 1;9 | | | 2;7 | fale (to do) |
| | 2;1 | tagliare (to cut) | | 2;8 | cecae (to look for) |
| | 2;1 | dare (to give) | | 2;10 | scendere (to go down) |
| | 2;2 | sclibele (to write) | | | |

From the grammatical point of view, one would not expect the participle and the infinitive to be used differently in the two languages. The participle is used to form the present perfect in both languages, with the aid of the auxiliary "to have" or "to be":

The lion pushes the bull (active)
The bull is pushed by the lion (passive)

The two constructions are equivalent in English and Spanish. Keller's bilinguals not only showed the same learning sequences in both languages; they also paralleled the development of the English-speaking monolinguals studied by Maratsos.

*Ich habe gemacht* (I have done) *Io ho fatto*
*Ich bin gegangen* (I have gone) *Io sono andata*

The infinitive is used principally for modal verbs:[8]

*Ich möchte rennen* (I want to run) *Io voglio correre*

But if we observe the development of the participle and the infinitive in monolingual children, we see that the Italian children come to use the participle extremely early and the infinitive later, while German children do the opposite [Antinucci, 1975; Mills, in press; Miller, 1976]. What is the reason for this difference?

According to Mills, the German child's early and frequent use of the infinitive stems from the adult's use. Mills found that adults who interacted with small children often used constructions with modal verbs in:

interrogative sentences: *Möchtest du Wasser trinken?* (Do you want to drink some water?)

indicative mood: *So, und jetzt wollen wir alles schön aufräumen.* (And now we want to tidy up everything.)

imperative mood: *Du sollst das nicht in den Mund nehmen.* (You must not put that in your mouth.)

Lisa and Giulia's main German interlocutor, their mother, often used constructions with modal verbs, and this would account for the children's early use of them. But since Italian adults also often use constructions with such verbs, this does not explain why the children did not begin to use the construction at the same time in both languages.

The difference between German and Italian usage is a bit more subtle; Germans emphasize the infinitive verb more when they speak to children:

1. *Wasser trinken ja?* (Water to drink, yes?)[9]
2. *So, und jetzt alles schön aufräumen.* (All right, now it's time to tidy up well.)
3. *Das nicht in den Mund stecken.* (This not in mouth put!)

In Italian, on the other hand, the modal verb is either emphasized (example 1), or not used at all (examples 2 and 3):

---

8 The infinitive is also used in forming the future tense in German, as in *ich werde rauchen* ("I will smoke"). However, at this age, children do not yet use the future.

9 It is important to remember the role played by the different ways in which Italians and Germans use a certain construction that children utter and hear quite frequently, i.e., "to want to have". In Italian, the desire to possess may be expressed by the modal verb alone, so that it is enough to say *io voglio* ("want"), and *avere* ("to have") is understood. But in German, *ich will* is not automatically understood to include *haben*. If the polite form *ich möchte* is used, the infinitive verb is even more necessary. In Italian, the polite form of "to want" (*vorrei*) can be used without the infinitive.

1. *Vuoi acqua?* (Do you want water?)
2. *Mettiamo a posto?* (We tidy up?)
3. *Non si mette in bocca!* (You don't put it in your mouth!)

As soon as the child begins to use these verb forms, the adult adapts himself to the child's speech, thus reinforcing it.

Because Italian children acquire the participle early and Germans acquire it late, we may suppose, by analogy, that Italians use it often whereas Germans do not. While Mills [in press], like Park [1974] and Preyer [1882], affirms that German children begin to use the participle at a late age, she does not give any indication of how German adults use it with children. Studies by Miller [1976], Cunze [1980], and Volterra [1972], as well as the study described here, all show that Italian and German adults use different tenses to describe the events in which children participate. For example, after a child has sat down, the Italian adult uses the present perfect, while the German uses the present.

Early use of the participle and the infinitive leads to early development of the structures which are connected to them, i.e., the present perfect and the modal predicate with infinitive complement. Lisa and Giulia acquired the present perfect in Italian first:

**G** (1;8): *Giulia ha detto Clistina blutta.* (Giulia has said Cristina ugly.)
**G** (2;2): *Giulia hat gemacht das hier.* Giulia has done this here.)
**L** (2;4): *La Mamma c'e schitto.* (Mommy [is written].)
**L** (3;0): *Mami hat gekauft für Lisa ein fazzoletto.* (Mommy has bought Lisa a handkerchief.)

In the same way, Lisa and Giulia acquired the modal verb with infinitive complement first in German, just as the German monolinguals learned it before the Italian monolinguals (see pp. 102 – 103 on implicit complex sentences). Early contact with the two languages enables the young bilingual to catch these subtle differences in the use of verb forms which may have similar or even identical functions, and thus he will give priority to certain forms, just as his monolingual counterparts do. For example, in German, the girls said

*Lisa Bleistift haben* (Lisa pencil to have)

and in Italian

*Lisa vuole penna* (Lisa wants pen)

Or:

*Mammi seduta* (Mami seated)

and:

*Giulia sitzt* (Giulia sits)

## 4.8 Pronouns and Gerunds

Still another example of the bilingual child's understanding of the peculiarities of each language can be seen in the correct omission of pronouns and the use of the gerund.

### 4.8.1 Omission of the Pronoun

In some Italian and German sentences, the pronoun may be omitted (see p. 61). However, there is not always equivalency between the two languages, and the pronoun may be omitted more often in Italian than in German.

Lisa and Giulia had no trouble distinguishing the sentences in which the pronoun may (or must) be omitted, as these examples show:

**L** (3;8) is with her father and G.

**L** [to G]: *Andiamo a cercare le telline.* (We're going to look for cockles.) [no pronoun]

**L** [to M]: *Wir gehen die Telline suchen.* (We're going to look for cockles.)

**L** [to M]: *Ich hab gebremst.* (I put on the brakes.)

**L** [to F]: *Ho frenato.* (I put on the brakes.) [pronoun in German; none in Italian]

**L:**    *Cerchiamo le telline.* (We're looking for cockles.) [no pronoun]

**L:**    *Ich such die Telline jetzt.* (I'm looking for cockles now.)

**L** (3;6)

**F:**    *Venite a mangiare.* (Come to eat.)

**L**    [to her mother, who does not react]: *Vieni?? Vieni?* (Are you coming?) [no pronoun]

**L:**    *Kommst du mit?* (Are you coming?)

**L** (4;2)    [as she takes a towel]: *Jetzt muß ich ein Moment sciugare.* (Now I must a minute dry.)

        [A few moments later]:

**L:**    *Adesso devo sciugare.* (Now I must dry.) [no pronoun]

### 4.8.2 Use of the Gerund

Although the gerund exists in both languages, it has quite different functions in each. In Italian it is often used to describe actions which are taking place (*Giorgio sta giocando* "Giorgio is playing", *sto cucinando* "I'm cooking", etc.), while in German it is rarely used in everyday language. Sentences such as *lächelnd begrüßte sie ihn* ("smiling, she greeted him") are found almost exclusively in literary works. Lisa and Giulia only acquired the gerund in Italian:

**L** (2;10): *Giocando qua Lisa.* (Playing here Lisa.)

**L** (3;4): *Cosa state facendo?* (What are you doing?)

**G** (2;6): *Lisa sta telefonando.* (Lisa is using the phone.)

**G** (3;0): *Sto aggiustando il gallo.* (I'm fixing the rooster.)

## 4.9 Understanding Subtle Differences

Not only in morphology, but also in the lexicon, the bilingual child perceives differences and subtleties in the meanings of words that appear to be equivalent but actually are more specific in one language. For example, Giulia distinguished between the German words *zum* and *für*, both of which are equivalent to the Italian *per*:[10]

**G** (2;3): *Das ist zum schleiben.* (This is for writing.)
**G** (2;3): *Quetto pe' sclibele.* (This is for writing.)
**G** (2;3): *Das ist für Giulia.* (This is for Giulia.)
**G** (2;3): *Quetto pe' Giulia.* (This is for Giulia.)

## 4.10 Superextension of Forms into Both Languages

During the organizational period (see p. 115) some forms which perhaps are more effective in one language are supergeneralized and applied to both languages. The Italian morphemes *ri, ci,* and *iamo* and the German morphemes *wir, aus,* and *ge* are some examples (see also Sect. 5.3). Lisa and Giulia attached the prefix *ri*, which means "once again", to German words, as in *rimachen, riholen, rinehmen,* etc. *Ci* is a pronoun which corresponds to the first person plural and may appear as a verb suffix (*portaci, dacci* "take us", "give us", etc.). Giulia said *bringci ein Tisch?* (*bringen* "to bring", *ein Tisch* "a table"). *Iamo*, the ending for verbs in the first person plural present indicative, was used by Giulia with German verbs, as in *gehndiamo, singhiamo*, etc.

However, it is not necessarily true that *iamo* is more effective than the corresponding German pronoun *wir*. For example, Cunze's daughter Dunia said *famea*, using the Italian root *fare* ("to do") with the German plural *wir* ("we"), which in Frankfurt dialect is pronounced *mir*. In German this pronoun is often used after the verb, as in *machen wir, gehen wir,* and pronounced *machenwa, gehenwa* and so forth, i.e., *machemea, gehenmea*.

The morpheme *aus* modifies the meaning of the verb. For example, *trinken* means "to drink", and *austrinken* means "to drink everything in the glass". Lisa (2;4 – 3;0) usually said *Giulia hat ausbevuto?* to ask if her sister had drunk everything, or *Hast du Milch ausbevuto?* to ask if she had finished drinking her milk.

The particle *ge* marks the participle in German, and the girls used it before Italian verbs as well:

1. (2;8) *Io ho gevinto.* (I *ge*won, i.e., from *vinto* "won")
2. (2;8) *Giulia hat gescappa in Bett.* (Giulia *ge*ran off to bed, i.e., from *scappare* "to run off")

---

10 See also Padilla and Lindholm [1976, p. 119], who found the Spanish equivalents *ahi, alli,* and *allà* for the English "here".

3. (2;6) *Hast du getolto, Mami?* (Have you *ge*taken off?, i.e., from *tolto*)
4. (3;9) *Lisa hat geballa.* (Lisa has *ge*danced, i.e., from *ballare*)

Examples 1 and 3 show the participle markings for both Italian and German. Such superextensions, which were not observed after 3;6 – 4;0, are of particular interest, because they show that the child has begun to understand the function of the morphemes and to detach them from the word roots. Thus, at a certain point in his development, the bilingual child learns one or more of the rules for expressing each function and then applies them to both languages. Only later does he learn that he must use rule X' only in language X and rule Y' only in language Y.

## 4.11 Negation, the Adjective, the Possessive, and Subject-Verb Inversion

The process described at the end of the preceding section was also observed in the acquisition of sentence position for negations, adjectives, and possessives, and for subject-verb inversion.

Let us look first at negation. In German, the negation follows the verb, whereas in Italian it precedes it: *Karl trinkt nicht,* but *Carlo non beve.* In an initial period, both girls used the typically infantile form of negation, which is to attach *no, non* or *nein* to the beginning or end of an affirmative sentence. [11] At the same time, however, they also produced negative sentences which corresponded to correct Italian. During a second period, the girls used both correct and "incorrect" word order in German and Italian negatives, while in the third period, only correct constructions were used. Tables 4.1, 2, which are divided according to the first, second, and third periods, give examples of negative sentences from the data for each of the girls.

Let us now consider the position of the adjective. In German the adjective precedes the noun, while in Italian it may precede or follow it, depending upon the adjective used (see Francesconi [1981]). For example, *ich kaufe ein enges Kleid* ("I'm buying a tight dress") as opposed to *Io compro un vestito stretto* or *ho visto una bella casa* ("I saw a nice house"). As Tables 4.3, 4 show, Lisa used the adjective in the "right" position until 3;2, and Giulia until 2;0. This was followed by a period in which both girls used it before and after the noun in both languages. Then, from 3;8 on (Lisa) and 3;4 on (Giulia), they went back to using it in the correct place.

Turning now to the possessive, we see that in German, it is usually expressed by means of the genitive or the preposition *von* ("of"), as in *Marias Haare* ("Maria's hair") and *die Haare von Maria.* In German dialect the construction *Maria ihre Haare* ("Maria her hair") is also used. The Italian possessive is always expressed using the preposition *di* ("of"), as in *i capelli di Maria.*

---

11 Monolingual children who speak other languages also express negation in this way; Klima and Bellugi [1966] call it the first stage of negation development.

**Table 4.1.** Negative constructions in the data on Lisa

| | German | | Italian | |
|---|---|---|---|---|
| | Verb + Negative | Negative + Verb | Verb + Negative | Negative + Verb |
| 1;5 | | | | Non c'è più eh! |
| 1;9 | Ta da daki noo! | | | Non è qua. |
| 2;4 | | | Fa pilli pilli no. | Io non vuole. |
| | | | Lisa cade no. | |
| 2;6 | | | | No, non vuole. |
| 2;7 | Lisa haia haia machen no. | | Giulia vuole haia no. | N'c'è più Lisa. |
| | Kein giogioletto kaputt nein. | | Questa non è la bottiglia no. | Questa non è la bottiglia no. |
| | Radio no, badi badi no. | | Lisa va da la no. | |
| | | | Questo è tuo no … lompe no. | |
| 2;8 | | | Non fa totò no. | Non fa totò no. |
| | | | | In vase non c'è più vase. |
| | | | | Quella non è a penna di Lisa. |
| | | | | No, no c'è più. |
| | | | | Quella non fa, non fa. |
| 2;9 | | | Non è morto Chicchi no. | Non è morto Chicchi no. |
| | | | Fa rompe no. | |
| 3;2 | Noch nicht gekommen. | | | |
| 3;3 | Giulia will nicht weiterschlafen. | Onkel Karlos nicht versteht Italienisch. | | Papi non è munto. |
| 3;4 | Lisa hat kein Topolino, kein Giogioletto. | | | Lisa non ha giogioletto. |
| | Papi ist nicht hier drinne. | | | |
| | Mami erzähl eine Geschichte no no no. | | | |
| 3;5 | Ist nicht Cremina. | | | |
| 3;6 | Ist nicht da. | Und nicht kommt Mami. | | Ecco non c'è l'auto. |
| | Ist nicht da die Sirene. | Nein, ich nicht will. | | Si, non c'è la pecora. |
| | Warum ich will nicht grün Blei-stift … | Ich nicht bin müde. | | Anch'io non la so contare. |
| | Lisa hat nicht Haare … und schwarze ist nicht da. | Ich nicht will der weisse Glas, ich will den grün Glas. | | Così anche non va bene. |
| | | | | Non ci sta dopo. |

**Table 4.1** (continued)

| | German | | Italian | |
|---|---|---|---|---|
| | Verb + Negative | Negative + Verb | Verb + Negative | Negative + Verb |
| | | Nicht geht das rein. | | |
| | | Ich nicht will eine Geschichte erzählen. | | |
| | | Nicht will in Haiabettchen gehen. | | |
| | | Ich nicht will das Fleisch. | | |
| | | Ich nicht will Käse aufessen. | | |
| | | Jetzt Papi nicht kommt? | | |
| 3;8 | Hab nichts gegessen. | Lisa nicht sitzt. | | Non far vedere a Mammi. |
| | Guck ist nicht kaputt. | Jetzt Papi nicht schimpft nicht mehr. | | Io non ci sto vedi? |
| | Lisa hat nicht eine Schleife. | Sonst ist nicht die Sonne da. | | Non ce n'è più. |
| | Dieses ist nicht eine Geldtasche. | Nicht sollst du machen. | | Non togliere, non toccare. |
| | Ich bin nicht so müde. | | | Non andare da Mamma. |
| 3;9 | ... tut nicht weh. | Papi nicht kommt? | | Tu non ci hai la cravatta. |
| | Man esst nicht alles. | | | Ma non rompere ... non c'è più la ... |
| | Ich will nicht studiern. | | | Se non mangi la minestrina non diventerai grande. |
| | | | | Io non lo so. |
| 3;11 | Ich weiss nicht die Geschichte. | | | Ma non c'è la porta ... |
| | Ist nicht da auf den Bild. | | | Papi non deve fare così. |
| | Auch dieses hier hat nicht Schwarzes. | | | Questo non sta fermo. |
| | Das ist nicht eine Blume. | | | Guarda questo grande non è. |
| | Ich weiss nicht jetzt. | | | Perché non devo fare il tetto. |
| | Aber das hier hat nicht Schwarzes. | | | Non voglio così. |
| | | | | Vedi che non c'è più. |

**Table 4.1** (continued)

| German | | Italian | |
|---|---|---|---|
| Verb + Negative | Negative + Verb | Verb + Negative | Negative + Verb |
| **3;11** | | | Quella non la ricerca. Non si entra che ... |
| **4;0** Das ist nicht ein Boot. Ist nicht so? Aber du musst nicht Portugiesisch sprechen. Ich weiss das nicht. Hat kein Brot. Wenn du das nicht machst nicht, dann ... | | | Non lo voglio io. Non devi andare là. Mamma non lo capisce. Non è da colorare. |

**Table 4.2.** Negative constructions in the data on Giulia

| German | | Italian | |
|---|---|---|---|
| Verb + Negative | Negative + Verb | Verb + Negative | Negative + Verb |
| **1;8** | | | N vuoi. |
| **1;9** Hin no. | | Tocca no. Pipì no. | Non è Mammi palla non è. Non è glande. Non è cip cip. Non so. Anina an è a casa. |
| **2;2** | Giulia nicht spukt da. Giulia nicht spuken. Mami nicht zum Schreiben das hier. | | Non è moletta. Giulia no se passa. |
| **2;3** Giulia macht aio nein. Giulia macht die Augen nein. Ich schreib aufm Papier nein. | Nicht hat dodoi. | | Quello no è la coda. Non può schreiben così. Giulia no può capace. |

**Table 4.2** (continued)

| | German | | Italian | |
|---|---|---|---|---|
| | Verb + Negative | Negative + Verb | Verb + Negative | Negative + Verb |
| 2;4 | Hab nicht soviele Blätter nein. Das hier malone nein. Das hier splecht nicht. | Giulia nicht Blot essen. Nicht spokelei. Nein spokelei. | Quetto parla non. | Vedi non cia fòide. Non ci sta vedi. Non si mangia. Non c'è piu. Quello non c'è la coda. non si scrive quello li. |
| 2;6 | Giulia kann nicht machen. Ist nicht zum Lachen. Giulia kann nicht anfassen. Mein Heft ist nicht da. Giulia nicht versteht nicht. | Giulia nicht schläft. Ich nicht mach kaputt diese Flasche. Nicht macht kaputt nein. Giulia nicht will dieses da. Giulia nicht versteht nicht. | | On cià le gambe. No metto. Non piange Gigi. Io non li conosco. … io non sono un bimbo. Non ce l'ho il leone. Non ce nè un altro elefante. |
| 3;0 | Ich zank nicht. Ich wein nicht. Ich hab nicht wehgetan hier. Ist nicht ganz egal. Ich will nicht studiern. Lisa hat nicht gehelfen. Geht nicht so. | Ich nicht bin ein Jungel. Ich nicht will mein Eierschlag. | | E anch'io non sono più böse. Così non si romperà. Io non mi tieno. Io non voglio dormire perché io non sono stanca. … poi non ci avevo paura. Questo non lo so. |
| 3;1 | Ich weiss das nicht. Nein, guck jetzt regen nicht. Womma nicht wieda anschaun. … geht nicht runta. Warum kann ich nicht. | Nicht läuft, fliegt? | | Guarda che non sa fare. Non c'è un'altra barca. Io non lo trovo. La figlia non rema. Così non è bene. |
| 3;2 | Ich hab nicht gelesen, nein. Kann man nicht reingehen. | | | Non si sputa. Adesso non c'è più. |

Table 4.2 (continued)

| | German | | Italian | |
|---|---|---|---|---|
| | Verb + Negative | Negative + Verb | Verb + Negative | Negative + Verb |
| 3;2 | Ist nicht da Pierina. Du passt nicht auf so sehr, ich ja. Schreibt nicht. Die Lumache sprechen nicht. Ich kann nicht. Ich will nicht Lisa dein Bleistift nimmt. | | | Non toccare la "garanza". Allora non voglio. Allora non facciamo ... Non mi devi tirare ... Le mie dita che non lo fanno fare. |

Table 4.3. Adjectival constructions in the data on Lisa

| | German | | Italian | |
|---|---|---|---|---|
| | Adj. + Noun | Noun + Adj. | Adj. + Noun | Noun + Adj. |
| 2;3 | Schöne Blume Schöne Blume. | | | |
| 2;4 | Ein schön Blum, Mama. | | | |
| 2;8 | Klein Ladio. Auch Lisa blaune Haare. Blonde Haale. | | | |
| 2;9 | | | Mangia ham buono la mela. Glande pescelino fa pipì. Guarda che bello sole, hai visto? | Cip, cip uno solo rosso. Pescelino glande. |
| 2;10 | Klein Boot. | | | |
| 2;11 | Die schön Schwein. Armes Schwein. | | | |
| 3;2 | | | | Pallone gran grande. |
| 3;3 | ... so viele Kinder. Papi hat kurze Haare. Ein kleines Haus. | Von Lisa klein klein. | | Questa è Lisa piccolina. |

**Table 4.3** (continued)

| | German | | Italian | |
|---|---|---|---|---|
| | Adj. + Noun | Noun + Adj. | Adj. + Noun | Noun + Adj. |
| 3;3 | Armer Federico. Klein Lisa. | | | |
| 3;4 | Da alles Haus. Ein grosser Vasino. Ein Buch mit so viele Ge-schichte. | | Questa tutta case. | |
| 3;5 | Armes Schwein, guck. Grün Meer, blau Meer. | | | |
| 3;6 | Der kleine Bade-zimmer. Ein hübsche Kandele. … grün Bleistift, ich will rot Bleistift. Der grosse böse Wolf. Ist die liebe Sonne da. Ein grosser Vasino. Der weisse Glas, der grün Glas. | Und die Zicklein marron und klein klein. Lisa will nur Schuhe dunkel-braun. Der Reis gut. | … tanti uomini Dov'è il grosso lupo? Il grosso lupo è … Quel bianco pecora … grande bastone. | … bambini tanti. Tanti, le donne tanti … Sì, le onde grandi. E lì un sole rosso rosso. Il riso buono. Io ho fatto due muri grandi. |
| 3;7 | Die grosse Musik … Ein klein böse Wolf. Arme Oma kranke. Was hat der kleine böse Wolf und der grosse böse Wolf? … eine rote Hose. Die arme Oma. Das kalte Was-ser … Die kleine Lisa hat soviele Haare Die kleine Giulia hat ein biss-chen Haare. | Es war einmal eine Geschichte hässlich. Eine Geschichte hübsch. Arme Oma kranke. Und die Oma kranke sagt ich will … | Una rossa palla. | Io ho fatto due muri grandi. Tu hai fatto due muri piccoli. Due muri belli. |

**Table 4.3** (continued)

| German | | Italian | |
|---|---|---|---|
| Adj. + Noun | Noun + Adj. | Adj. + Noun | Noun + Adj. |
| **3;8** Guck dieses blaue Wasser | | | Son capelli biondi. |
| Es war einmal ein kleines Mädchen. | | | Io sono un cacciatore felice. |
| Ein grosses Vasone für mich. | | | Una carta rotta ... perché è una scarpa blu. |
| Ein klein Baum und ein grossen. | | | Tanti capelli belli. |
| Lisa macht ein kleines Flugzeug. | | | |
| Das ist die kleine Schere? | | | |
| **3;9** Eine grosse Sonne. | | La brutta cattiva favola. | ... e il penello grande? |
| Der alte schwarze Kaugummi. | | | Ce l'ha la maestra nera. |
| ... ein hübsches Knoten. | | | Tu ci hai una cintura nuova dell'olologio. |
| Ein klein Fisch, ein blau Fisch, ein rosa Fisch. | | | La favola brutta. |
| Ein grosses Blatt, eine kleines Blatt. | | | |
| Guck die ganz kleine Bäume. | | | |
| Eine ganz große runde Birne. | | | |

**Table 4.4.** Adjectival constructions in the data on Giulia

| German | | Italian | |
|---|---|---|---|
| Adj. + Noun | Noun + Adj. | Adj. + Noun | Noun + Adj. |
| **1;8** Gos Fisch. | | E due alanci. | |
| Klein Kinda. | | Glande plano. | |
| | | Solo babau. | |
| | | Uno babau. | |
| | | Solo afante. | |
| **1;9** Gos gos Haiabettchen a Lisa. | | | |
| Gos a Mamma. | | | |
| Klein Zeh! | | | |

**Table 4.4** (continued)

| | German | | Italian | |
|---|---|---|---|---|
| | Adj. + Noun | Noun + Adj. | Adj. + Noun | Noun + Adj. |
| 1;9 | Anche Lisa klein Zeh! Auch Giulia gos Haia. | | | |
| 1;11 | Gos gos Zeh! Klein klein Zeh! A Giulia kleine Cleme. Giulia klein Kinda. | | Mamma glande cleme. Giulia piccolo cleme. | |
| 2;1 | Mami Giulia will klein klein klein Farbe. Von glosse Flau. Kleine Flau ge- schlieben: grosse Flau. Auch kleine Flau ein Stlich. | Ja, Mami, eine Schele bianco eine Schele lote. Das, hier eine Bürste für Giulia glosse. | | Giulia ci ha mani porche perché. |
| 2;4 | Das hier kleine Bliefe? ... kleine Blätter. Guck glosse Füsse. | Das ist der Stock klein klein | Fa: brutto l'acqua bella l'acqua. | Io faccio una pupi piccola. Guarda bambino piccolo. |
| 2;6 | Mach ein gros Haus. Eine kleine Sonne. Ein klein Knopf. | | Piccolo lattino. Glande lattone. | Questa la gonna lunga. |
| 2;9 | Ein kaputten Zahn. Ich will ein klein Blatt. Eine kaputte Gummi. | Füsse mutsig. | Piccolo armadio. Ci ho un rotto dente. Ah! che sporca acqua. Dov'è il mio nero capello? | Anch'io ci ho un dento rotto. |
| 2;10 | Will viel Geld ham. | | | E poi un film brutto. |
| 3;0 | So ein grosses Kind. Ich will zwei kleine Biciclet kaufen. Ein grün Bon- bon. Ist ein bisschen gros diese Susanna. | | | |

**Table 4.4** (continued)

| | German | | Italian | |
|---|---|---|---|---|
| | Adj. + Noun | Noun + Adj. | Adj. + Noun | Noun + Adj. |
| 3;0 | Ich hab weisse Hände. | | | |
| 3;1 | Ich hab gegeben zwei Decken für diesen Kind. Ein klein Blatt. Ganze Blumen, so Blumen. | Die Bonbon ganz viel. | Perché sono rotonde caramelle. | Adesso pipì lungo. Tante gomme rotonde. |
| 3;2 | Hübschen Boot hast du mal gemachen. ... ein paar Buntstifte. Ein grosser Kopf. | | | Una mano nera. |
| 3;4 | Wie dicker Buch. So ein grosses Ast. | Ich bin Zicklein krank. Und das is dein Wörterbuch klein. | | E io con la coda bella. Guarda anche fiocco giallo. E le bimbe piccole. E la gomma lunga. E i capelli neri. |
| 3;6 | Mein hübschen kleinen Ski. Das ist ein kleines Sack. Guck soviele Worte ... Ich will ein hartes Hocker. | | | Non è l'acqua sporca. Prendo il bichiere pulito. Prendo la matita colorata. Voglio i pantaloni corti. |
| 3;7 | Und dann das kleine Zicklein geht spazieren. Schöne Flöte. | | | I faggiolini lunghi mangio. |

At first, Lisa and Giulia used possessor-possessed sequences in both German and Italian, but without the genitive s, the prepositions *di* or *von*, or the above-mentioned construction with the possessive pronouns *ihre* or *sein*. They also used two-noun utterances which could be completed with verbs such as "to have", "to belong", etc. In a second period, they began to use *von, ihre,* and *sein* in German and *di* in Italian, and to make sentences using both forms, as in:

*Questo è di Giulia libro.* (This is of Giulia book.)
*Golfino von Armios.* (Sweater of Armio's.)

In a third period, they used only the *di* form in Italian and the genitive or *von* in German.

Both girls first expressed the possessive in German using the dialect form. When their mother, who quite often used that form, noticed this, she began to replace it with the genitive or the preposition *von*. [12] This occurred when Lisa was 3;7 and Giulia 2;6. As Tables 4.5, 6 show, two months after this adult pattern was abandoned, the girls abandoned it as well. It is important to point out that their mother did not begin to correct their speech; she merely dropped a consistent input pattern. This loss of the dialect form demonstrates the fundamental importance of a pattern given by the adult to the child for a certain function. In order for a pattern to be acquired, the input must be clear, constant, and continuous. The fact that the child has already begun to use certain structures does not necessarily mean that those structures have been learned. On the contrary, the rapid loss of the possessive pronoun shows how slowly and gradually children acquire speech, and how much they depend upon structural patterns received from adults.

Other authors have reported results which support the acquisition sequence observed in Lisa and Giulia. Bergman [1976, p. 87] analyzed the appearance and use of the possessive in Spanish and English in Mary, who at first (1;2 – 1;6) used the correct forms in both languages:

1. *Son las botas de Papa.* (Those are Daddy's boots)
2. That's Mommy's coffee.

Later, toward 2;3, she began saying things like:

3. *Es de Mamma's.* (Is of Mommy's)
4. *Es bebito de Paula's.* (Is baby of Paola's)
5. *Es Annie's libro.*

Forms 1 – 5 coexisted until about 2;5, after which the child used the standard form in each language, with occasional mistakes of the type shown in example 5.

Bergman thinks her analysis of the possessive confirms the hypothesis that there are two independent linguistic systems from the outset. She holds forms 3, 4, and 5 to be the consequence of a linguistic setting which did not establish a clear distinction between the two languages. Twice a week Mary visited a Chicano family with four children who interacted in Spanish. Once, when Bergman noticed that the children's mother used the construction *es Jennifer's?* she asked the woman if she used it often, and received the reply that it had been picked up from the children.

---

12 It should be remembered that the girls' mother was their principal and often only German interlocutor.

**Table 4.5.** Possessive constructions in the data on Lisa

| German | | | Italian | |
|---|---|---|---|---|
| Noun + (s) + Noun | Noun + Posses- sive pronoun + Noun | Noun + (von) + Noun | Noun + Noun | Noun + (di) + Noun |
| 1;8 | 1;8 | 1;8<br>Kita Kita Giulia | 1;8 | 1;8 |
| 1;9<br>Giulia Buch.<br>Giulia ...<br>  Beine. | 1;9 | 1;9 | 1;9 | 1;9 |
| 1;10<br>... Giulia haia<br>  haia.<br>Guia Beille.<br>Mamma nyam<br>  nyam cotta. | 1;10 | 1;10 | 1;10<br>Miao bua.<br>Mamma, Paola<br>  tita. | 1;10 |
| 2;1<br>Mami Baby. | 2;1 | 2;1 | 2;1<br>Giulia popo. | 2;1 |
| 2;3<br>Giulia Buch.<br>Lisa Schuhe.<br>Giulia Hand. | 2;3 | 2;3 | 2;3<br>Giulia agiama. | 2;3 |
| 2;4<br>Giulia Dodoi. | 2;4 | 2;4 | 2;4<br>Guarda Giulia<br>  bua.<br>Lisa bibicletta. | 2;4 |
| 2;6<br>Nein, Lisa Ar-<br>  beit.<br>Lisa fertig Lisa<br>  Arbeit.<br>Giulia camicina<br>  blau.<br>Mami Nase.<br>Giulia Nase.<br>Tante Hanny<br>  macht Lisa<br>  Hose.<br>Tante Hanny<br>  Lisa Hose<br>  macht.<br>Lisa Buch.<br>Lisa Baum. | 2;6 | 2;6 | 2;6<br>Mammi bot-<br>  tone.<br>Giulia attenta<br>  bua Lisa<br>  letto.<br>Giulia penna ... | 2;6<br>Quetto da<br>  Giulia.<br>Da Mamma<br>  questto?<br>Da Mamma. |

**Table 4.5** (continued)

| German | | | Italian | |
|---|---|---|---|---|
| Noun + (s) + Noun | Noun + Possessive pronoun + Noun | Noun + (von) + Noun | Noun + Noun | Noun + (di) + Noun |
| 2;8<br>Lisa Arbeit. | 2;8 | 2;8<br>Shappen Lisa. | 2;8<br>Lisa gomma. | 2;8<br>… a penna di Lisa. |
| 2;9<br>Giulia Buch.<br>Di Lisa Haare. | 2;9 | 2;9<br>Quetto von Giulia. | 2;9<br>Quetto è di Giulia libro. | 2;9<br>Quetto è di Giulia.<br>Quetto libro di Giulia, di Lisa.<br>Quetta è di Giulia.<br>Sono i capelli di Lisa. |
| 2;10 | 2;10 | 2;10<br>E qui von Mami. | 2;10 | 2;10<br>Sai quella è la stellina di nonna.<br>Ricordi stellina di nonna.<br>Testa di Giulia.<br>La favola di Lisa. |
| 3;0<br>Nur Lisa Mami Baby, Giulia Mami Hund. | 3;0 | 3;0 | 3;0 | 3;0 |
| 3;2 | 3;2<br>Giulia hat Feige Lisa ihren gegessen.<br>Lisa ihren Schlappen sind gross.<br>Wo ist Lisa ihren Regenschirm? | 3;2 | 3;2 | 3;2 |
| 3;3<br>Lisa Schlappen. | 3;3 | 3;3<br>Von Lisa klein klein. | 3;3 | 3;3 |

**Table 4.5** (continued)

| German | | | Italian | |
|---|---|---|---|---|
| Noun + (s) + Noun | Noun + Possessive pronoun + Noun | Noun + (von) + Noun | Noun + Noun | Noun + (di) + Noun |
| 3;4<br>Sonst Lisa Strümpfe schmutzig. | 3;4<br>Mami ihr Strickzeug nicht anfassen.<br>Guck das Händchen sein Paola.<br>Lisa ihren Bett hat Pierina ...<br>Giulia isst nicht Giulia ihren Reis.<br>Oh! Mami in Lisa ihren Bett!<br>Ja, Lisa ihren Geburtstag.<br>Mami Lisa ihren Tochter. | 3;4<br>Die Schale von Lecaleca.<br>Ein Stock von Lecaleca.<br>Papi von diese kleine ... | 3;4 | 3;4 |
| 3;5 | 3;5 | 3;5<br>Wo ist die Puppe von Weihnachten?<br>Mama ist die Mami von Lisa.<br>Kommen nur die Kinder von Mami. | 3;5 | 3;5 |
| 3;6 | 3;6<br>Luise ihren Mami ist im Auto drinne. | 3;6 | 3;6 | 3;6 |
| 3;7<br>Wo sind Giulia Strümpfe?<br>Ist das Giulias Strümpfe? | 3;7<br>Und Papi ihren Federica hat nicht ein Bart.<br>Wo ist Pongo ihren Alessandra? | 3;7<br>... im Bett von die Oma.<br>Ich hab Wasser von die Flasche getrinken. | 3;7 | 3;7 |

**Table 4.5** (continued)

| German | | | Italian | |
|---|---|---|---|---|
| Noun + (s) + Noun | Noun + Possessive pronoun + Noun | Noun + (von) + Noun | Noun + Noun | Noun + (di) + Noun |
| 3;7 | 3;7<br>Ist das Giulia ihre Krone? | 3;7 | 3;7 | 3;7 |
| 3;8<br>Giulias Geburtstag mit zwei<br>. . .<br>Wo sind Giulias Mohrrüben?<br>Papis Tasche.<br>Und Giulias Mami. | 3;8<br>Ist runtergefallen Papi ihre Tasche.<br>Papi seine Tasche.<br>Mein Name und Giulia ihr Name. | 3;8<br>Die Geschichte von die Milch . . .<br>Das ist der Igel von Zicklein. | 3;8 | 3;8 |
| 3;9<br>Giulias Hose.<br>Auch Giulias Blue Jeans sind zu kurz.<br>Ein Kissen von Adrianos Boot. | 3;9 | 3;9 | 3;9 | 3;9 |
| 3;10<br>Weil ist Mamis Geburtstag.<br>Nach Mamis Geburtstag. | 3;10 | 3;10<br>Honig ist drinne in Bauch von die Biene.<br>Das Bild von Urgrossmutter.<br>Das ist das Haus von die Schnecke.<br>Ich hab die Schale von Piselli genommen. | 3;10 | 3;10 |

**Table 4.6.** Possessive constructions in the data on Giulia

| German | | | Italian | |
|---|---|---|---|---|
| Noun + (s) + Noun | Noun + Possessive pronoun + Noun | Noun + (von) + Noun | Noun + Noun | Noun + (di) + Noun |
| 1;8<br>Julia Haus.<br>Mami Arbeit.<br>Giulia Boot. | 1;8 | 1;8<br>Buch Mami.<br>Buch Giulia.<br>Gos Haiabett-<br>chen a Lisa. | 1;8 | 1;8<br>La cucu di<br>mamma.<br>A mano<br>Antonio.<br>Auto a Vanna.<br>Mbaca a Giulia. |
| 1;9<br>Julia Buch.<br>Giulia Schuhe.<br>Giulia Lock.<br>Mami Haale. | 1;9 | 1;9 | 1;9 | 1;9 |
| 2;2<br>Dies ist von<br>Giulia<br>Schuhe. | 2;2<br>Guarda Giulia<br>ihre Zähne.<br>Mami Birne sein<br>Giulia das<br>hier? | 2;2<br>Dies ist von<br>Giulia<br>Schuhe. | 2;2<br>Quetto a Giulia<br>atito. | 2;2<br>Capello a<br>Giulia. |
| 2;4 | 2;4<br>Papi ihren<br>Haarekem. | 2;4<br>Das ist die<br>Strasse von<br>Giulia. | 2;4 | 2;4<br>Letto di<br>Mamma.<br>Lettino di<br>Giulia.<br>Bocca di<br>Giulia.<br>Capelli di<br>Mammi.<br>Pulcino di<br>Nonna. |
| 2;6 | 2;6<br>Bambino ihren<br>Haare macht<br>so. | 2;6 | 2;6 | 2;6<br>L'amichetta di<br>Luca. |
| 2;7 | 2;7<br>Wie Laura ihren<br>Schlappen.<br>Des beide is<br>Nonna Tina<br>ihren. | 2;7<br>Der Schal von<br>Aerosol.<br>Die Schachtel<br>von Mami.<br>Eine Riga von<br>Palloncini ist<br>im Baum. | 2;7 | 2;7<br>La pancia di<br>Papi. |

**Table 4.6** (continued)

| German | | | Italian | |
|---|---|---|---|---|
| Noun + (s) + Noun | Noun + Possessive pronoun + Noun | Noun + (von) + Noun | Noun + Noun | Noun + (di) + Noun |
| 2;7 | 2;7 | 2;7<br>Ein klein Palloncino von eine Riga von Filo.<br>Ein klein Knopf von Giulia von capotto. | 2;7 | 2;7 |
| 2;8 | 2;8 | 2;8<br>Wo ist der Amico von Babau.<br>Das ist die Mami von das Mädchen. | 2;8 | 2;8 |
| 3;0<br>Pallina ist unter Nonna Tinas Bett gegangen. | 3;0 | 3;0<br>Ich bin die Mami von Giulia. | 3;0 | 3;0 |
| 3;4<br>... golfino von Armios. | 3;4 | 3;4<br>... Golfino von Armios. | 3;4 | 3;4 |
| 3;6<br>Mein Rio di Janeiros Rock.<br>Ich hab geschrieben mit Mamis Kugelschreiber. | 3;6 | 3;6 | 3;6 | 3;6 |

Without excluding the possibility that the use of the English genitive in Spanish by the Chicano mother reinforced Mary's own sentences, it would nonetheless appear that the process of possessive acquisition described on p. 141 was at work in Mary, and thus her usage was correct during an initial period. But when, during a second period, she learned the function of 's and *de*, she did not yet know that 's is used only in English and *de* only in Spanish.

Mary's monologues during this period made it clear that she was undergoing a phase of reflection and reorganization [Bergman, 1976, p. 87]. They included constructions such as *es de Paula's bebito, el bebito es de Paula's,* and *es de Paula el bebito,* and also some instances of self-correction, as in *es Annie's libro* − *libro de Annie.*

In a third and final period, Mary used each morpheme with its respective language.

We now direct our attention to subject-verb inversion. In some German sentence structures, for example those beginning with an adverb, the subject must be moved from its usual position before the verb to a position after it. For example:

*Ich gebe dir eine Blume.* (I give you a flower.)
*Jetzt ( ) gebe ich dir eine Blume.* (Now ...)[13]
*Ich möchte dir eine Blume geben.* (I want ...)
*Jetzt ( ) möchte ich dir eine Blume geben.* (Now ...)
*Ich habe dir eine Blume gegeben.* (I gave ...)
*Gestern ( ) habe ich dir eine Blume gegeben.* (Yesterday ...)
*Ich schiebe die Tür zu.*
*Jetzt ( ) schiebe ich die Tür zu.* (Now ...)

This displacement is called inversion, and also appears in German interrogative sentences:

*( ) Gibst du mir eine Blume?* (Are you giving me a flower?)
*Was ( ) gibst du mir?* (What are you giving me?)

In Italian, there is no inversion, because except in a few cases (e.g., for emphasis), the subject is omitted:

*Ti dò un fiore.* ([I] give you a flower.)
*Ora ti dò un fiore.* (Now [I] ...)
*Ti voglio dare un fiore.* ([I] want ...)
*Ora ti voglio dare un fiore.* (Now [I] want ...)

Giulia and Lisa began to use inversion in German at about 2;6 and 3;2, respectively. For about six months their inversions were always correct, but then they began to use inversions when they were not necessary or to omit them when they were. They also sometimes forgot to drop the subject from the beginning of the phrase when they did invert.[14] These "errors" appeared for a while and then disappeared altogether (see Table 4.7, p. 150).

---

13 The dashed circle indicates the pronoun's original position in the noninverted sentence, and the arrow its subsequent position.
14 Cancino et al. [1978] observed six Spanish-speaking children who were learning English as a second language, and found that they went through much the same learning sequence.

**Table 4.7.** The appearance and initial development of utterances with correct and incorrect inversion

| Lisa | | | | | | | | |
|---|---|---|---|---|---|---|---|---|
| 3;2 | 3;4 | 3;6 | 3;8 | 3;10 | 4;0 | 4;2 | 4;4 | |

| | correct inversion |
|---|---|
| ├────────────────────────────→ | correct inversion |
|        ├──────────────┤ | missing inversion |
|          ├──────────┤ | incorrect inversion |
|          ├──────────┤ | inversion with double subject |

| Giulia | | | | | |
|---|---|---|---|---|---|
| 2;6 | 2;8 | 2;10 | 3;0 | 3;2 | 3;4 |

| | correct inversion |
|---|---|
| ├────────────────────────────→ | correct inversion |
|      ├────────────┤ | missing inversion |
|     (no examples) | incorrect inversion |
|      ├─────────────────┤ | inversion with double subject |

Some examples of correct inversions were:

**G** (2;6): *Jetzt kommt Virginia.* (Now Virginia is coming.)
**G** (2;8): *Hast du Brot gekaufen?* (Have you bought bread?)
**G** (3;0): *Wie macht man?* (How does one do it?)
**G** (3;0): *Kann ich ruhig eintunken?* (Can I dunk it without problems?)
**L** (3;2): *Wollen wir Hände waschen, Mami?* (Want we hands wash, Mommy?)
**L** (3;4): *Und auch Joghurt hat Lisa gegessen.* (And also yogurt has Lisa eaten.)
**L** (3;10): *Ein bisschen Wasser will ich.* (Some water I want.)
**L** (4;4): *Jetzt wollen wir nicht mehr lesen.* (Now want we no longer read.)

Some examples of missing inversion were:

**L** (3;9): *Jetzt das Haus geht kaputt.* (Now this house breaks.)
**L** (4;2): *Sonst ich weine so doll.* (Otherwise I cry so much.)
**G** (3;0): *Dann ich bin böse.* (Then I am angry.)

There were only a few instances in which inversion was used when it was not called for:

**L** (3;0): *Hast du gesagt: nachher diese!* (Have you said: after this one!)

Examples of inversion with double subject were:

**G** (3;0): *Du möchtest du sehen?* (You want you to see?)
**G** (3;1): *Du musst du hier bleiben.* (You must you always stay here.)

**L** (3;9): *Du bist du gross geworden, zu gross.* (You are you big become, too big.)

**L** (4;1): *Du schläfst du heute mit mir?* (You sleep you today with me?)

It should be noted that these sentences were uttered with no pause after the first subject, and thus it is clear that it was not used for emphasis or to get an adult's attention.

The monolingual German children who were observed also used the inversion incorrectly or forgot to drop the first subject. For example:

**Jana** (2;5):    *Kann man die hinsetzen.* (Can one set those down.)

**Mara** (3;6):    *Du kannst du mir das Buch vorlesen?* (You could you read the book to me?)

**Malte** (3;11):  *Mami, du weiss du wo diese Julias Mutter wohnt?* (Mommy, you know you where this Julia's mother lives?)

**Verena** (4;1):  *Ich kann ich das aber nicht.* (I can't I do this.)

An analysis of German-speaking monolingual and bilingual children shows that there is a quantitative difference between the two: the monolinguals use few mistaken inversions, while Lisa's errors amounted to about 40% Giulia's to 20%.

In his verbal test, Roeper [1973] found that only 3 out of 75 German children use incorrect inversion in interrogative sentences.

On the other hand, American children [Menyuk, 1964; Bellugi, 1971], who, like German children, must invert the subject and the verb in interrogative sentences, but unlike Germans, must not do so in other constructions, make systematic errors. Several of the sentences uttered by Bellugi's subject Adam [1971, p. 100] greatly resembled Lisa's and Giulia's, in the sense that they used both inverted and noninverted sequences in the same sentence:

What shall we shall have?
Did I didn't mean to?

With Adam, as with Lisa and Giulia, the period during which numerous interrogatives appeared without inversion came before 4;0.

According to Roeper, German children do not make many mistakes in subject-verb inversion because it is used in several constructions in German, and thus has a much wider-ranging function than in English. It is also for this reason that it is learned early.

Roeper does not base his statement on the concept that more frequent usage of a certain structure results in more thorough learning, as Park does. He bases it upon the innatist concept which Chomsky called LAD (Language Acquisition Device). In other words, Roeper considers one of the features of the deep structure of German to be "verb second transformation," which means that the child makes his first transformation at the deep structure level by changing one typical German structure to another: the verb is moved from the final position to the second position.

But because Roeper's subjects were at least 4 years old when he gave them the test, and thus were well into the period when verb-subject inversion is almost never wrong, neither in monolingual nor in bilingual children, his results do not adequately support the statement that German children do not often use this sequence incorrectly. This subject could profit by further research.

At any rate, another possible approach to the problem of correct and incorrect usage of subject-verb inversion may be proposed. In the vast majority of cases, the subject which is moved in inversion is not a noun but a pronoun:

*Möchtest du?* (Want you?)
*Will ich?* (Want I?)

In German phrases such as *machen wir, gehen wir,* or *mache ich,* the two words are not pronounced separately, but as though they were one unit, i.e., *machenwa, gehnwa,* and *machich.* Thus it is extremely improbable that the child perceives the verb and the pronoun as two distinct elements from the very outset. It would appear that the child considers the verb to be a verb root and the pronoun to be a verb ending. This means, for example, that the child perceives

*machenwa*   in the same way as   *facciamo* (let's do)
*gehnwa*     in the same way as   *andiamo* (let's go)

Thus, sentences such as:

1. *Jetzt willich rausgehen.* (Now I want to go out.)
2. *Willste rausgehen?* (Do you want to go out?)
3. *Wie willste rausgehen?* (How do you want to go out?)

would be perceived in the same way as their Italian equivalents:

1. *Adesso voglio uscire.*
2. *Vuoi uscire?*
3. *Come vuoi uscire?*

One possible indication that bilinguals consider *facciamo* and *gehnwa* to be exactly equivalent can be seen in several examples of Dunia's and Giulia's speech (Sect. 4.10), in which they use the Italian ending *iamo* with a German root to form words such as *gehndiamo,* or the German pronoun ending *mir* or *wir* with an Italian verb root to form *famea.*

If this is the case, then:

1. *Du sollst du das machen.* (You must you do this.)

is equivalent to:

2. *Tu devi fare questo.* (You must do this.)

In the same way,

3. *Du willst **du** das haben?* (You will you have this?)

is equivalent to:

4. *Tu vuoi questo?* (Do you want this?)

But the linguistic setting does not accept or promote constructions 1 and 3, and thus the child will rapidly set them aside.


## 4.12  Word Order

The preceding four categories have brought us to the acquisition of syntax, i.e., word order in sentences. This aspect will be examined here in three different types of sentences:
a) two-word sentences;
b) sentences with modal verbs and participles;
c) sentences with secondary clauses.

It is of utmost importance that children learn correct word order, because the native speaker does not accept such sentences as:

*Ich habe gegessen Brot.* (I have eaten bread.)
*Ich will essen Brot.* (I will eat bread.)
*Maria ha il pane mangiato.* (Maria has the bread eaten.)
*Maria vuole il pane mangiare.* (Maria wants the bread to eat.)

The most noticeable difference between German and Italian word order is unquestionably that of verb position. Among the components of the main clause, the finite German verb (i.e., verb root + tense and personal ending) usually occupies the second position, while an uninflected verb (i.e., participle or infinitive) occupies the last position. [15] For instance:

1a. *Maria **isst** Brot.* (Maria eats bread.)
1b. *Maria **mangia** pane.* (Maria eats bread.)
1c. *Maria **geht** in die Wohnung **rein**.* (Maria goes to the house in.)
2a. *Maria **möchte** Brot **kaufen**.* (Maria wants bread to buy.)
2b. *Maria **vuole comprare** il pane.* (Maria wants to buy bread.)
3a. *Maria **hat** Brot **gekauft**.* (Maria has bread bought.)
3b. *Maria **ha** comprato **pane**.* (Maria has bought bread.)

This happens in all affirmative sentences, but not in subordinate clauses, in which the finite verb takes the last position and the infinite verb the next-to-

---

15  The gerund is not taken into consideration here.

last position. Furthermore, the separable particle of German verbs (i.e., *rein* in *reingehen*, as in Example 1c above) is not detached from the finite verb in sentences containing an auxiliary or modal verb or in subordinate structures. For example:

4a. ... *weil Maria Brot gekauft hat*. (... because Maria bought bread has.)
4b. ... *perché Maria ha comprato il pane*.
5.  ... *weil Maria in die Wohnung reingeht*. (... because Maria in the house enters.)

Examples 1b, 2b, 3b, and 4b show that in Italian, the finite and infinite verbs are always together in the word sequence. Examples 1a and 1b are the only ones in which the verbs are in the same position in both languages. The German verb has three different positions: in Example 1a, it is between the subject and the object; in 1c, 2a, and 3a, the finite verb is between the subject and the object and the infinite verb (or particle) is at the end; in 4a and 5, the finite verb is at the end. In Italian, on the other hand, the verb is always in the same place, between the subject and the object.

### 4.12.1 Two-Word Sentences

Let us begin our analysis of word order at the simplest level, that of the two-word sentence. Because we are interested in the position of the verb with respect to the subject and the object, we will only consider two-word sequences which contain a verb and subject or object, thus excluding sentences which have no verb. [16]

In the first two-word sentences, the order was the same for both languages: verb + object, subject + verb, or object + verb, with the latter group predominating slightly. [17]

---

16  When the predicate is missing from incomplete nuclear sentences, the arguments that refer to the subject and the object may be placed in either first or second position. In the examples that follow, the predicate was found by means of "rich interpretation" [Brown, 1979], which is based upon the context and the interpretation of the child's interlocutor. The sentences marked (a) have the predicate "is of" (i.e., "belongs to"), and those marked (b) have the predicate "to be".

| **G** (1;2 to 1;8) | *Italian* | *German* |
|---|---|---|
| | Mamma tita (a) | Mami Arbeit (a) |
| | (mother pencil) | (mother work) |
| | Pedi Giulia (a) | Buch Mami (a) |
| | (feet Giulia) | (book Mommy) |
| **L** (1;7 to 2;3) | *Italian* | *German* |
| | *Cheo qui* (b) | *Giulia Beine* (a) |
| | (water here) | (Giulia leg) |
| | *Qui miao* (b) | *Beine Paola* (a) |
| | (here cat) | (leg Paola) |

17  The present data might also be analyzed in terms of topic-comment. I have chosen here to make a more formal analysis. This does not mean, however, that verb, subject, and object are categories which the child analyzes as adults do.

**Table 4.8.** Two-word German sentences in bilingual children. [a]

| $V_f$ + O | S + $V_f$ | O + $V_{inf}$, O + $V_{sp}$ |
|---|---|---|
| Ting Milch | Duck badi | Giulia sehnja? |
| Guck Teppich | Plina arbeit | Schuhe anziehen |
| Sitzi Haiabettchen | Mami nimm | Stumpfe aus |
| Guck die Tasche | Mami pilli pilli | Schleife binden |
| Weg Haare | Mami macht | Kaki machen |
| | Mami sitzi | Ball mit |
| | Lisa sitzi | Hose aus |
| | Der weint | Lock aus |
| | Mami komm | Baubau machen |
| | Giulia macht | Hopa Hopa machen |
| | Lisa spielt | |
| | Lisa friert | |
| | Giulia lest | |

| S + $V_{inf}$, S + $V_p$ |
|---|
| Giulia nicht spuken |
| Giulia erzählen |
| Lisa zumachen |
| Mami anziehen |
| Lisa gegeben |

[a] Key to Tables 4.8 – 11: 

V — Verb  
O — Object  
S — Subject  
f — Finite  
inf — Infinite  
sp — Separable particle  
p — Participle  

During a second period, the subject + verb order was present in both languages, with object + verb prevailing in German and verb + object prevailing in Italian (see Tables 4.8, 9).

It would seem that the bilingual child already uses a distinct order for each of the two languages when uttering two-word sentences. This order resembles the one used by monolingual children in the respective language. Park [1974], Ramge [1975], and Miller [1976] have shown that German children initially use different orders in such structures and that very early on, the object + verb and subject + verb structures become predominant (Table 4.10). Italian monolinguals undergo a similar development: after a short initial period in which various word orders are used, they begin to use the verb + object and subject + verb structure more than the others (Table 4.11).

Brown and Bellugi [1971, pp. 468, 469] analyzed spontaneous imitation in the first sentences produced by their subjects, Adam and Eve. They observe that "the first thing to note is that this imitation conserves the pattern sentence's original word order . . . .

**Table 4.9.** Two-word Italian sentences in bilingual children[a]

| $V_f + S$, $V_p + S$ | $V_f + O$, $V_p + O$ | $S + V_f$, $S + V_p$ | $O + V_f$ |
|---|---|---|---|
| Chiu tata | Da (re) Mamma | Giulia fa | Acqua vuoi |
| Galato Nonna | Ti (ra) palla | Julia penda | Pentola vuoi |
| Cade Giulia | Fa bibi | Joia cade | Bicicletta lascia |
| Guarda Mamma | Ade Mamma | Lisa fatto | Capse chiama |
| Butta Mamma | Pende Lisa | Lisa cercato | Mò mò fa |
| Itto Mammi? | Butta a Lisa | Lisa cade no | Afante a penda |
| Attona Papi | Guarda Giulia | Lisa ha tolto | |
| Tiene Lisa | Guarda pipi | Lisa legge | |
| | Da (re) bacetto | Giulia allabbia | |
| | Fa la barchetta | Mani mette? | |
| | Fale l'acqua | Julia a butta | |
| | Non fa toto | Julia cerca? | |
| | Chiudi capuccio | Julia a penda | |
| | Guarda aeroplano | Mammi guada | |
| | Ricordi il nonno? | Giulia fa | |
| | Tieni Lisa | Giulia non se passa | |
| | Visto Giulia | Giulia ha dormito | |
| | Vuoi mela | Mammi aple? | |
| | Fatto la bua | Io cerco | |
| | Tocca no pipi no | | |
| | Lascia penna | | |
| | Chiaciato piedi | | |
| | Fa din don | | |

[a] For key to the abbreviations, see Table 4.8.

**Table 4.10.** Two-word sentences in German children[a] – Meike [Miller, 1976][b]

| $V_{inf} + S$, $V_{sp} + S$ | $V_{inf} + O$, $V_{sp} + O$ | $S + V_f$ | $O + V_{inf}$, $O + V_{sp}$ |
|---|---|---|---|
| Schlafen Maxe | Finden Sachen | Teddy schlaft | Schule hol |
| Sitzen Pupa | An Puschen | Puppe schlaft | Sack raus |
| Abmachen Mama | Raus den | Mone weint | Stiefel an |
| | Um Wagen | | Mütze auf |
| | | **$S + V_{sp}$** | Kaka suchen |
| | **$V_f + O$** | | Sofa fahrn |
| | | Mama mit | Häschen mit |
| | Hol Auto | Maxe weg | Jacke an |
| | | | Wauwau festhalten |
| | | **$S + V_f$** | Lala suchen |
| | | | Wanne suchen |
| | | Mone klingelt | Balla holn |
| | | Baby isst | Kaka suchen |
| | | Pferd laft | Flugzeug sehn |
| | | Beide laft | Saft holn |
| | | Puppe weint | Auge zu |
| | | Ulli kommt | Milch trinken |
| | | Flugzeug kommt | Auto rein |
| | | Oma kommt | |

**Table 4.10** (continued)

| $V_{inf} + S, V_{sp} + S$ | $V_f + O$ | $S + V_{inf}$ | $O + V_{inf}, O + V_{sp}$ |
|---|---|---|---|
| | | Mone schlafen | |
| | | Mone heia | |
| | | Puppe turn | |
| | | Mama lafen | |
| | | Mama sitzen | |
| | | Teddy reiten | |

[a] For key to the abbreviations, see Table 4.8.
[b] See also the sentences produced by Simone, Miller's other subject; they are similar to Meike's. The same tendency was also observed by Park [1974].

**Table 4.11.** Two-word sentences in Italian children[a] — Francesco[b]

| $V_f + O$ | $V_f + O, V_p + O$ | $S + V_f$ | $O + V_f$ |
|---|---|---|---|
| Ape Checco | Oio a pappa | Checco batte | |
| Vuole Checco | Ammo papa | bache c'è | |
| Totto popo | | | |
| Pendo io | Acceso motore | Io (ac) cendo | |
| Metto io | Poto via pappa | Io chiudo | |
| | Peso a pappa | Io torno | |
| | | Io monto | |
| | | Io pendo | |
| | | Io volto | |
| | Cia un bastone | A mucca | |
| | Fatto un botto | domme | |
| | Detto mamma | | |
| | Vado a bimbo | | |
| | Gio a vite | | |
| Teni Inni | Itta a luce | Io aggiusto | |
| | Facciamo a popo | Io l'ammazzo | |
| | Faccio popo | A macchina ipate | |
| | Pendo a popo | | |
| | Metto a mucca | | |
| | Pulisci camion? | | |
| | Metto garage | | |

[a] For key to the abbreviations, see Table 4.8.
[b] These constructions are similar to those of Claudia, the other monolingual Italian child observed.

The children often omitted words in their imitations, but the order was always that of the pattern." They give these examples to support this:

| *Pattern sentence* | *Child's imitation* |
|---|---|
| Daddy's briefcase | Daddy briefcase |
| Fraser will be unhappy | Fraser unhappy |
| He's going out | He go out |
| It's not the same dog as Pepper | Dog Pepper |

The data on Lisa and Giulia supports the hypothesis that the child acquires word order by imitating the patterns heard from the adults who interact with him, and that these patterns are different in Italian and German (see Sect. 4.11 on the fundamental role played by imitation in the acquisition of morphology and syntax by children).

With regard to the possible pattern structures of incomplete nuclear (two-word) sentences, several recent studies [Snow, 1972; Fraser and Roberts, 1975] show that adults do not use complex constructions when addressing a small child, but tend instead to adapt their language to the child's age and abilities. Effective communication depends greatly upon such flexibility, and it is not surprising that adults use clear and simple statements and many repetitions so that their children will understand them. As the child's ability to speak increases, the adult's speech becomes more complex. Although children are exposed to both normal and simplified speech, the latter appears to be more tangible for them. In fact, often even the adult who starts by addressing the child in long and difficult constructions simplifies his speech as soon as the wants to be understood. [18]

Let us take a brief look at this process. The mother of a two-year-old girl stares impatiently at some pans which her child has just taken out of a cabinet.

**M**: Why did you take all the pans out again? I already told you not to! Where will we end up if I put things away and you pull them out again?

The woman then bends down and starts to put the pans away, looking straight into her daugther's eyes.

**M**: The pans stay inside! Understand? Inside! Don't touch! No, no! Don't do that, no, no! It's bad, very bad! The next time a smack, get it? A smack on Marta's behind, that's what!

**C** [staring seriously at her mother and touching her bottom]: Hurt.

**M** [getting up and addressing the other adult present]: Well, I'm thrilled she understood.

---

18  Children as young as 4 and 5 years of age modify their speech, and use brief, simple sentences when they speak to smaller children [Shatz and Gelman, 1973; Sachs and Devin, 1976; Gleason, 1973].

Thus pattern sentences should be sought from utterances which are not too complex, such as sentences consisting of a subject, an object, and a verb, sentences containing a participle, and sentences with modal verbs (see Examples 1a, b, 2a, b, 3a, b, p. 153).

A close look at verb + object and object + verb sequences used by both bilinguals and monolinguals reveals that the German sequences are (see Tables 4.8, 10):

Object + separable verb particle (O + sp)
Object + infinitive verb (O + $V_{inf}$)
Object + particle + infinitive verb (O + sp + $V_{inf}$).

The sequences in Italian for monolingual and bilingual children are (see Tables 4.9, 11):

Finite verb + object ($V_f$ + O)
Participle + object ($V_p$ + O)

The subject + verb sequence found in both languages is:

Subject + finite verb (S + $V_f$).

The subject + verb sequence found in Italian only is:

Subject + participle (S + $V_p$).

The subject + verb sequences found only in German are:

S + $V_{inf}$, S + sp, S + sp + $V_{inf}$.

As Figs. 4.1, 2 show, these sequences are found in the word order of the German sentences 1a, b, 2a, and 3a, and the Italian sentences 1b, 2b, and 3b on p. 153.

Modal constructions are not recognizable in the children's Italian sentences, while in their German sentences, past participle constructions cannot be discerned.

What we do find in the sentences of Italian children are two-word utterances whose elements follow the S + $V_f$ + O order and the S + $V_{aux}$ + $V_p$ + O order. The two-word utterances of German children follow the S + $V_f$ + O, the S + $V_f$ + $O_{sp}$, and modal sequences. As was explained at the beginning of this chapter (Sect. 4.7), this happens because Italian adults often use participial constructions when addressing children, while German adults often use modal sentences.

## 4.12.2 Participial

In view of the data presented in the preceding section, it is not surprising that German-speaking children begin to use modal sentences first and Italian chil-

(a) Simple nuclear sentences

(b) Sentences with participle

(c) Modal sentences

$$S + V_{mod} + V_{inf} + O$$

Fig. 4.1. Word orders (denoted by enclosed areas) used \ by Italian-speaking children (monolingual and bilingual)

(a)  Simple nuclear sentences

$$(S + V_f) + O$$

(a1)  with particle

(b)  Sentences with participle

$$S + V_{aux} + O + V_p$$

(b1)  with particle

$$S + V_{aux} + O + {}_{sp}V_p$$

(c)  Modal sentences

(c1)  with particle

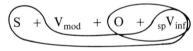

Fig. 4.2. Word orders (denoted by enclosed areas) used by German-speaking children (monolingual and bilingual)

dren participial sentences, and that bilinguals do the same in the respective languages. Tables 4.12, 13 show Lisa's and Giulia's development in this respect. Almost no mistakes were made in the word order for these structures.

One would expect heavy interference, since the bilingual child uses the modal construction in German before he does in Italian, and vice versa for the participle. There is a great temptation to explain the lack of interference by the fact that the child forms such structures by stringing together short sequences he has already learned (see Grimm, 1973: *Additionsregel,* i.e., the rule of addition). This would mean that in German the child might join sequences as follows:

S + V   and   O + V

to obtain the result:

S + V + O + V,

**Table 4.12.** Lisa's initial use of the past participle

| Italian | German |
|---|---|
| 2;4 | 2;4 |
| *La Mamma c'è schitto* (Mommy is written) | |
| | |
| 2;10 | 2;10 |
| *Ha fatto Mamma la medicina* (Mommy has made the medicine) | |
| *Adesso è andata a letto* (Now she's gone to bed) | |
| *Tutto s'era rotto* (Everything had broken) | |
| *La mosca è venuta sai?* (The fly has come, you know?) | |
| *Cosa ha fatto Mammi?* (What has Mommy done?) | |
| *Quetto ha fatto bua a Lisa* (This has hurt Lisa) | |
| | |
| 3;0 | 3;0 |
| *Lisa ha tolto quetto* (Lisa has taken this off) | *Mami hat gekauft für Lisa ein fazzoletto* (Mommy has bought a handkerchief for Lisa) |
| *Cosa c'è schitto li?* (What is written there?) | |
| *Mamma ha compato per Lisa* (Mommy has bought for Lisa) | |
| | |
| 3;2 | 3;2 |
| *La maestra ha preso la bambola* (The teacher has taken the doll) | *Ist Papi gekommen?* (Has Daddy come?) |
| *Hai visto il dirigibile?* (Have you seen the blimp?) | *Lisa hat ein Fritate gemacht* (Lisa has made an omelet) |
| *Io l'ho tagliata invece* (I have cut it instead) | *Lisa hat die Tür zugemacht* (Lisa has closed the door) |
| | *Und auch Joghurt hat Lisa gegessen* (And Lisa has also eaten yogurt) |
| | *Lisas Blatt hat Pierina weggenommen* (Lisa's leaf has Pierina taken away) |
| | *Und auch Lisa hat nicht ein Buch genommen* (And Lisa has also not taken away a book) |

which is typical of modal sentences, participial constructions, and verbs that use the particle.

In Italian, this process might be:

$$S + V \quad \text{and} \quad V + O =$$
$$S + V + V + O$$

But this is not the case, because as Fig. 4.1 shows, the two-element sequences never correspond to the sum of the elements within the sentence. There were no $S + V_{aux}$ sequences in Italian, nor were there $S + V_{mod}$ sequences in German. Surely, as Brown and Bellugi [1971] point out, the child

**Table 4.13.** Giulia's initial sentences with an object and with modal and infinite verbs

| Italian | German |
|---|---|
| 2;2 | 2;2<br>*Giulia will Kaki machen* (Giulia wants to go to the bathroom) |
| 2;4<br>*Voglio dare totò alla pupi* (I want to spank the doll) | 2;4 |
| 2;6 | 2;6<br>*Musst Kraft machen* (Must make effort)<br>*Giulia kann nicht machen* (Giulia cannot do)<br>*Ich möchte ein bisschen sauber machen* (I want to clean a little bit)<br>*Ich möchte ein bisschen Wasser haben* (I want to have a little bit of water) |
| 2;8<br>*Perché io voglio fare una barchetta* (Because I want to make a boat)<br>*Perché io posso prendere la palla* (Because I want to get the ball)<br>*Posso prendere anche la bicicletta?* (May I take the bike, too?)<br>*Perché non puoi andare là?* (Why can't you go there?) | 2;8<br>*Ich will die Haare waschen* (I want to wash my hair)<br>*Giulia will dieses malen* (Giulia wants to draw this)<br>*Giulia kann nicht anfassen* (Giulia cannot touch)<br>*Ich will schlafen in dein Bett* (I want to sleep in your bed)<br>*Ich will dich kämmen* (I want to comb you)<br>*Ich will nicht studiern* (I don't want to study)<br>*Ich will drei Biciclet kaufen* (I want to buy three bikes) |

extrapolates the words having a richer content from the sentence, while preserving the adult pattern. As his linguistic skills improve, he inserts the missing elements into the sentence.

Starting with the incomplete nuclear structure, we have seen how the child selects an object or subject which is linked to the verb particle, the participle, or the infinitive, but not one which is bound to an auxiliary or modal verb.

In fact, in German verbs with a particle it is the particle which expresses the most specific content:

*aufmachen* ( = to open, i.e., *auf* = open, *machen* = to do);
*zumachen* ( = to close, i.e., *zu* = close, *machen* = to do);
*reingehen* ( = to enter, i.e., *rein* = in, *gehen* = to go);
*rausgehen* ( = to go out, i.e, *raus* = out, *gehen* = to go);
*rausholen* ( = to take away, i.e., *raus* = out, *holen* = to take).

And in fact, Giulia translated "open" with *auf*:

**G** (1;11): *Mami, api.* (Mommy, open.)
**M:**      *Ja?*
**G:**      *Mami auf.*

In modal sentences, it is the infinitive verb which carries the principal meaning. The modal verb expresses the speaker's intention rather than what the action or event will be.

In participial constructions, the auxiliary verb indicates the tense and person and thus serves a syntactic purpose, while the participle expresses the content of the event.

### 4.12.3 Subordinate Clauses

As was shown at the beginning of Sect. 4.12, the word order in subordinate clauses is different in Italian and German. [19] Thus, in Italian the word order is the same in a subordinate clause as it is in an independent clause. The two independent clauses:

*Mario ride.* (Mario laughs.)
*Giovanni racconta la barzelletta.* (Giovanni tells the joke.)

become, when linked by a subordinating conjunction:

*Mario ride perché Giovanni racconta la barzelletta.*

In German, on the other hand, the components of the second sentence change their order when it becomes a subordinate clause. Thus,

*Mario lacht.* (Mario laughs.)
*Johan erzählt den Witz.* (Johan tells the joke.)

become, when connected as above by a subordinating conjunction:

*Mario lacht, weil Johan den Witz erzählt.*

When the existing relationship is one of coordination, the word order does not change. It should be recalled that it is always the finite verb which is moved to the end of the sentence. This is a new rule for children who are learning German, because initially they only learn sentences with the infinite verb in the final position. This new word order is presented to the child only when the existing relationship between two phrases is made explicit by means of the connective. As long as the connective is not used by the child, the cause-effect relationship between the two phrases is expressed only by the meaning of those phrases; the word order remains the same, and the child does not place the finite verb in the last position. As we saw in Chap. 3, the child first

19 German word order also differs from that of Italian in relative and explicit connected constructions.

utters structures without connectives, and adds the connective at a later date. Structures without connectives are nothing new for the child, and they appear at the same time in the Italian and German of monolinguals, and both languages of bilinguals.

The development of Lisa's and Giulia's Italian was identical to that of Italian children as regards structures with the connective. The subordinates and coordinates appeared at the same time and the word order was correct.

In German, however, Lisa's and Giulia's development was only partially the same as that of monolinguals. Whereas Jana, Oliver, Mara, Verena, Julia, Malte, and Florian used correct word order as soon as they began to use the connective, Lisa and Giulia did not immediately do so. Instead, they used the sequence: main clause + connective + main clause (see Taeschner and Testa [1978] for subordinate sentences). For instance, Lisa said:

1. *Ein Schwein für mich ist das weil du hast ein Schwein.* (A pig for me is this because you have a pig.)
2. *Ich weiss nicht wo ist die Decke.* (I know not where is the blanket.)
3. *Wenn hast du alles das hier gelesen, kriegst du das hier.* (When have you all this here read, receive you this here.)
4. *Joghurt ist so kalt weil ist in Eisschrank hingetan.* (Yogurt is so cold because it is in the refrigerator kept.)

It should be noted that the word order in these sentences is not a reproduction of the equivalent sentences in Italian. It is, instead, the result of a general rule that enables the child to form connected subordinate phrases by simply using the connective between (or in front of) two main clauses. Sentences 3 and 4 do not reflect the Italian word order, but that which would be found in German if the two main clauses stood alone.

What Lisa and Giulia did was to apply the word order rule, i.e., main clause + connective + main clause, to both languages, without realizing that it was not valid for German. It took them a while to abandon this rule in German and begin placing the finite verb in the last position when necessary. The acquisition of a subordinate structure complete with main and secondary clauses and all the word order changes that this implies is a very gradual process. At first, the girls simply began to place the finite verb at the end of the sentence without making the necessary inversion:

**G (3;2):** *Wenn ich klein war (ich) hab getanzt.* [20] (When I little was I danced.)

**G:**     *Mami, wo ich klein war (ich) bin in Brasilien gegangen.* (Mommy, when I little was I went to Brazil.)

The correct order together with the correct inversions did not appear until later:

---

20  The dashed circle shows the incorrect position, and the dashed arrow the correct one.

**L** (4;5): *Wenn du es sagst, nächstes Mal, Giulia macht es kaputt, dieses Bild, dann werde ich böse.* (If you say, next time, Giulia breaks it, this picture, then I will get mad.)

Various factors contributed to Lisa's and Giulia's initial misuse of subordinates with the connective. The first was the direct superextension of an Italian rule to both languages. This rule does not exist in German, except in dialect.

The second factor was the intrinsic difficulty of moving the finite verb to the end of the sentence. According to Lehman [1973], the verb and the object form a sort of perceptive *Gestalt* which resists any separation. In SOV languages, of which German appears to be one (although linguists are divided on this point), this *Gestalt* has the OV sequence. In SVO languages, one example of which is Italian, the sequence is VO. Lehman hypothesizes that the child perceives and acquires the verb and the object within one sentence sequence as a single, inseparable entity which tends to have rigidly fixed, side-by-side positions and to resist any attempt to come between or separate its elements.

From the point of view of child development, it might be that the first such inseparable entities in German are not the OV sequences (where the V refers to the finite verb) but:

1. $O + V_{inf}$
2. $O + V_{sp}$
3. $V_f + O$
4. $V_f + V_{aux}$
5. $V_f + V_{inf}$

In Italian, they might be:

6. $V_f + O$
7. $V_p + O$
8. $V_f + V_{aux}$
9. $V_f + V_{inf}$

In planning the order of the components in a sentence, the child will not break up these inseparable entities. In learning to place the finite verb at the end of the subordinate sentence, he must learn to break the inseparable entities 3, 4, and 5 into their single elements and make new entities of them, to be used alongside the old ones. The new groups will be exactly the opposite of the old:

3a. $O + V_f$
4a. $V_{aux} + V_f$
5a. $V_{inf} + V_f$

Placing the finite verb in final position is not only an entirely new sequence for the child, but also entails the break-up of entities which during the entire previous period of language acquisition have been considered inseparable. This break-up and rearrangement requires a certain period of time, for monolingual as well as bilingual children. While Francesco, Lisa, and Giulia acquired coordinates and subordinates with the connective simultaneously in Italian, Jana, Oliver, Lisa, and Giulia did not learn to use the connective with subordinates in German until two or three months after they had been using it with coordinates (see Tables 3.1, 2, 4, 5, 8 – 10).

This would seem to suggest that it takes longer for children to learn to construct subordinates with the connective in German than it does in Italian. However, further research should be conducted on the subject, because Sara, the other Italian monolingual observed in this study, developed these sequences in the same way as the German children. For the time being, it may only be said that the bilingual child cannot help but superextend the rules he learns to both languages, because generalization is a cognitive process which applies to both languages. Adult speech then quite rapidly teaches the bilingual child that some rules are only valid in one of his two languages.

## 4.13 Summary

Based on the complex conditions of interaction described at the beginning of this chapter, and bearing in mind the evolution from initial, correct use to frequent mistaken use and, finally, frequent correct use, we may formulate the morphosyntactic development of the simultaneous bilingual as follows:

The child begins using morphology and syntax like native-speaking monolingual children. Thus, if the two languages have identical grammatical markers and if the adults use them identically, they will appear at the same time. If this is not the case, these aspects will branch off to parallel the development of the respective monolinguals. The process is the same for morphological aspects which exist in one language alone.

According to Slobin [1978, p. 181], "If a given meaning receives expression at the same time in both languages of a bilingual child, this suggests that the formal devices in two languages are similar in complexity. If a given semantic domain receives expression earlier in one of the two languages, a difference in formal complexity is suggested."

While the data presented here confirms Slobin's first statement, it does not confirm the second. Although some structures may be identically complex in Italian and German, they do not appear simultaneously in the bilingual child, because adults use them differently in the two languages. Thus the appearance of structures is affected not only by the complexity of their form, but also by the way adults use them.

With the child's newly gained ability to analyze the speech he has already acquired and to restructure it, he begins to use rules in constructing utterances. At first, he believes that both languages have the same rules, and sometimes uses all the alternatives available to him in one interaction:

G is crying because she wants to be first to play in a domino game, having won the last one.

**G** (2;7): *Io ho vintato!* (I have wonned!)

No one answers her.

**G:**     *Io ho gevinto, ah!* (I gewon!)

**M:**    *Giulia, sag mal: Io ho gevinto.* (Giulia, say, "I gewon.")

**G:**     *Ich hab gewonnen!* (I won!)

As Karmiloff-Smith [1979a, p. 94] points out, there "is an important macro-developmental difference between juxtaposing a number of adequately working procedures versus subsequently seeking coherence amongst the procedures themselves. Thus, younger children juxtapose various procedures they have available ... they point out the concrete extra-linguistic referent .... Older children [in contrast] make intra-linguistic reference ... so that the intra-linguistic system remains crucial."

At first, the morphosyntactic marker is used correctly, because the child's speech is based substantially on imitation and not yet on rules. However, this fundamental imitative strategy is applied creatively [Clark, 1977], and this might lead one to believe that the child is using rules. But as Roeper states [1973, p. 189], "Children often seem to be able to control the sentence types of an inflected language before they have mastered inflections." Later, these markers are used much more frequently as the child tries to identify the rules for their use.

Slobin [1975, p. 17] hypothesizes that "each of the two languages maintains its lexical material, but the position of grammatical markers results from application of a single set of production rules for both languages" (see also Imedadze [1967]).

However, this is only true for the initial period of rule acquisition. During the second period, the child very gradually realizes that the rules involved in linguistic processing must be separated. This process of distinction undoubtedly continues throughout the entire period of language acquisition.

It is important to point out that the bilingual child does not develop these markers late; he merely has more work cut out for him in organizing and rearranging certain aspects, especially those which have no coherent justification or are not very meaningful. In the beginning, the rule systems are not yet bound to their respective languages, and some of the rules are superextended to both. [21] In a beneficial linguistic environment, these hardships are gradually overcome, and the bilingual's linguistic competence in each language will eventually resemble that of native-speaking monolinguals.

---

21 Kessler [1976, p. 131] concludes her study on the syntax development of Italian-English bilingual children from 6;0 – 8;0: "The pattern of sequential arrangements of structures from all phases of the investigation gives credibility to the theory that a bilingual's two languages are not encoded separately and that rules held in the common core are stabilized approximately in the same order and at the same rate."

# 5. Interferences

## 5.1 Definitions

Interference is the transferral of elements from one language to another. Here, the concept of interference will also be used in the more general sense of errors caused by a situation in which two languages are in contact with each other.[1]

There are interferences which involve not only single words, but entire phrases. Thus, if an Italian-German bilingual says the word *Tisch* ("table"), there is no interference. But if *Tisch* is inserted into an Italian sentence, as in *io mangio sul Tisch di Mamma* (I'm eating on Mommy's table), it is an interference. Interferences at the sentence level can be lexical, syntactical, or prosodic, while at the word level they can be morphological, semantic, or phonological.

Lexical interference occurs when a sentence in one language contains words from another language:

1. **G** (2;4): *Questa luce non fa **Licht an**.* (This light doesn't make light on.)

Here *Licht* and *an* are German lexical interferences in an Italian sentence. In a sentence such as the following

2. **G** (1;11): *Giulia **gemacht** a casetta per a **böse Wolf**.* (Giulia made [a] house for [an] angry wolf.),

it is not clear which language is interfering with which. The sentence is termed mixed, because it contains a relatively equal number of words from both languages.

Syntactical interference occurs when the word order of one language is used in the other:

3. **G** (2;7): *Ich nicht will.* (I not want.)

instead of *Ich will nicht*. The German sentence has been constructed with Italian word order. In the sentence which follows, there are two syntactical interferences:

---

1 The term "error" is used here to mean a dynamic force which helps the child learn more, defined as an intermediate state between not knowing and knowing [Nickel, 1972].

**4. G** (2;7): *Ich nicht mach kaputt diese Flasche.* (I do not make broken this bottle.)

The correct German word order would be, *Ich mache diese Flasche nicht kaputt.* A sentence of type 4 is considered German despite its Italian word order, because the words are the elements which determine whether a sentence belongs to one language or the other or to the mixed group.

Prosodic interference occurs when the intonation, cadence, or rhythm of one language is partly or entirely replaced by that of the other. This type of interference will not be dealt with here.

Semantic interference is incorrect generalization of the meanings of the words of one language to the other. For instance, it is easy to find interference between the Italian verb *studiare* and the German correspondents *lernen* and *studieren.* These two German words have distinct meanings; the first refers to the activity of the student, and the second to that of the scholar. Italian-German bilinguals often use the word *studieren* for the meaning of *lernen* as well.

Phonological interferences occur when the words of one language are pronounced using sounds typical of the other. A classic example of this is the glottal stop[2] used in German for certain words that begin with vowels, which German speakers are apparently unable to discard when learning Italian.

In morphological interferences, only part of a word comes from the other language. This part is not the word root itself, but the morpheme, i.e., the prefix, suffix, ending, etc.:[3]

**5. L:** *Das ist ein Fischone.* (This is a big fish.)

The German *Fisch* is thought to be enlarged by the addition of the Italian augmentative ending *one.*

In this chapter, the types of interferences used by simultaneous bilingual children are identified, and the circumstances under which these interferences occur are investigated. This investigation is based entirely on the interference observed in Lisa and Giulia, that is, in German-Italian bilinguals. It should also be noted that these are interferences which appeared in the speech of children, and thus may differ from those found in adult bilinguals.[4]

---

2 "The glottal stop is performed by completely closing the vocal chords and thus keeping them from vibrating and not allowing the air to pass freely. When this occlusion of the vocal chords is released, the air escapes all at once" [Canepari, 1979, p. 71].

3 Weinreich [1974, p. 50 foll.] follows Bloomfield in distinguishing between bound morphemes (described above) and free morphemes, which are in reality prepositions and adverbs. Thus, for example, the superlative is expressed in German using a suffix (bound morpheme): the root *schön* (beautiful) + the suffix *er* = *schöner.* In Italian, the same superlative is expressed by means of a free morpheme and an adjective, giving *più bello.* In this work, free morphemes are treated as lexical interferences.

4 For ample treatment of adult interferences in various languages, see Weinreich [1974]. However, Weinreich uses a classification which differs slightly from that used here. What are here termed semantic interferences are considered by him to be lexical interferences, and he does not consider lexical interferences as they are defined above.

From birth until the present (Giulia is 9 and Lisa is 10) the two girls have never stopped producing sentences with interferences,[5] alongside correct Italian and German sentences. However, over the years these interferences have undergone important changes which are worthy of examination.

## 5.2 Lexical Interferences

The most frequently encountered interferences are of lexical type. What should be noticed first (see Fig. 5.1) is that the production of lexical interferences tends to decrease as the child progresses through the second lexical stage (see Chap. 2 for a definition of the lexical stages).[6] For the most part, the lexical interferences which do occur in this period result in mixed sentences:

1. **L** (2;9):  *Lisa vuole **schaun**.* (Lisa wants to see.)
2. **L:**      *Lisa **specht** di là.* (Lisa talks there.)
3. **L:**      *Edi Lisa **gemacht**?* (See Lisa did?)
4. **G** (2;9): *Ich **hat trovato** un schwarze **capello** von **nere** Haare.* (I found a black hair of black hair[s].)

For further examples, see the mixed sentences in Tables 3.1, 2.

During this early period, interferences are a direct consequence of the process of acquisition of equivalents. As was noted in Chap. 2, from the first stage of their linguistic production, bilingual children have only one lexicon, made up of words from both languages with no equivalents. During the

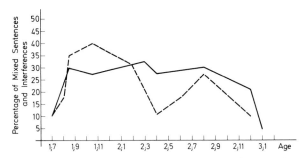

**Fig. 5.1.** Lisa's mixed sentences (————) and Giulia's mixed sentences

---

5 On this subject, Rosenzweig says [1963, p. 64], "It should be taken as an axiom that there is no bilingualism without interferences."

6 On this subject, see Redlinger and Park [1980], who also observed that the speech of their bilingual subjects contained fewer and fewer instances of lexical and mixed interference as they grew older.

second stage, equivalents begin to appear gradually and over a prolonged period. Of course, when the child is in the first stage or at the beginning of the second, these equivalents cannot yet be termed interferences, inasmuch as the two languages are for the most part still used as one. As time goes on, the mixed and short sentences decrease to the vanishing point. Later, these sentences are uttered in either one language or the other. Mixed, long sentences such as Example 4 above were an exception in Lisa and Giulia's speech. It was only after they had begun using the two languages distinctly that they produced true examples of interference, i.e., sentences of one language containing one or more words from the other. Of the 1500 sentences Lisa uttered from 3;9 to 4;5, only 89 contained interference. This shows that at this age, Lisa preferred to speak in one language or the other, trying not to mix the two lexicons. This preference can be seen in several corrections that she made, such as:

5. **L:** *Hat **codini** ... Schwänze.* (Has pigtails.)
6. **L:** *Guck das ist ... Questa è una figurina.* (Look this is a figurine.)

In Example 6, Lisa did not know the German word for *figurina*, and preferred to say the whole sentence in Italian rather than mix the two lexicons. In Example 5, Lisa was in a German context, and immediately replaced the Italian *codini* with its German equivalent. Giulia also made such self-corrections:

7. **G** (3;0): *Das ist eine **mutandi**/ ... eine Hose.* (This is a *mutandi*/ ... a panty.)

We should note that Giulia stopped herself halfway through the word, as though it had been a lapse. At times, she even gave explanations to justify her mistake:

8. **G** (2;6): *Ich will **pet** / ... kämmen. Mami, **pettinare** ist auf italienisch, kämmen ist in deutsch.* (Mommy, *pettinare* is in Italian, *kämmen* is in German.)

At other times, she even went so far as to ask for the word she didn't know before she began her sentence:

9. **G** (2;9) [in bed, opening and shutting her mouth]:
   *Wie sagt man "allora" auf deutsch?* (How do you say *allora* in German?)
   **M:**  *Dann.* (Then.)
10. **G:**  *Wenn Giulia macht den Mund auf, dann ...* (When Giulia opens her mouth, then ...)
    **M:**  *Dann?*
11. **G:**  *Dann macht wieder zu.* (Then she closes it again.)

Of Lisa's 89 sentences with interference, 77 contained only one word in the other language, 11 contained two interfering words, and only one had three words from the other language. Of the 77 one-word examples, 70% were nouns and 30% verbs, adverbs, prepositions, adjectives, and pronouns. Thus, it was by far more common to use the nouns in the other language than to use any other parts of speech.[7]

It is interesting to note that when the interfering noun was accompanied by an article, the article did not belong to the language of the noun but to the language of the rest of the sentence. In other words, the interferences always took the form *Hier ist die sabbia*, and never the form *Hier ist la sabbia* ("Here is the sand"). Thus only the noun was involved, and not the entire noun phrase. But while the noun and article belonged to different languages, they always agreed with each other:

12. **L:** *Wo ist ein **biberon** mit ein bisschen Wasser?* (Where is a baby bottle with a bit of water?)

*Biberon* is masculine, while the German correspondent, *Flasche*, is feminine. Lisa did not say *un biberon*, but *ein biberon*, using the masculine article in accordance with the noun it accompanied. In this example,

13. **L:** ... *ist eine **bicicletta*** (... is a bicycle)

*una bicicletta* is feminine and *ein Fahrrad* is neuter. Lisa said *eine bicicletta,* thus making the German article agree in gender with the Italian word. In a later example,

14. **L:** ***Bicicletta** ist ein Fahrrad,*

Lisa used the article and the noun in correct agreement, but this time both were in German. In Example 12 above, Lisa purposely made the German article agree with the Italian noun. In

15. **L:** ... *und hier ist die **sabbia**,*

*la sabbia* is feminine and *der Sand* is masculine. Lisa did not say *la sabbia* or *der sabbia*, but instead placed the German article in agreement with the Italian noun. The same process took place when German words interfered with Italian sentences:

16. **L:** ... *e un porcellino suona la **Flöte**.* (... and a little pig plays the flute.)

Here, *die Flöte* is feminine and *il flauto* is masculine.

Often the gender is the same in the two languages, in which case there is no problem of agreement:

17. **L:** *Tut weh die **vaccinazione**.* (The shot hurts.)

---

7 Almost all authors who have considered this subject (see the authors quoted by Weinreich [1974], and Swain and Wesche [1975]) have found that the nouns are the part of speech most often called upon to substitute in another language.

Here, both *la vaccinazione* and *die Impfung* are feminine.

This type of interference shows that the cohesion between article and noun does not seem to be strong enough to keep the noun phrase from being split between the two languages.[8] It also shows that Lisa was already able at this age to analyze the article and the noun as two separate entities. On the other hand, when she was younger and had just begun to use articles, the article and the noun appeared to form one entity which was always pronounced together, as in *Doè a palla, doè?* (Where the ball, where?), or *Wo a palla, Mami?*

However, this did not occur with other types of phrases which Lisa probably was not yet able to analyze as separate elements. In fact, the sentences with two-word interference usually contained phrases of this type, i.e., verbal, prepositional, or adverbial phrases:[9]

18. L: *... hat **ieri sera** wo Paola kommt?* (... has last night where Paola come?)
19. L: *Der läuft **in piedi** ein bisschen.* (That [one] walks by foot a bit.)
20. L: ***Ti ricordi** du hast den Kuchen gebradt?* (Remember, you have fried the cake?)
21. L: *Zum **finta**? **Finta** ist ... ist ...* (For pretend? Pretend is ... is ...)

Example 21 is one of the very few in which the child split the cohesion of a phrase, in this case a prepositional one. This is probably because the strength of the phrase lies in its semantic aspect rather than in its syntax. In the prepositional phrase *zum finta*, the bearer of meaning is the word *finta*, just as the noun bears the principal meaning in the noun phrase. On the other hand, in the phrases *in piedi, ti ricordi,* and *ieri sera,* both elements carry meaning, but often, when together, they have only one meaning.

Lexical interferences may continue even after the age of 5. For instance:

22. L (5;8):  *Nein ich will eine **femmina** sein.* (No, I want to be a girl.)
23. G (7;11): *Weisst du wo meine **zoccoli** warn? Im Schrank!* (Do you know where my clogs were? In the wardrobe!)

Now let us examine the circumstances under which lexical interferences occur. The available data show that Lisa used lexical interference when: (a) she could not remember the word in the language she was speaking and used its equivalent in the other language rather than interrupt the sentence to look for a synonym:

---

8 Swain [1973] also observes that Michael used two languages to express one noun phrase, but unlike Lisa, Michael also transferred entire noun phrases to the other language.

9 There was only one example where the words were separated, but both words were nouns in this case:

   L: *Mami hat mich keine **punta** so mit die **unghie**.* (Mommy didn't [make] prick it with the nails.)

24. **L:** *Quello non è il bagno ma è* **Badewanne.** *Come si dice* **Badewanne** *in italiano?* (That's not a bathroom, it's a *Badewanne.* How do you say *Badewanne* in Italian?)

and (b) when a certain word is actually used only in one language and there is no suitable equivalent in the other:

25. **L:** *Jetzt gebe ich Giulia eine totò.* (Now I give Giulia a spank.)

The word *totò* is much more frequent than the German equivalent *Klaps*, and even Lisa's mother used *totò*.

26. **L:** *Ist nicht* **mica** *so.* (That's not at all right.)

The word *mica* has no adequate equivalent in German.

Examples of this type imply an obvious attempt to achieve the clearest communication possible. Lisa's one three-word interference also may be considered part of this category:

27. **L:** *Tu eri qua con me, il medico anche, non ha fatto* **picksi in Popo,** *ti ricordi?* (You were here with me, and so was the doctor, and he didn't make an injection, remember?)

*Picksi im Popo* is one entity; furthermore, the act of receiving an injection was always expressed this way, even by the girls' father.

Lisa appears to have followed very precise linguistic behavior patterns where lexical interferences were concerned. These patterns can be summarized as follows:

a) The two lexicons must be kept separate.

b) A word from the other language is inserted in the sentence only when necessary to keep from interrupting the flow, and as few words as possible should be inserted.

c) Words from the other language may be inserted as long as they do not disturb the grammatical rules that the child has developed for each of the languages.

The appearance and maintenance of pattern (a) was surely furthered by Lisa's linguistic environment, where everyone always tried to speak without using interferences. As for pattern (b), the desire to keep up a flow of words is very commonly felt. One's listeners are often impatient, and will start to guess or come to premature conclusions when there is even the slightest pause. This compels us to be mental, verbal, and gestural acrobats in order to finish our sentence by ourselves. Pattern (b) would prevail over (a) when Lisa did not remember or know the word she wanted to use in the language she was speaking. This would also explain why Lisa said *die sabbia* instead of *la sabbia* or *der sabbia*. In saying *die sabbia* instead of *la sabbia,* she was respecting pattern (b) faithfully by inserting as few words as possible. Her reason for saying *die sabbia* instead of *der sabbia* (i.e., in accordance with the masculine gender of the German *der Sand*) was logical: she could not remember the word *Sand*, and thus could not remember the gender either, since gender is not an intrinsic quality of the object. Pattern (b) was used with pattern (c) in mind. In other words, the sentence had to conform to the child's grammatical rules, and thus the interfering word(s) must upset the other language's normal formation as little as possible. Some of Lisa's interfering words were even Germanized or Italianized, as in:

28. **L** (3;7): *Und Giulia rest hier.* (And Giulia stays here.)

Here, Lisa cut off the typical Italian final vowel, so that the Italian word *resta* (third person singular present indicative of *restare*) took the ending of the German verb, which always ends with *t* in this conjugation (*sie singt, geht, macht, raucht, tanzt, lacht,* etc.).

29. **L:** *Die Ente holen wir aber is zuficile.* (We get the duck, but it's too difficult [from the Italian *difficile*])

Lisa could not remember the word *zu schwer*, although it is used quite often in German, and so she introduced a new word, *zuficile*, which is neither Italian nor German.

## 5.3 Morphological Interferences

Examples 28 and 29 have taken us into the realm of morphological interferences. Such interferences occur fairly infrequently and sporadically, and their purpose is to make lexical interferences conform to the language into which they are inserted. For example:

30. **G** (2;8): *Mami guck, ein filen bitte in der Müll.* (Mami look, a thread please in the garbage.)
31. **L** (3;8): *Ti ricordi Giulias Geburtstag mit zwei candelen?* (Do you remember Giulia's birthday with two candles?)
32. **G** (3;2): *Zwei sopraciglien.* (Two eyebrows.)

Just like Bovi's *Sturmtruppen*, the girls added a typical German ending, *en*, to Italian roots such as *fil* (*filo* "thread"), *candel* (*candela* "candle"), and *sopraciglie* ("eyebrows").

33. **L** (4;7): *Oh! Che bel fingherinco!* (Oh, what a beautiful ring!)
34. **G** (3;0): *Io trinko, io esso* (I drink, I eat.)

Here, the German words *Fingerring, trinken,* and *essen* were Italianized by adding a final vowel or modifying it. If the girls wanted to Germanize an Italian word, they added *en* (Examples 30, 31, 32) or omitted the final vowel as in the following example (see also Example 28):

35. **G** (3;0): *Ich will drei biciclet kaufen.* (I want to buy three bicycles.) [correct Italian would be *biciclett*]

Camouflaging a foreign word by adapting its morphological features is a strategy that almost all bilinguals use. In bilingual communities, where the morphological transferrals of all speakers combine to become a part of common usage, bilingual speakers end up unable to determine which language certain words belong to, and thus a new terminology is coined. [10] Examples 30 through 35 show us that these interferences start at a very young age in bilingual children.

Other morphological interferences are the result of superextension, which the child employs after realizing that the morpheme may have a meaning distinct from that of the word root (see examples in Sect. 4.10). [11] Such interferences were quite frequent for a certain period of time, but later disappeared altogether. This strategy of using the morphemes of one language with the word roots of the other led to several strange misunderstandings:
G takes a towel, unrolls it, and stretches it out on the floor.

36. **G** (3;1):   *Aspetta che debbo fare un bel legato.* (Wait, I have to make a nice "tied".)
37. **L**:   *La spiaggia è lì, vero?* (The beach is there, isn't it?)
38. **G**:   *Sì, aspetta che debbo fare ...*
39. **L**:   *... un bel legato. Lo so. Va bene? Fai il legato, fai il legato, e poi ci leghiamo, no?* (... a nice "tied". I know. Okay? Make your "tied" and then we'll "tie" ourselves up, right?)

As soon as G finishes unrolling the towel, the two girls lie down on it and pretend they are at the beach, sunbathing.

Or **G** lies down on the bed.
40. **G** (3;8): *Mi voglio legare.* (I want to "tie" myself up.)
She invites her sister to lie down.
41. **G**:   *Leghiamoci?*
42. **G**:   *Ah! Sto bene qui legata!* (Ah, I feel great here "tied" up!)
She sees her sister lie down elsewhere.
43. **G**:   *Ti leghi lì?* (Are you "tying" yourself up there?)

In Examples 36 – 43, Giulia used the boldfaced words to mean "lie down", making an acoustic-semantic transferral based upon the German word *hinlegen* ("lie down"), which has nothing to do with the Italian verb *legare* ("tie up"). The girls never used the Italian word *legare*, but preferred to express its meaning with the German equivalent *binden*, Italianized, if necessary:

---

10 One interesting example is "Blumenauer Deutsch", which has not yet been sufficiently described, although it is mentioned in Lenard [1970].
11 Interferences using *ge* were observed by Weinreich [1974] in adult subjects as well.

44. **G** (3;8): *Lo vuoi bindare?* (Do you want to tie it up?)
45.        *Ich muss das binden.* (I must tie that up.)
46.        *Uh! Kann das bindare?* (Ah! Can tie this?)

The child said Sentences 44 – 46 while trying to tie the laces of a bag. In these sentences, the girls considered the root *bind* to be a neutral word (such as *basta!* "enough!", *bravo*, etc.) which could be used in either language with the respective endings.

Another transferral similar to the *legare-hinlegen* one was performed with the words *anlehnen* ("to lean") and *allenare* ("to train"). The girls used Italian conjugations with this German root:

47. **G**       [wanting to tell her sister to lean back on the car seat]: *Allenati, allenati!* (Train yourself!)

And:

48. **L** (3;3):   *Lisa ist munter.* (Lisa is awake.)

Then:

49. **L** [looking at her father, who is asleep]: *Papi non è munto.* (Daddy is not "milked", i.e., past participle of *mungere*, Italian for "to milk")

They also Germanized the verb *scegliere* ("to choose"), transforming it into *scelen* (*schälen*), which is very similar to the German verb *abschälen* ("to peel"):

50. **G** (5;6): *Was schälst du? Dieses oder dieses?* (Which do you peel? This or this?)
51. **L** (7;2): *Nein ich schäl das nicht.* (No, I don't peel this.)

The bilingual child's production of interferences also depends upon the languages which his interlocutor is able to speak. He may be interacting with other bilinguals or with monolinguals, and he is more likely to produce interferences in the former case.

Later, we will examine the way the girls used the two languages when they were with Italians, Germans, and bilinguals, and the types of interference which arose in each situation. When Lisa and Giulia talked to each other (i.e., interaction between bilinguals) they generally used Italian, sometimes with German interferences:

52. **L** (4;5): *Giulia, tu devi fare il **Waschbecken**, il **Waschbecken** lì sotto.* (Giulia, you have to do the sink, the sink down there.)
53. **G** (5;2): *Lisa, mi dai il **Frosch**?* (Lisa, will you give me the frog?)

When they spoke German to each other, there were instances of interference:

Lisa is cutting a hand out of paper.
54. **L** (4;4): *Ich mach den Daumen. Guck ich hab schon den Daumen ge-macht. Guck das ist* **pollice.** *Nein, das ist nicht* **pollice.** *Das ist den Daumen.* (I'm making the thumb. See, I've already made the thumb. This is the *pollice.* No, this isn't *pollice,* it's the thumb.)
55. **G:** *Lisa! Schnell! Sofort!* (Lisa! Fast! Hurry!)
56. **L:** *Wir ham gemacht den Daumen.* **Mignolo** *ist ein kleines Mädchen, kleiner Finger.* (We have made the thumb. *Mignolo* is a little girl, a little finger.)
57. **G:** *Ma Lisa!* (But Lisa!)
58. **L:** *Daumen, Daumen. Ich mach* **coriandoli!** (Thumb, thumb. I'm making cutouts!)
59. **G:** *Ich will machen.* (I want to make.)
And she takes the scissors from Lisa's hands.

In the girls' interactions with their mother (and thus again with a bilingual), they used German with some Italian interferences:

60. **L** (3;11): *Ich hab die Schale von* **piselli** *genommen.* (I took the pea shells.)

In the tapes of interactions between the girls and their father or their Italian friends (i.e., monolinguals) they used Italian. There were no observed lexical interferences in these recordings.
In tapes where the girls were playing with a German monolingual they used German with few Italian interferences, as in:

61. **L** (4;11): *Ja, aber der Esel hat nicht Füsse, hat* **zampe,** *hat nicht Füsse wie ham wir. Hast du verstanden?* (Yes, but the mule doesn't have feet, it has hoofs, it doesn't have feet like us. Do you understand?)

Or:

62. **L** (4;11): *Ich bin die Oma, ja? Die Oma geht (einkaufen) und sagt: "Hm, ich will mich was kaufen ja! dann soviele Spielsachen ... dann ein paar von* **Robiola.** **Robiola** *ist ein Käse, ein Käse viel guter ... und auch* **Nutella.** **Nutella** *ist mit mit ... gemacht mit Scho-kolade. Will ich auch kaufen, Nutella, Brot und Äpfel weil da in Eisschrank ist nichts da ..." Hast du verstanden?* (I am grand-ma, right? Grandma goes (shopping) and says, "Hm, I want to buy something, yes! Then lots of toys, then two Robiolas. Robiola is a cheese, a much gooder cheese ... and also Nutella. Nutella is with with ... made with chocolate. I want to buy Nutella, bread and apples because there's nothing in the re-frigerator." Do you understand?)

These examples clearly show the child's fear of being misunderstood. She is perfectly aware that she is using Italian words, and thus when her listener is a German monolingual she feels she should explain the meaning of the interfering words and then ask if she's been understood. [12]

But this lexical awareness is not matched at the level of syntax. In fact, word order interference did not decrease when the girl spoke with monolinguals, and the tapes showed no instances of hesitation or self-correction. [13] When the children were recorded' speaking to their father and mother together, both languages were spoken in alternation and interferences were observed in both languages. [14] For example:

63. **L** (4;5)   [ to F]: *Posso portare Giulia? Ai giardinetti, in tanti posti?* (Can I take Giulia to the park, to lots of places?)
**M:**          *Wo willst du Giulia hinnehmen?* (Where do you want to take Giulia?)
64. **L:**       *In soviele **giardini**, soviele **posti**.*

Or:

The entire family is together.
65. **L**       [to F]: *Questa è una **Maus** elegante.* (This is an elegant mouse.)

In such situations, the child is forced to change lexical codes continually, and the likelihood of interferences greatly increases. [15] In interactions between bilinguals, the child is more relaxed in choosing his words, and he may even happen to use equivalents in the same exchange:

66. **L** (4;7): *Nachher muss ich noch mehr nähen. Ich weiss schon **cucire**.* (Later I have to sew even more. I already know how to sew.)
67. **G** (3;7): *Und dann die Sonne **cammina** und geht sie in sein Haus.* (And then the sun goes and goes home.)

Observation of Lisa and Giulia showed that the simultaneous bilingual produces more lexical interferences if his interlocutor is bilingual and fewer or even none if the other person is monolingual. But as the child grows, he has

---

12 Lisa does not know that Robiola and Nutella are international brand names and thus are known in Germany, too.

13 See Sect. 5.4 for word order interferences in 500 utterances made by Lisa when speaking with a German monolingual.

14 As Gumperz and Chavez [1972, p. 88] rightly note, "one might, by way of explanation, simply state that both codes are equally admissible in some contexts and the code switching is merely a matter of the individual's momentary inclination". With respect to this "momentary inclination", Schönpflug [1977] is correct in saying, "We must not forget the weariness and stress which cause the person to make interferences he would ordinarily never make".

15 Swain and Wesche [1975, p. 18] came to the same conclusion in their analysis of Michael's interferences: "The necessity of communicating almost simultaneously with unilingual speakers ... clearly resulted in considerably more linguistic interference in the child's speech than was exhibited in unilingual situations in either language".

more and more experiences which are related circumstantially to one linguistic context alone, and because he does not learn the equivalents for these words, he is at times forced to use interference. [16] This category would include words learned by Lisa and Giulia at Italian nursery school and elementary school, on trips with monolingual friends of both languages, from books, cartoons, television, etc.


## 5.4 Interferences in Word Order

Word order interferences appear to depend upon:

(a) the level of development achieved in syntax acquisition in both languages;

(b) the word order of sentences which the child has said first and then translated.

Let us look first at (a). As we saw in Sect. 4.15, it takes the Italian-German bilingual child a while before he is able to use the respective word orders correctly. In particular up to the age of 4, there is interference in the positioning of the possessive, negation, and the adjective. After that age Lisa and Giulia, at least, rarely exhibited such interference, though interference in the structures analyzed in Sect. 4.11 was frequent (subject-verb inversion, participial and modal sentences, and placement of the verb in the final position in subordinate clauses).

When Lisa was about 5, a series of recordings was made of her speech while she played with a German monolingual adult. Of 500 German utterances, only 32 exhibited word-order interference. These sequences were considered to contain such interference because the verb was not placed in the final position, and thus in one way or another, the sentence resembled Italian word order. However, by analyzing the constituents of such sentences one by one, we can see that the word order does not entirely correspond to the Italian. [17] For example, the sentence:

**L** (4;6): *Ja guck was ham die gemacht.* (Yes look what they have done.) [the correct German word order is: Ja guck was die gemacht ham]

bears more resemblance to an inserted explicit sentence structure juxtaposing a verb with an interrogative sentence:

---

16 In her analysis of the interferences made by her Italian – English bilingual son Adriano (6;5 – 8;0), Foster-Meloni [1978] observed the same results as those observed for Lisa. On the whole, Adriano used few interferences, and most were lexical; nouns were transferred more than other parts of speech. The lexical interferences occurred in interaction with his mother (a bilingual), and depended upon the language the words were normally used in.

17 The concept of *Zwischensprache* ("intermediate language") described by Zydatiss [1976, p. 9] could also be applied to simultaneous bilinguals: "It seems that the $L_2$ learner blends the rule systems of three different sources. $L_1$, $L_2$, and one which does not belong to $L_1$ or $L_2$".

**Table 5.1.** Oral translation test. The girls were asked to repeat in German what the adult said in Italian. Lisa was 9;0 and Giulia 7;11. The adult pronounced the sentences very clearly, but only once. The girls did the exercise separately.

Example 1.　*Il bambino che è bello è andato al cinema.* (The child who is beautiful went to the cinema.)
　　　**G:**　*Das schöne Kind ist in Kino gegangen.* (The beautiful child went to the movies.)
　　　**L:**　*Das Kind ist schön und geht ins Kino.* (The child is beautiful and goes to the movies.)

Example 2.　*Lo sai dove andrò domenica?* (Do you know where I'll go Sunday?)
　　　**G:**　*Weisst du wo ich Sonntag geh?* (Do you know where I go Sunday?)
　　　**L:**　*Weisst du wo ich Sonntag hingehe?* (Do you know where I go Sunday?)

Example 3.　*Voglio andare al cinema perché il film mi sembra bello.* (I want to go to the movies because the film seems beautiful to me.)
　　　**G:**　*Ich möchte ins Kino gehen weil ich das Film schön find.* (I want to go to the movies because I find the film beautiful.)
　　　**L:**　*Ich will in Kino gehen weil das Film schön ist.* (I want to go to the movies because the film is beautiful.)

Example 4.　*Il palloncino verde è scoppiato.* (The green balloon exploded.)
　　　**G:**　*Der grüne Luftballon is geplatzt. Pum!* (The green balloon exploded.)
　　　**L:**　*Der grüne Luftballon ist geplatzt.* (The green balloon exploded.)

Example 5.　*Il bambino sapeva che non doveva prendere le caramelle di nascosto.* (The child knew he shouldn't steal the candies.)
　　　**G:**　*Der Junge wusste dass er nicht die Bonbons di **nascosto** nehmen sollte.* (The boy knew that he shouldn't steal the candies.)
　　　**L:**　*Das Kind wusste dass er nicht die Bonbons in Versteck nehmen darf.* (The child knew that he was not allowed to steal the candies.)

Example 6.　*Quando sarò grande potrò guardare tanta TV quanta voglio.* (When I'm big I'll be able to watch as much TV as I want.)
　　　**G:**　*Wenn ich gross bin dann kann ich viel Fernseh anschaun, wieviel ich will.* (When I'm big I can watch all the TV, so much as I want.)
　　　**L:**　*Wenn ich gross werd dann darf ich Fernseh anschauen, soviel wie ich mag.* (When I'll be big I'll be allowed to watch all the TV, as much as I wish.)

Example 7.　*Il padre, che è sempre così buono, si è dimenticato di portare un regalino alla figlioletta.* (The father, who is always so good, forgot to bring his small daughter a little gift.)
　　　**G:**　*Der Vater der immer sehr gut ist, ist sich vergessen das kleine Geschenk den Kindchen bringen.* (The father who is always so good, had forgotten himself to bring a small gift to the little daughter.)
　　　**L:**　*Der Vater der so gut ist hat sich vergessen das Geschenklein für das Kind zu bringen.* (The father who is always so good, had forgotten himself to bring a small gift for the child.)

*Ja guck + was ham die gemacht*

than it does to an Italian sentence. As a matter of fact, in the Italian explicit structure the pronoun must be placed in final position:

*Sì guarda cosa hanno fatto quelli*

and a word-by-word translation would be:

*Ja guck was ham gemacht die.*

Table 5.1 shows the results of an oral translation test performed by the girls when they were 7;11 and 9 respectively. By that time, even the type of word-order interference mentioned in the above example had disappeared. Thus, it is very likely that word-order interferences are initially the result of the bilingual acquisition process and that overcoming them depends largely upon the degree of linguistic organization the subject has achieved.

The second case described at the beginning of this section occurs when the child says something in one language and then immediately translates it into the other, keeping the original word order, and thus translating word for word:

**G (2;8)**   [to M]: *Lavare i capelli.* (To wash hair.)
**M:**        *Wie?* (What?)
**G:**        *Mami, ich will waschen die Haare.* (Mommy, I want to wash the hair.)
              [correct German word order: *Mami, ich will die Haare waschen.*]
**G (2;9):**  *Piedi sporchi che schifi!* (Dirty feet what a mess!)
**M:**        *Wie Giulia?* (What, Giulia?)
**G:**        *Diese sind Füsse mutzig.* (These are dirty feet.)
              [correct German word order: *Diese sind schmutzige Füsse.*]
**G (2;9):**  *Dov'è il dento rotto? Io vado a vedere allo specchio.* (Where is the broken tooth? I'm going to look in the mirror.)
**G**         [returning]: *Un dento rotto, anch'io ho un dento rotto!* (A broken tooth, I have a broken tooth, too!)
**M:**        *Was hast du?* (What do you have?)
**G**         [opening her mouth]: *Hah! Ein kaputten Zahn* [correct German order for "a broken tooth"]
**M:**        *Ein kaputten Zahn?*
**G:**        *Ja.*
**G**         [to F]: *Anch'io, io c'ho un rotto dento, vedi? Come te.* (Me too. I have a tooth broken, see? Like you.)
              [correct Italian word order: *Io c'ho un dente rotto.*]
**G (2;10):** *Io lo dico alla Mamma che io non sono un bimbo.* (I'm going to tell Mommy that I'm not a boy.)

**G**          [to M]: *Ich nicht bin ein Jungel.* (I'm not a boy.) [correct word order: *Ich bin nicht ein Jungel.*]

**G (3;7):**   *Cerco la mia matita rossa. Mami, wo ist meine matita rossa?* (I'm looking for my red pencil. Mami, where is my red pencil?)

**M:**         *Wie bitte?*

**G:**         *Mein Bleistift rot, wo ist er?* (My red pencil, where is it?) [correct German word order: *Mein roter Bleistift, wo ist er?*]

**M:**         *Wollt ihr in Mamis Schule gehen?* (Do you want to go to Mommy's school?)

**G** and **L:** *Ja!*

**G (4;4)**    [to Nun]: *Io vado a Mamma scuola.* (I'm going to Mommy's school.) [correct Italian word order: *Io vado alla scuola di Mamma.*]

**L (3;4)**    [seeing Giulia's rice fall on the floor]: *Il riso buono!* (The good rice!)

**M:**         *Wie bitte?*

**L:**         *Der Reis gut!* [correct word order: *Der gute Reis.*]

**L (3;7)**    [to M]: *Giulia hat kurze Haare.* (Giulia has short hair.)

**L**          [to G]: *Tu c'hai corti capelli.* [correct word order: *Tu c'hai capelli corti.*]

**L (3;10)**   [to M]: *Kann ich Brot essen?* (May I eat some bread?)

**M:**         *Ja.*

**L**          [to F]: *Posso ... posso ... pane mangiare?*

**F:**         *Certo.* (Of course.) [correct Italian order: *Posso mangiare il pane?*]

**L (5;4)**    [has helped her mother make lunch]: *Hm, Mami, wir haben ein schön gemacht?* (Hm, Mommy, have we made it well?)

**L**          [to F]: *Abbiamo un bel pranzetto fatto.* (We have made a nice lunch.) [correct word order: *Abbiamo fatto un bel pranzetto.*]

**G (4;9)**    [to M]: *Mi dai il cucchiaino per prendere lo zucchero?* (Will you give me the spoon for the sugar?)

**M:**         *Wie bitte? Hab nichts verstanden.* (What? I didn't understand.)

**L (5;10):**  *Der Löffel für nehmen den Zucker.* [correct German order: *Den Löffel, um den Zucker zu nehmen.*]

Such interferences are typical interlanguage errors caused by the subject's contact with both languages. [18] The form they take can be traced to the way in which sentences are planned in the other language. Since the sequence of a sentence just said or heard is still fresh in the child's mind, and since this sequence forms a perceptive Gestalt (see Sect. 4.12, p. 165), the child is merely replacing items from lexicon A with items from lexicon B, and leaving the structure intact. Monolingual children also demonstrate this strategy of syntax pattern acquisition, but in one language, so that it is less evident. In the literature on child speech there are countless examples which clearly show how

---

18  Such errors must be distinguished from errors of maturation, which are a consequence of the ongoing linguistic development of the child, and are also made by monolinguals.

children use an utterance just produced by their interlocutor. They repeat the entire sequence just as it was, without taking it apart, and merely add an item or two to express their utterance. Clark [1974, pp. 3, 4] gives the following examples:

Adult: We're all very mucky.
Child: I all very mucky, too.

Adult: Do you want to get off?
Child: No I want to get off.

McWhinney [1980] believes that such sequences provide "evidence for short-term memory syntactic rote and [are among] the various kinds of strategies used by monolingual children in order to acquire syntax."

Thus, these interferences are part of the normal process of speech acquisition and are due to factors of linguistic organization. After Lisa and Giulia had passed out of the stage in which they were learning word order, this type of interference was no longer observed. This is an interesting case, then, of an intralanguage acquisition strategy occurring within the interlanguage sphere.

## 5.5 Semantic Interferences

The recordings of Lisa's and Giulia's speech contained almost no instances of semantic interferences, i.e., interferences which occur when the meaning of a word in one language is superextended to a seeming or partial equivalent in the other. For example, *hören* and *sentire* are equivalents for "to hear". However, *sentire* has additional meanings which *hören* does not. It can also mean "to taste", "to smell", and "to feel", both literally and figuratively. Lisa and Giulia gave this same range of meanings to *hören*:

L (3;4) [giving her mother a flower to smell]: *Hör mal, hör mal.* (Listen, listen.) [19]
G (3;8) [stroking velvet]: *Hör mal; ganz ganz weich!* (Listen, very very soft!)

Another interference of this type involved *aushalten* and *tenere*. *Tenere* corresponds to *festhalten* or *halten* ("to hold on", "hold"). *Aushalten* corresponds to *sopportare* ("to bear", "put up with"). The girls connected *aushalten*

---

19 Cunze's subject Dunia [1980] produced examples which were identical to those of Lisa and Giulia for *hören* and *sentire*. In addition, Dunia used *böse* and *cattivo* ("bad") as exact equivalents, although *cattivo* can refer to animate and inanimate objects, while *böse* refers only to animate objects.

Dunia turns to her friend and says, *"Cattiva!"* and then, *"Lisa böse"*. So far, so good. But later, when she is eating pine nuts, she says, *"Cattivo pinoli"* ("bad pine nuts") and then *"böse pinoli"*, when she should have used *schlecht* instead of *böse*.

with *tenere*, thus translating the German expression *Ich kann das nicht mehr aushalten* with the Italian sentence *Non posso più tenere* ("I can't hold it any longer") instead of *Non posso più sopportare* ("I can't bear it any longer"). Giulia's mother explained to her that this was wrong, and that *tenere* does not mean *aushalten* but *festhalten*. Giulia seemed to have understood, and as soon as her sister used the incriminating construction, she wasted no time in correcting her:

**G** (4;4): *Sai Lisa, me l'ha detto Mamma; tenere non è una parola italiana e allora bisogna dire, Non posso piu **aushalten**.* (You know, Lisa, Mommy told me that *tenere* isn't an Italian word, and so you have to say, I can't *aushalten* any more.)

Semantic interferences may also be caused by acoustic or phonological similarities between words which have little or no resemblance in meaning in the two languages. For example, while the Italian word *bravo* means "well done" or "clever", as well as "obedient", the German word *brav* only means "obedient". But Lisa and Giulia used *brav* for both meanings:

**G** (7;5): *Giuliana ist die alla bravste.* (Giuliana is the cleverest.)

However, as there are few such words in German and Italian, interferences of this kind were rare.[20]
Another important phenomenon related to semantic interferences and probably attributable to Lisa's and Giulia's contact with two languages was the elision of the separable particle in German verbs. The girls omitted only the locative particles, but did so with remarkable regularity. For example, the verbs:

*hingehen* = to go there
*hinsetzen* = to sit there
*hinlegen* = to lie down there
*hingucken* = to look there
*angucken* = to look in the direction
*hintun* = to put there

were used by the girls in the following manner:

**L** (4;4): *Ich weiss nicht wo das geht. Wo geht das?* (I don't know where this is going. Where is this going?) [instead of *Ich weiss nicht wo das hingeht. Wo geht das hin?*]

---

20 Such interferences are quite frequent between two Romance languages, such as Portuguese and Italian. As Ervin and Osgood state [1954, p. 17], "Interference is most likely to occur when the languages are closely related". See also Zydatiss [1976], who deals with the subject at length.

**L** (4;11):   *Ich guck hier, aber ich* ... (I look here, but I ...) [ instead of *Ich guck hier **hin**.*]

**L** (6;5):   *Ich guck die Ameisen.* (I look the ants.) [instead of *Ich guck die Ameisen **an**.*]

**G** (7;11):   *Aber wo tu ich das?* (But where do I put this?) [instead of: *Aber wo tu ich das **hin**?*]

In the above examples, the specific forms *hingucken* and *angucken* have been absorbed into the generic verb *gucken*; the same has happened with *hintun* and *tun*.

A few such elisions are also observable in German monolingual children:

**Mara** (3;8): *Meins setzt sich noch da.* (Mine sits down there again.) [instead of *Meins setzt sich noch dahin*]

Nonetheless, I think Lisa and Giulia were more likely to omit the particles *hin* and *an* because there are no semantic equivalents for these particles in Italian. I asked the girls to tell me the difference between the two forms.

**L** (9;0):   ... *gucken ist dasselbe wie guardare, und angucken ist dasselbe wie* ... *dasselbe wie* ... (... *gucken* is the same as *guardare*, and *angucken* is the same as ... the same as ...)

Lisa grins, unable to add anything, so Giulia comes in.

**G** (7;11):   *Angucken ist più perfetto, ist più perfetto Mami; ich weiss nicht wie ich sagen soll, angucken ist so* ... *hm* ... *so* ... *einfach più perfetto!* (*Angucken* is *più perfetto* [more perfect], it's more perfect ... I don't know how to say it, *angucken* is so ... hm ... so ... simply *più perfetto!*)

Although Giulia managed to intuit the difference, it is clear that the meaning of *hin* and *an* is vague in the girls' minds. If we add this to the fact that there is no equivalent in Italian, it is not surprising that their use of such particles was not constant. Other verb particles with richer meanings, such as *auf* ("open"), *rein* ("in"), and *raus* ("out"), were not omitted.

It seems probable that this is not so much the result of direct transposition from one language to the other, but of the process of equivalent acquisition. In other words, bilingual children continue to build up their system of equivalents between the ages of 4 and 8, and this process extends to other levels besides the lexical as they comprehend, acquire, and perfect the equivalences between the two languages. In the example which follows, Lisa is dissatisfied with her mother's translation, which seems to her to be ambiguous and not exactly what she wanted to say.

**L** (3;3):   *Tanto tanto tanto.* (Lots lots lots.)

**M:**       *So ganz viel.* (So very much.)

**L:**       *Tanto tanto tanto.*

**M:** *So ganz viel.*
**L:** *Nein, viel, viel viel!*

The next four examples show Lisa pointing out that the German equivalent of *gola* ("throat") is not *Hals,* and it is clear that her mother's incorrect translation has left her doubtful.

**L** (4;7): *Und meine **Gola.*** (And my throat.)
**M:** *Hals.* (Neck.) [The correct German word for "throat" is *Rachen.*]
**L:** ***Collo** ist Hals. So sagt man, hm? **Collo** wie Hals.* (Neck is *Hals.* That's how you say it, hm? Neck like *Hals.*)
**M:** *Ja.*
**L:** *Und **gola?***
**M:** *Auch.* (Also.)
**L:** *Warum?* (Why?)
**M:** *Weil so.* (Because it is.)

In favorable social and cultural conditions, it is certainly true, as Stern says [in Weinreich, 1974, p. 104], that "the difference between the languages leads not only to the associative aspect of interferences, but it is also a powerful stimulus towards developing individual thought, comparisons, differentiations, and perception of the breadth and limits of concepts, and towards understanding subtle differences in meanings." [21]
Swain and Wesche [1975, p. 11] give a very good example to illustrate this point. The reflection and arrangement which precede Michael's utterance are quite clear: [22]

**M:** Marcel's going to be ... *Marcel va être le payeur.*
Adult: What?
**M:** Marcel's go ... *Marcel va être le payeur.*
Adult: What?
**M:** Marcel's going to be the *payeur.* Let's wait.
Adult: Why?
**M:** Because Marcel's going to be the man who ... who pay.

In the following examples, Lisa has associated the candy brand TicTac with German, and has trouble believing that it has the same name in Italian.

**L** (3;6): *In italiano come si dice?* (How do you say it in Italian?)
**M:** *Auch TicTac.* (Also TicTac.)
**L:** *TicTac auf deutsch. In italiano come si dice?* (TicTac in German. How do you say it in Italian?)

---

21 According to Titone [1981, p. 92], "the social and economic level of the subject is an aspect of crucial importance in any investigation of bilingualism". For further treatment of this aspect, see Peal and Lambert [1962], and Viera [1976].
22 See also examples 9 and 10, p. 171, and the example in Sect. 5.6, p. 190.

**M:**    *Auch TicTac.*
**L:**    *Nein! TicTac auf deutsch! In italienisch?*

The child's need to know the equivalent at any cost is part of his job of arranging the two languages. The meanings and functions which prove to exist in both languages, thus enabling the child to make comparisons, are reinforced. But functions which exist in only one language are considered to be of little importance and allowed to disappear, especially if they have little or no meaning for the child.

It was also noted that *sein* and *essere* ("to be"), *haben* and *avere* ("to have") were not always used correctly. Sometimes the use of these words is reversed in German and Italian. For instance, age is given with *sein* in German and with *avere* in Italian, and the expression "to hurt oneself" calls for *haben* in German and *essere* in Italian. The following examples show that Lisa and Giulia often used *haben* and *sein*, and *essere* and *avere* indiscriminately.

**L (3;6):** *Io sono finita.* (I am done.) [instead of *Io ho finito.*]
**G (2;6):** *Papi, sei finito?* (Daddy, have you done?) [instead of *Papi, hai finito?*]
**G (4;6):** *Ich hab 4 Jahre.* (I have four years.) [instead of *Ich bin 4 Jahre.*]
**G (5;2):** *Io sono 5 anni.* (I am five years.) [instead of *Io ho 5 anni.*]
**G (4;6):** *Ich bin mich hier weh getan.* (I hurt myself.) [instead of *Ich hab mich hier weh getan.*]

However, their use of these verbs in one language did not always reflect the correct usage in the other. It might be more suitable to say that some words have an ambiguous meaning for the bilingual child; there are even instances when "to be" and "to have" appear to be equivalents. In the following sentences, the correct verb is "to be" (and not "to have") in both languages:

**G (2;5):** *Nein, Mami hat gewesen.* (No, Mami has been.) [instead of *Nein, Mami ist gewesen.*]
**L (3;2):** *Lisa hat krank.* (Lisa has sick.) [instead of *Lisa ist krank.*]
**L (3;6):** *Hai caduto dal mobiletto.* (You have fallen from the chest.) [instead of *Sei caduto dal mobiletto.*]
**L (3;8):** *Und er hat runtergefallen.* (And he has fallen down.) [instead of *Und er ist runtergefallen.*]
**L (3;0):** *Vedi Lisa hat müde?* (See Lisa has tired?) [instead of *Vedi Lisa ist müde?*]
**L (6;0):** *Und der Fuchs hat gefallen.* (And the fox has fallen.) [instead of *Und der Fuchs ist gefallen.*]

Italian monolingual children are also confused by *essere* and *avere*, and they make mistakes such as *Io ho andato* ("I have gone"), instead of *Io sono andato*. As many scholars in the field of bilingual education point out,[23] such

23  See Richard [1971], Nemser [1971], Corder [1971], Selinker [1972], Dulay and Burt [1974a], Schönpflug [1977], and Schachter and Celce-Murcia [1977].

errors should not be called interference when bilinguals make them; "interference from one's native language is not a major factor in the way in which bilinguals construct sentences and use language" [Richard 1971, p. 59]. Dulay and Burt [1974a] found that of the errors made by 179 English-Spanish bilinguals between the ages of 5 and 8 tested with the Bilingual Syntax Measure, only 5% were interlanguage errors, while 87% were intralingual.


## 5.6 Phonological Interferences

The literature on the acquisition of phonology has shown that children have an articulatory and phonatory flexibility which enables them to learn all the sound presented to them, and learn them with perfection. This is the most important advantage in learning more than one language at a very early age, and a new phonological system is the hardest obstacle to overcome when learning a language as an adult. After analyzing the speech of 243 Hungarian subjects over the age of 16 who had taken intensive German lessons, Juhász [1970, p. 11] noted that "phonetical interferences are significantly more frequent than grammatical interferences".

Asher and Garcia [1969] came to the same conclusions in their experiments with 71 subjects who were learning a second language between the ages of 7 and 19 and found that the youngest children had weaker accents than the others. According to Locke [1981, p. 63], "... older children and adults typically do better [in learning a second language] ... or at least as well as younger children, except for the area of phonology." Baetens-Beardsmore [1982] says, "Perhaps the most difficult area of all for the avoidance of interference is that of phonology, though often the child or early bilingual has no problems here." And many other authors agree.

The bilingual has to learn only a few sounds more than the monolingual, and these sounds do not usually cause greater problems than those generally caused by phonology acquisition. The small bilingual's real problem is not that of acquiring these sounds, but of sorting them into two distinct codes. In Chap. 1 it was noted that several authors observed phonological interferences in the languages of their subjects, while others did not. Detailed studies on Lisa's and Giulia's phonological development have not yet been made, but intuitive observation points to a lack of phonological interferences in their speech. This is supported by the fact that when they entered Italian nursery school at about 3, German nursery school at $4\frac{1}{2}$ and $5\frac{1}{2}$, and Italian elementary school at 6 years of age, their teachers and schoolmates did not realize that they were bilingual. It was only when they spoke the foreign language with their mother or father that the others found out.

Lisa and Giulia imitated their father's Northern Italian accent perfectly, and as they grew older, were also influenced by the Roman accent they heard around them. Both girls were able to distinguish the phonological system of

Italian and German at the levels of production and metalinguistics, and could tell one regional subsystem from another within each of their languages:

**L** (4;5):   *Tré.* (Three.)
**F:**         *Si dice trè.* (It's: trè [i.e., open *e*])
**L**          [smiling]: *Lusce. Quando si dice tré si dice lusce and quando si dice trè si dice luce.* (When you say *tré* you say *lusce* and when you say *trè* you say *luce.*)

Here, Lisa is referring to the difference between Roman and Northern Italian pronounciations; Romans say *Tré* and *lusce* (light), while Northerners say *trè* and *luce.*

The girls used their mother's German pronunciation, except when they went to Heidelberg for five months. Within only two or three months, they picked up the pronunciation and cadence used by their schoolmates. When they returned to Rome, it took them only another two or three months to begin using their mother's pronunciation and cadence again (see Sect. 6.3, p. 217). It is likely that the phonological interferences observed in the speech of simultaneous bilinguals are caused by the dominance of one of the languages. This same situation is also described for the children of De Matteis [1978], Murrell [1966], and Burling [1971] (Sect. 1.3). However, when there is a fair balance between contact with and production of the two languages, phonological interferences are rare or nonexistent. (Sect. 1.3: Pavlovitch [1920], Ronjat [1913], Oksaar [1971], Raffler-Engel [1964b], etc.). It is also possible that the child does not immediately perceive the two phonologies as distinct systems, and thus may use typical sounds of one language in the other, as when Leopold's daughter [1978] used the German glottal stop in English as well. However, after a while she stopped using it incorrectly. On the whole, the acquisition process appears to be the same for phonology as for lexicon, i.e., there is an initial period with no distinction, and then the child gradually begins to differentiate. Phonology and lexicon are closely related, so it is likely that the distinction between the two phonological systems is made at the same time as it is for the lexical systems. At any rate, a thorough study of this topic might reveal the extent to which the phonological (and prosodic) distinction precedes the lexical one, and show how it influences, aids, and acts as an indicator in the distinction between the child's two languages (see Chap. 7).

## 5.7 Summary

We have observed that the different types of interference are caused by different needs. Morphological interferences are a consequence of the child's need, once it has moved out of the period of superextension described in Sect. 4.10, to make lexical interferences conform as much as possible to the language with which they are interfering.

Lexical interferences are the result of the child's experiences in each of the languages, his memory, the language used by his interlocutor, and whether that person is monolingual or bilingual. The parts of speech which are most often subject to interference are nouns, probably not only because there are more nouns to be memorized than verbs, adverbs, etc., but also because nouns can be inserted without causing great damage to the sentence, while other parts of speech often require at the very least a change in word order.

Word-order interferences apparently stem from the habit of putting the pieces of a concept together in a certain way. Learning to use two languages in which equivalent sentences have different arrangements for their constituents disrupts the sentence *Gestalt* and leads to word-order interference.

Semantic interferences are slightly different from the other types, in that they are caused by unusual associations, partial equivalencies, interlingual hyponymy, and phonological resemblances that are not matched at the level of semantics.

The majority of "errors" made by bilinguals in early childhood cannot be blamed upon the interference of one language with the other, but are the result of normal speech acquisition. And, finally, Lisa and Giulia showed no phonological interference in their speech.

# 6. A Bilingual Upbringing

**Lisa** (3;2): *Tante Hanny, Onkel Carlos nicht versteht Italienisch; Tante Hanny, Onkel Carlos spricht Portugiesisch.* (Aunt Hanny, Uncle Carlos doesn't understand Italian; Aunt Hanny, Uncle Carlos speaks Portuguese.)

**Lisa** (3;4): *Ja, und Lisa la chiude. Lisa hat die Tür zugemacht. Lisa spricht auf deutsch wie Marco, ja?* (Yes, and Lisa shut it. Lisa shut the door. Lisa speaks German like Marco, yes?)

**G** (2;6): [meditating]: *La suora parla in italiano, sì, sì. Anche Luca, anche Camilla, sì, sì.* (The nun speaks Italian; Luca too; Camilla too, yes, yes.)

**G** [to M]: *Ich auf italienisch, sprech mit Luca.* (I, in Italian, speak with Luca.)

**M:** *Ja, du sprichst Italienisch mit Luca. Und mit Mami?* (Yes, you speak Italian with Luca. And with Mommy?)

**G** [smiling]: *Auch ...* (Also ...)

**G** [gets up and speaks, apparently to no one]: *Io parlo italiano come Papi, e basta!* (I speak Italian like Daddy, and that's that!)

Not all children who grow up in bilingual families become bilingual. Learning two languages as a child is not as simple or spontaneous as is sometimes thought; but neither is it as difficult or traumatic. In any case, it is not impossible. The undeniable need to communicate is sufficient motivation to make the child speak one or more languages, but it is also absolutely indispensable. Given this motivation, it is practice which leads to a more or less thorough and perfect knowledge of the two languages. The bilingual needs practice in speaking his two languages, just as an athlete needs to train, and a pianist needs to play. The question of whether a child becomes bilingual or not depends upon the quantity, form, and quality of this practice.

This chapter describes the relationship between linguistic input and linguistic output in Lisa's acquisition of German and Italian. The results of this examination can be considered to apply to Giulia as well, because for the most part her linguistic environment was the same as Lisa's.[1]

---

1 For a detailed description of the linguistic environment of other bilingual children, see Cunze [1980], Bizzarri [1978b], and El-Dash [1981].

## 6.1 The First Stage: The Role of the "Sole" Interlocutor

Lisa has always lived in Rome, a monolingual city, but most of the time she is taken care of by her mother, who speaks only German to her. However, when Italians are present, Lisa's mother speaks Italian, while her father speaks only Italian, even when German monolinguals are present. Both parents understand everything the child says. Her father spends his evenings and weekends with her. During the week, she spends two hours a day with the family's Italian domestic helper. She has other, less regular contact with Italian and German at the park, on walks, and with her Italian or bilingual Italian-German friends.

None of Lisa's relatives lives in Rome, so that she comes into contact with them only on visits, which vary in duration. She spent four weeks with her maternal grandparents, and thus in close contact with German, when she was six months old, and her maternal grandmother and uncle visited her again for the same period when she was 18 months old. She has seen her paternal relatives more often but for shorter periods of time, for a week when she was 11 months old and three weeks at the age of 13 months. Both times, her mother was absent, so the environment was exclusively Italian. Again, at the ages of 14, 21 and 23 months, she spent ten days with her paternal grandparents, but this time her mother was with her.

Lisa spent two or three hours every afternoon with an Italian neighbor from the age of 1;7 to 1;11, after which she again spent the afternoons with

**Table 6.1.** Summary of the relationship between Lisa's linguistic contact and linguistic output from birth to the age of 2 years

| Age | Linguistic contact | Linguistic output |
|---|---|---|
| 0 – 2;0 | M is the most important German interlocutor | |
| | F, the domestic helper, and neighbors are the most important Italian interlocutors | |
| 0;6 – 0;7 | Intense contact with German | |
| 0;11 – 0;11,8 | Intense contact with Italian | |
| 1;1 – 1;2 | Intense contact with Italian | |
| 1;6 | | Equal output in both languages |
| 1;6 – 1;7 | Intense contact with German | |
| 1;9,5 – 1;9,15 | Intense contact with Italian | |
| 1;7 – 1;11 | Afternoon visits with Italian neighbor | |
| 1;11 | | Slight dominance in Italian |
| 1;11,10 – 1;11,25 | Intense contact with Italian | |
| 1;11 – 2;0 | Afternoons with M | |
| 2;0 | | Equal output in both languages |

her mother for two months. Since Lisa was 13 months old, her mother has also spoken only German with her sister Giulia (see Table 6.1).

The recordings and observations show that at 1;6 Lisa had a total of 18 words, of which 6 were German, 6 Italian, and 6 neutral, i.e., acceptable in both languages, such as *Mamma, caca,* etc. This count includes only the actual words, not the different meanings the child gave to each one. For instance, *ja* counts here as one word, but for Lisa it meant affirmation and also the act of finding something; *daki* meant the act of thanking as well as giving and receiving, etc. for further explanation, see Chap. 2. On the other hand, Lisa did not have more than one word for each meaning. In fact, apart from the word game *kuckuck da* or *cucu tetè* ("peek-a-boo"), which she played willingly in both languages, she possessed a form of language which is peculiar to children, being neither monolingual nor bilingual, but consisting of a single lexicon made up of words from both languages.

By 1;11, Lisa used 100 words, of which 46 were Italian, 34 were German, and 20 were bivalent (e.g., the names of people); thus Italian dominated slightly.[2] At this time, she normally spent three hours a day with her father, two or three with the Italian neighbor, and two sleeping in the afternoon. This left an average of four hours a day of exclusive German contact with her mother. It was during this period that her Italian grandmother and aunt came to stay with her, thus reinforcing her contact with Italian. By 2;0, her mother was spending more time with her, and from a total of 98 utterances, 36 were German, 27 Italian, 3 mixed, and 21 bivalent. From this description, it is clear that there is a close relationship between the amount of contact with each language and the child's linguistic output; the quantity of contact the child had with each language determined the quantity of words she learned. When Lisa had more opportunities of speaking Italian, her Italian output increased, and the same was true of German. Thus, if a child is to learn both languages, he must have continuous exposure for several hours daily.

It should be remembered that Lisa's is a bilingual family living in a monolingual community. In addition, within the family itself, the one-sided bilingual situation has tended to favor Italian, because while the girls' mother speaks both Italian and German, their father speaks only Italian. But up to 2;0 – 2;6, this situation is not a determining factor in bilingual acquisition. During this first stage, even one person is enough to establish a true linguistic environment. The child needs a great deal of individual care: his meals take place before or after the others; he is usually washed and changed by one of

---

2 Here, "dominant language" means the language which the bilingual uses most frequently, in the sense which Dodson (in Baetens-Beardsmore, 1982) calls "preferred language". As Dodson says, the "dominant"-"preferred" distinction is useful above all when considering late bilinguals, who may use the second (preferred) language more often, for contingent reasons, while they nonetheless have better grammar in the first (dominant) language. Dodson's distinction is not used here, because the simultaneous bilingual differs from the late bilingual in this respect. Nor is the term "preferred" used, because it may easily be minsunderstood to mean that the bilingual likes, admires, or has less difficulty with one of the two languages.

his parents, and almost never in the presence of others. While it is true that his play with other children is intense at the level of motor activity, it involves little or no linguistic production.

The fundamental factor is that the child's field of interest is limited to the people who are normally around him, and any contact he may have with others does not take place at the linguistic level, but involves other forms of communication, such as looks, smiles, hugs, caresses, and so on. In consequence, if during this first period there are many speakers of one language and only one of the other, this does not hinder the child's bilingual acquisition as long as the person we might call the "sole" interlocutor is in contact with the child for no less than three or four hours a day and interacts verbally with him, not limiting the exchanges to gestures and actions.

A positive relationship with someone who is not one of the child's parents will also give him the chance to learn more than one language. But if this relationship is negative, this will surely influence the child's bilingualism.

Many parents wonder about the right age to begin speaking a second language to their child. It is often thought that the ideal age is around 2, because the child is not too young and already knows how to speak. However, this does not appear to be the best age, for a number of reasons. First, it quickly becomes habit to speak one language with a certain person, so that the parent should begin speaking the language he has chosen as soon as the child is born, primarily so that he will become accustomed to doing so. This way, the child will hear him speak, and the parent will see the child's gradual reactions to his monologues; the child will also be given the chance to listen for a year or so before his first attempts at speech. It is no easy task for the adult to change languages after this point, and because the child has always interacted with the parent in the first language, he will not accept a sudden change at the age of 2. At the very least, the parent will seem strange to him.

Second, it is not true that a 2-year-old already knows how to speak. He has only begun the process of language acquisition, and possesses at most a lexicon of 150 to 200 words, even in the most precocious of cases. He has just begun to overcome the greatest obstacles of phonology and pronounce words fairly well. At this point, he is ready to begin a second process, that of learning morphology and syntax. He might not be at all pleased to have to repeat the hardships he has already overcome once. Also children whose families move to another country at this point, thus placing them in conditions of almost total language immersion, have shown that they do not like to start all over again, and that they need an initial period just for listening. Itoh and Hatch [1978] describe the acquisition of English by a $2\frac{1}{2}$-year-old Japanese boy who refused to speak the new language for an initial period, only beginning after he had been in nursery school for several months.

## 6.2 The Second Stage: The Child Begins to Speak the Language of the Majority

At about the time when Lisa reached the age of 2, her parents considerably modified their linguistic behavior: her father began to understand less and less of what she said to him in German, and when Lisa was 2;9, her mother began to pretend she didn't understand what the girl was saying to her in Italian. What is more, she began the practice of speaking to the child in German even when there were Italians present, despite the difficulty this often entailed.

Apart form these changes, Lisa's life continued more or less as it had been in the first stage: her mother spent more time than anyone else with Lisa and her sister; her father spent his evenings and weekends with her, the domestic helper spent two hours each weekday with her, her friends were Italian or Italian-German bilinguals, and she spent an average of one afternoon a week with her Italian neighbors.

During this period, Lisa had two kinds of intense contact with Germans: First, she spent two months (2;0 – 2;2) with her maternal grandparents, and a month (3;1 – 3;2) with her aunt and uncle. This latter visit took place during vacation, when her Italian friends were out of town, and her aunt and uncle spent a great deal of time with her. Second, at the age of 2;11 she met a monolingual German woman to whom she immediately took a great liking. Although she saw her only four times over a period of a week, this was an important event for Lisa, because it made her realize that people other than her mother spoke German. And, in fact, she repeated again and again, *"Tante Arco spricht Deutsch, ja Mami?"*

When Lisa returned from her two-month visit with her maternal grandparents, German was clearly dominant: of 134 utterances, 65 were in German, 18 in Italian, 12 mixed, and 39 bivalent. The same thing happened a month later, when 80 of her 141 utterances were German, 17 Italian, 11 mixed, and 33 bivalent. The influence of German was unquestionably very strong during her stay with her grandparents, but it must also be remembered that this was a period of intense linguistic development for Lisa: it was at this time that her sentences with two or more words increased rapidly, shooting from 23% (i.e., 23 out of 98) at 2;0 to 50% (i.e., 67 out of 134) at 2;3.

At 2;6, Lisa's German was still dominant, with 53 of her 123 utterances being German, 36 Italian, 19 mixed, and 15 bivalent. But only one month later, her Italian had caught up: of 122 utterances, only 11 were German, while 67 were Italian. This pattern continued into the next month, when only 22 of her 134 utterances were German, while 71 were Italian.

During this period, Lisa had intense contact with Italian when she, her mother, and her sister visited her paternal grandparents for two weeks, one at 2;7 and again at 2;9. In addition, she spent a month at the seaside with her mother and a friend at 2;10. Thus, from 2;7 to 2;10, her contact with Italian increased enormously.

It was at this point that her mother began to alter her linguistic behavior, and this undoubtedly furthered the development of Lisa's German, although the results were not evident in the first two months; when the child was 2;9, she produced 15 German and 109 Italian utterances out of 183, and at 2;10, 45 in German and 90 in Italian out of a total of 167. But after two- or three-month effort, the recordings showed a very different pattern: at 2;11, 51 of Lisa's 135 utterances were German and 75 Italian; at 3;0, 34 out of 79 were German, and 40 were Italian.

Italian was always the dominant language, but remarkable progress had been made in German. When her aunt and uncle came to visit for a month (3;1), the child's interest in German picked up considerably. Lisa was amazed, often repeating, *"Tante Hanny spricht Deutsch, ja Mami? Und Onkel Carlos auch, ja ja."* She made rapid progress, so much so that at 3;2 she was able to speak almost entirely in German with German monolinguals, and of her 131 utterances at this point, 82 were German, and only 16 Italian.[3] However, this does not mean that Lisa had replaced her Italian with German. As the recordings made with Italian monolinguals show, she was able to speak almost entirely in Italian: only 7 of her 81 utterances in these recordings were German, while 57 were Italian. Thus, in this period Lisa had achieved almost equal bilingualism (see Table 6.2).

**Table 6.2.** Summary of the relationship between Lisa's linguistic contact and linguistic output from the age of 2;0 to 3;6

| Age | Linguistic contact | Linguistic output |
|---|---|---|
| 2;0 – 3;6 | M is the principal German interlocutor | |
| | F, the domestic helper, neighbors, and friends are the principal Italian interlocutors | |
| 2;0 – 2;2 | Intense contact with German | |
| 2;2 | | German dominates |
| 2;6 | | German is slightly dominant |
| 2;6 – 2;10 | Increased contact with Italian | |
| 2;9 | M begins not to understand Italian | |
| 2;10 | | Italian dominates |
| 3;0 | | The two languages are almost equal |
| 3;1 – 3;2,15 | Intense contact with German | |
| 3;3 | | The two languages are equal |
| 3;3 | Italian nursery school begins | |

3 The recordings on which these figures are based were made either with German monolinguals, Italian monolinguals, or people who spoke both languages.

During this stage, as in the first, the most important factor is the amount of contact with each language. But there is one significant difference between the two stages: up to 2;0 – 2;6, the child only needs intense contact with one person in order to be bilingual, because this contact is enough to establish a true linguistic environment for him. Up to this point, the child does not realize he is speaking two languages, and therefore does not differentiate between them. He lives in an environment where everyone uses a certain language, and he does the same, speaking the language he has been able to learn on the basis of what the environment has given him. [4] But after this age, many things begin to change. The child's interest in his peers grows and he becomes increasingly independent, making more and more social contacts of all types. His speech makes noticeable progress, because the child now shows a real desire to communicate with words. Every person he meets and speaks with provides stimulus for communication. At this time, the child begins to distinguish between the two languages and realize that he, too, is speaking with two different linguistic codes. [5]

For the bilingual, this is when the richness of the linguistic environment becomes the decisive aspect in speech acquisition. Here, "wealth of the linguistic environment" refers specifically to the number of people who steadily interact verbally with the child. [6] Thus, it is now the language which is spoken by the greatest number of people that dominates, and the language of the "sole" interlocutor may even be lost. [7] This is the classic type of rejection, and it happens to most bilingual children. According to El-Dash [1981, pp. 2, 3], who analyzed the speech of his bilingual Portuguese-English son Neale, "During the time that his basic socialization was with his parents, English was the predominant language lexically, but even then Portuguese dominated structurally. But at 2;9 he was enrolled in a nursery school in which Portuguese was spoken. For the first few days he acted as if he didn't understand anything and did not participate in group activities. But within a couple of weeks, he was participating in everything and insisted on speaking only Portuguese, even at home. There was a rapid increase in the quantity and complexity of his Portuguese, accompanied by a voluntary rejection of all attempts to get him to use

---

4 Leopold [1939, p. 179] says, "While she was a small child, Hildegard's speech was not yet aiming at this ideal (of bilingualism). Bilingual conditions were not yet permanent: her speech was still striving to make one unit of the split presentation. That is why the list of bilingual synonyms is so short. Incidentally, it omits all instances of single forms which were the result of bilingual models."

5 Leopold [1939, p. 159] says, "This is the course of development which was to be expected under the circumstances. As the child grew up, her circle of English-speaking friends widened. Playmates and their mothers, maids, etc. ... reinforced the English element. The importance of the father, the only significant German speaker in Hildegard's world, became absolutely and relatively smaller."

6 As defined by Titone (private communication).

7 Leopold [1939, p. 163] says, "German words continued to be acquired, but their constancy was much inferior, because most of them did not stand up against the English competition for long."

English. The fact that both parents understood when he spoke in Portuguese facilitated this transition, and even their insistence and encouragement to use English had no effect. After a few months in the school, Neale no longer used any English expressions, his English being limited to isolated content words such as 'butterfly' and 'airplane', which were extremely important in his world. This phase of total rejection of English lasted for over a year, although the family continued to speak only English to him."

For precisely this reason, that is, to keep Lisa's and Giulia's bilingualism active and to ensure that they would not refuse to speak one of their two languages, the girls' mother resorted to a tactic which is described in the next section.

### 6.2.1 An Educational Tactic: "What Did You Say? I Didn't Understand ..."

Many years ago the linguist Grammont advised his friend the French linguist Ronjat, who had married a German woman and wanted to bring up his son Louis as a bilingual (see Sect. 1.2, pp. 6 – 8), to follow the *"une personne, une langue"* principle, that is, to have each parent speak to the child in his own language. Lisa and Giulia's parents used this strategy, which caused no problems during the first two years, because the children's speech was still so limited that everyone could understand everything they said. Even the Italian neighbors and relatives understood, helped as they were by the context, or because they, too, had meanwhile learned the few words and short sentences uttered by the children.

However, after the age of 2, the girls' lexicon increased rapidly and their monolingual friends and relatives were no longer able to understand everything they said, so the adults were often forced to ask questions such as, "What? What did you say? ... Whatever could she be trying to say?"

Sometimes even the girls' father did not understand them:

**G** (2;2): *Dov'è Schlappen?* (Where is slippers?)
**F:**      *Cosa vuoi?* (What do you want?)
**G:**      *Dov'è pantofole?* [This time G has said "slippers" in Italian.]

It did not take the children long to realize that some words were more effective than others, and that everyone understood Italian, while almost no one understood German. They were being conditioned to consider only one of their languages effective – the language which belonged to their environment and was spoken by the majority. Slowly, but systematically and steadily, Lisa and Giulia began speaking less and less German. A word which had been spoken in German one day was replaced with its Italian equivalent the next. Although their mother purposely intensified her contact with them, this did not have a decisive effect on their output. Even though they perfectly understood everything that was said to them in German, they tended to answer in Italian. If they were asked to repeat the word in German, they obeyed reluctantly or not at all.

It should be stressed that the girls' behavior was not the result of a negative attitude toward a bilingual upbringing on the part of others. On the contrary, the approval of Lisa's and Giulia's bilingualism by their acquaintances was an important factor which positively affected their personalities and bilingual acquisition. None of their relatives, neighbors, or friends ever raised any objections to their bilingualism, because their mother was a foreigner in Italy, and bilingualism was considered a natural, logical consequence. Furthermore, the girls were continually exposed to remarks such as, "How clever you are! I wish I could speak German, too. Will you teach me?" – and this greatly encouraged them. When they were a bit older, from the ages of 7 to 9, one of the accomplishments they were most proud of showing off was their ability to speak a second language, and they never missed a chance to do this, whether it was with a dinner guest, new friends, or simply casual acquaintances. Even if the environment was exclusively Italian, they always managed to say something to their mother in German, often about a subject that had nothing to do with the topic of conversation, for the express purpose of being heard by the others. And when the visitor inevitably responded with wonder, and their mother explained that they were bilingual, because she spoke only German with them, Lisa and Giulia were entirely satisfied. At that age, one of their favorite pastimes was to talk to their parents' friends in the two languages.

But let us return to the child of 2 or 3 years who is replacing his active bilingualism with a passive one. While he was previously able to understand and speak two languages, he now understands both but speaks only one. In order to promote active bilingualism at this point, there must be parity between the two languages, not only with respect to the adults' production, but also to their understanding of the child's speech. If the child has contact with a certain number of people who speak and understand Italian but not German, he must also be able to interact with people who speak and understand German but not Italian. If this is not the case, the situation will be asymmetric and the child will not be able to develop equal bilingualism. His acquisition of speech will necessarily reflect this disparity.

When Lisa and Giulia were about 2 or 3, their mother decided to try to create the same conditions for Italian as they had experienced with German, and began pretending not to understand most of what they said in Italian. When they spoke to her in German, she answered immediately and fulfilled their desires. But when they spoke to her in Italian, she answered *Wie bitte?* ("What, please?"), or *Was hast du gesagt?* ("What did you say?"), or simply *Was? Wie?*. In the beginning, the children thought their mother was merely a bit deaf and would repeat the same words at a louder pitch, sometimes even shouting. But their mother would cover her ears and ask *Wie?* again,[8] so the girls began to replace their shouting with the use of equivalents. The following example is a lovely illustration of this point:

8 It should be recalled that the girls were already using equivalents as a strategy for other purposes (Sect. 2.2).

**G** (2;4): *Mami aple.* (Mommy open.)
**M:**       *Wie bitte?*
**G:**       *Mami aple.*
**M:**       *Wie bitte?*
**G:**       *Mami aple.*
**M:**       *Wie?*
**G:**       *APLEEEEEEE!!!!*
**M**        [covers her ears] *Wie bitte?*
**G:**       *Aufmachen?* (Open?)

When they saw that their wishes would be fulfilled if they spoke German, the girls quickly realized that their mother's *Wie?* meant only that they were to switch language. After a while, in order to avoid having to say the same thing twice, they began to speak to her directly in German.

The child should not be subjected to this *Wie?* tactic before he has reached a certain level of linguistic organization. It would be wrong to start while the child is still in the first stage, because at this time he does not yet possess equivalents, and the *Wie?* strategy clearly calls for them. Nonetheless, the child may sometimes happen to be asked for an equivalent he does not yet possess.

**G** (2;1): *Das da **per tagliare**.* (This here for cutting.)
**M:**       *Was ist das?* (What is this?)
**G:**       ***Per tagliare.***
**M:**       *Wie heisst das?* (What's it called?)
**G:**       ***Per tagliare unghie.*** (To cut fingernails.) [G pretends to be cutting her nails.]
**M:**       *Das ist eine Schere.* (These are scissors.)
**G:**       *Eine Schele, ja Mami, eine Schele **bianca**, eine Schele **lote**.*

In this phase, if a word which the child has acquired after considerable effort and with obvious joy and pride is not understood by the adult, condition may arise which could easily block his linguistic production. Not only will he be unable to understand what the adult wants, and thus insistently repeat the word he knows, but he will also be led to believe that this word does not communicate anything. This happens quite clearly in the following example, where Giulia finally disqualifies the communication:

**G** (1;11): *Ancoa.* (More.)
**M:**        *Was Giulia?*
**G:**        *Ancoa.*
**M:**        *Was ist?*
**G:**        *Ancoa acqua.* (More water.)
**M:**        *Was willst du?* (What do you want?)
**G:**        *Ancoa acqua.*
**M:**        *Was?*
**G:**        *Ancoa acqua?*

**M:**     *Mami hat dich nicht verstanden.* (Mommy doesn't understand you.)

**G:**     *Ancoa acqua.*

**M:**     *Was?*

**G:**     *Babau, babau.*

Let us imagine for a moment that we are dealing with a child who possesses about 50 words, of which one half belong to one language, and one half to the other, with almost no equivalents. There are monolingual interlocutors who often do not understand the child. If not even the bilingual interlocutor understands what the child is saying, his speech will be incomprehensible too often. If the child is also unlucky in guessing which language to use for a certain person, the number of incomprehensible utterances will be too high. At this point, the child will realize that his speech does not impart meaning and for a while, at least, he will give up wasting his efforts in that direction.

Let us add to this the fact that the child is as yet unable to distinguish the language to which his words belong. If there are words which could belong phonologically to both languages, we have examples like the following one, in which Giulia was reading a magazine.

**G** (2;2): *Uno donna.* (A woman.)

**M**     [pointing to the picture of the woman]: *Was ist das?*

**G:**     *Uno donna!*

**M:**     *Was ist das hier?*

**G:**     *Uno donna!!*

**M:**     *Auf deutsch?*

**G:**     *Uno donnaaaa!!!*

**M:**     *Ach ja? Auf deutsch uno donna?* (Oh yes? In German *uno donna?*)

**G:**     *Ja!* [9]

Giulia was convinced that what she was saying was correct. But two months later, when she listened to this recording, her attitude changed:

**G** (2;4): *Auf deutsch eine Frau, non una donna.* (In German *eine Frau*, not *una donna.*)

When the child has developed a richer lexicon with various equivalents, when he realizes that he is dealing with two distinct languages and begins to replace the words of one language with those of the other, the *Wie?* strategy becomes extremely important. These three conditions appeared in Lisa and Giulia about six months after the beginning of the second lexical stage, i.e., when Lisa was 2;9 and Giulia 2;4.

Lisa and Giulia had both begun to distinguish the two lexicons at the beginning of the second lexical stage, and it was soon apparent that they tended to speak one language with one person and the other with another.

---

9 The German word for "thunder", *Donner*, is pronounced "donna". The child might have been confused by this similarity.

**G** (1;9) [looking at a very small pencil]: *Non è glande, piccolo, piccolo.* (Not big, small, small.)

**M:**  *Ist der Bleistift gross?* (Is the pencil big?)

**G:**  *No no gloss, klein klein.* (No no big, small small.)

Lisa wants to eat her dessert before the fruit.

**G**  [eating her fruit]: *Dopo Kuchen dopo.* (Dessert later.)

**G**  [to **M**]: *Her.* [i.e., *nachher* = later]

This spontaneous tendency to speak to each person in his own language was gradually lost by the girls as they began to speak Italian most of the time, even with their mother. This was not, however, because they had difficulty speaking German or did not possess the equivalents; on the contrary, they could usually express themselves in both languages, often using two terms alternatively.

**G** (2;2): *Mami, das hier **per sclibele**?* (Mommy, is this here for writing?)

   G shows her mother the pencil she's holding, and then picks up a blunt pencil.

**G:**  *Mami, nicht zum Schreiben das hier?* (Mommy, this here's not for writing?)

The girls spoke German and Italian in the tapes with their mother, and only Italian with their father, although they had been using both languages with him as recently as two months. Now they realized that they could not continue to do so with their father, while with their mother they could. This was the appropriate moment for the *Wie?* stategy to begin.

But how did the girls react to their mother's new behavior? In general, they reacted positively. As soon as they realized that what she wanted was a different language, they gave it to her, and communication continued as before.

**G** (2;3): *Metti tavolo di Giulia.* (Put Giulia's table.)

   G wants to move the cup and saucer from L's table to hers.

**M:**  *Wo soll ich's hintun?* (Where should I put it?)

**G:**  *Das da, das da auf Tisch von Giulia.* (That there, that there on Giulia's table.)

**G** (2;3)  [crying because she doesn't like her tummy to be uncovered]: *Guck Mami, la pancia fuoli.* (Look Mommy, my tummy's out.)

**M**  [points to G's tummy]: *Was ist das da?*

**G:**  *Bauch.* (Tummy.)

**M:**  *Und wo ist der Bauch?* (And where is your tummy?)

**G:**  *Laus.* (Out.)

**G** (2;6)  [wants permission to tear off a piece of paper]: *Mami un foglio.* (Mami, a piece [of paper].)

**M:**  *Was ist?*

**G:**  *Ein Blatt? Ist schlecht dies hia.* (A piece of paper? This is bad.)

**G** (2;8): *Lavare i capelli.* (Wash hair.)
**M:**      *Was?*
**G:**      *Lavare i capelli.*
**M:**      *Was möchtest du?* (What would you like?)
**G:**      *Mami, ich will waschen die Haare.* (Mommy, I want to wash the hair.)
            Lisa did the same:
**L** (2;9): *Mani porche, mani porche, Lisa ce l'ha mani porche.* (Dirty hands, dirty hands, Lisa has dirty hands.)
**M:**      *Wie sind deine Hände?* (What are you hands like?)
**L:**      *Hände mutzig.* (Hands dirty.)
**L** (2;9) [holding paper and pencil; she wants to draw]: *Lisa fa sole?* (Lisa makes sun?)
**M:**      *Was?*
**L:**      *Lisa fa die Sonne?*
**M:**      *Mami versteht dich nicht.* (Mommy doesn't understand you.)
**L:**      *Lisa macht die Sonne?*
**L** (3;3): *Mammi, fai una casetta?* (Mommy, will you make a house?)
**M:**      *Was?*
**L:**      *Mami mach ein Haus, ein kleines Haus.* (Mommy, make house, a little house.)
**L** (3;5) [having fixed the broom]: *Bene così?* (Is this okay?)
**M:**      *Hm?*
**L:**      *Richtig so?* (Okay like this?)

It didn't take the girls long to reaccustom themselves to speaking only German with their mother, and they often went so far as to interrupt themselves to change to the other language:

**M:**      *Hast du Schuhe an?* (Have you put your shoes on?)
**G** (2;4): *Io ... Ich hab die Stlenfe.* (I have my stockings.)
**G** (2;5): *Ich will **pettinare**.* (I want to comb.)
**M:**      *Wie bitte?*
**G:**      *Ich will pett/ ... kämmen. Mami, **pettinare** ist auf italienisch, kämmen ist in deutsch.* (I want to pett/ ... comb. Mommy, *pettinare is in Italian and **kämmen** is in German.*)
**M:**      *Ja.*
**G** (2;6): ***Quello è wie un ... ein Teller, è wie ein Teller.*** (That's like a ... like a plate.)

However, even though they were at the right age, Lisa and Giulia were not always willing to accept their mother's strategy unconditionally. And of course some moments were more opportune than others for using it. For instance, it was not used when the girls were telling about things they had experienced almost totally and/or very frequently in the other language. Although they usually were not patient enough to describe to their mother things that had happened to them at nursery school, and often responded to her questions with a laconic *nichts* ("nothing"), this was not due to bilingualism. Monolingual children also often have no desire to talk about school, and answer in the same way. On days when something interesting had happened at school, Lisa and Giulia enthusiastically began to tell about it. Here, it was found that a dry interruption of their euphoria with a metalinguistic *Wie?* or *Was?* did not give good results. Usually the girls stopped, used one or two German words and several "ahs" and "uhms", and then either continued the story in Italian, dropped it altogether, or, most frequently, got irritated and gave vent to their nervousness with expressions of malcontent.

The *Wie?* strategy is ineffective when the subject carries emotive connotations. When the child is relaxed and happy or when there's no hurry, the interaction is not compromised or disturbed by the brief *Wie?* interruption. But if the child is crying because he is unsatisfied, anxious, or angry, or if he is in a state of euphoria, the *Wie?* interruption is an indication that the parent is more interested in the child's language than in his unease, or that his participation in the child's joy must pass through the filter of the language that has been used. Children do not like this type of behavior, and express their dislike by clearly rejecting the tactic. If the child has a problem, the parent must understand him, or he will only be adding one more problem. The child's small problems demand immediate solutions, and any attempt to put them off only makes the child more impatient than he already is.

The *Wie?* tactic is less likely to succeed in interactions where it is primarily the adult who is interested in the conversation. But when the child is the more interested participant, this strategy is at its best.

The *Wie?* tactic also proved inadvisable when the group included other people who spoke only Italian. For example:

> Lisa is at the table with her parents and paternal grandparents. Her mother interrupts her Italian to ask, *Wie?*

**L** (4;6): *Io parlo a tutti.* (I'm speaking to everyone.)

Finally, it is always a good idea to reflect a moment before using the *Wie?* strategy, because it offers the child a chance for revenge, if he is in the mood.

> M is studying and G is sitting next to her.

**G** (2;10): *Ich will ein klein Blatt. Kann Giulia schreiben? Kann Giulia machen? Kann Giulia nehmen?* (want a small piece of paper. Can Giulia write? Can Giulia do? Can Giulia take?)

**M:** *Ein Moment Ruhe, jetzt schreib ich.* (A moment of silence, I'm writing now.)

**G** [to L]: *Lisa, mi accompagni con la pistola piccola?* (Lisa will you come with me with the little gun?)

> Lisa follows her into the other room. They start to play. When their mother hears them speaking Italian, she shouts into the other room.

**M:** *Was? Was habt ihr gesagt?* (What? What did you say?)

**G:**     *Nein, du schreibst du. Nicht sprechen! Nicht hören!* (No, you're writing you. Don't speak! Don't hear!)

Giulia was more interested in getting revenge for her wounded pride than in making her mother happy.

The *Wie?* tactic is effective in modifying the child's lexicon and teaching him to switch codes, but it does not correct errors in morphology and syntax. Thus, at a time when they were not yet placing the verb at the end of German subordinate clauses (see Sect. 4.12.3), their mother tried a few times to correct Giulia:

**M:** *Non si dice: weil ist die Bluse schön **ma si dice** weil die Bluse schön ist.* (You don't say *"weil ist die Bluse schön"*; you say *"weil die Bluse schön ist."*)

But the child continued to say the sentence the way she had before. Her mother then told her to speak correctly, or she wouldn't understand her. Giulia tried again by improving her lexicon and adding, *"Du musst verstehen?"* ("You must understand!"). Another time, she excused herself with *"ich weiss nicht, Mami"* ("I don't know, Mommy").

While it is easy for the child to distinguish between the two lexicons and connect them to the right person, it is more complicated to elaborate and distinguish morphological and syntactic rules, and it is useless to supply corrections until the child has extrapolated the rules for himself and learned to apply them correctly to each language. Thus, errors due to the process of linguistic organization were not influenced by correction, and the only effective method was repeated presentation of the right pattern. When Lisa and Giulia's parents attempted to correct their grammatical errors, the girls insisted that their way was correct:

**L** (3;6): *Weil ich bin zia.* (Because I the aunt am.)
**M:**     *Weil ich zia bin, sagt man.* (You say, *"weil ich zia bin".*)
**L:**     *Nein, weil ich bin zia, sag ich.* (No, I say, *"weil ich bin zia".*)
**L** (3;4): *Ho mettato lì.* (I put there.)
**F:**     *Si dice messo.* (You say, *"messo".*)
**L:**     *No, è brutto messo, è mettato.* (No, *messo* is ugly. It's *mettato*.)

This rejection of grammatical corrections made by adults is not limited to bilinguals; as part of the general process of speech acquisition, it is also characteristic of monolinguals. Clark and Clark [1977, p. 336] point out that "... adult approval is not contingent on the grammaticality of what children say, and adults do not correct their children's grammar in the early stages of acquisition".

But when the adult uses *Wie?*, does the child really believe that his parent doesn't understand? This is a difficult question. It may be that the child does not ask himself this, but merely accepts this new aspect of reality, i.e., that

Mommy speaks and understands only German. Observation of Lisa's and Giulia's behavior suggests that at first they did believe this, despite the fact that they heard their mother speaking Italian with others every day.

**L** (4;2) [to G (3;1): *La sai che la mamma parla italiano?* (You know Mommy speaks Italian, don't you?)

**G** [with conviction]: *No!*

Towards the age of 3 or 4, the girls began to realize that their mother's *Wie?* was nothing but a strategy and that she understood Italian perfectly. In fact, at about 3;3 Lisa often asked her father, "Why is Mommy speaking Italian?" However, in the meantime, they had become accustomed to speaking to her in German, and had taken the presence of *Wie?* for granted; by then it had become much less frequent anyway.

In addition, they accepted their mother's German as one of the many phenomena of life, and experienced it almost as though it were a physical attribute such as hair or eye color. Just as the small child does not like it if his mother, who has long blond hair, shows up one day with short, dark hair, so the child who is used to having his mother communicate with him in language X will not like it if she suddenly addresses him in language Y. If the girls' mother did happen to speak to them in Italian, they immediately reacted with surprise:

**L** (3;11) is going to nursery school.

**M:**    *Fai la brava!* (Be a good girl!)
    Lisa nods and goes to the elevator with her father.

**L** [to F]: *Perché Mamma mi parla in italiano?* (Why is Mommy speaking Italian to me?)
    Lisa (4;3) is having a good laugh telling her sister (3;2) that she talked to her mother in Italian and her mother answered, *"Ja"*. Ten minutes later, Giulia goes to her mother and speaks Italian, but receives no answer. Disappointed, she returns to Lisa.

**G:**    *Con me non parla italiano!* (She doesn't speak Italian with me!)

    M wants to make a recording.

**M** [into the microphone]: *Siamo appena tornate dall'asilo; adesso mangerete la paste asciutta.* (We've just come back from nursery school; now you'll have some pasta.)

**G** (3;4): *Parla in italiano con noi!* (She's speaking Italian with us!)

**L** (4;5): *Si, si!*

When they play make-believe, they use the *Wie?* strategy as one of the features of the mother:

    Lisa is the mother, Giulia the daughter.

**G** (2;7): *Stringhe, due stringhe.* (Laces, two laces.)

**L** (3;8): *Was?*

| | |
|---|---|
| **G:** | *Capotare, vedi?* (Turn over, see?) |
| **L** | [lecturing]: *Was? Der Jäger pip piip!* (What? The hunter pip piip.) |
| **G:** | *No, der Jäger macht **la tromba**.* (No, the hunter makes a trumpet.) |
| **L:** | *Der Jäger macht pip piip, sagt man.* (The hunter says pip piip, is how you say it.) |

At times, the girls even used the *Wie?* strategy themselves, but it was for reasons other than linguistic-didactic ones.

> **L** (3;7) has taken a spoon and is eating the pudding left in the serving bowl. When **G** (2;6) sees her, she goes to get another spoon for herself, but Lisa won't let her near the bowl.
>
> **G:** *Lisa, ich hat auch cucchiaino.* (Lisa, I have a spoon too.)
> **L** doesn't answer.
> **G:** *Lisa! Ich hat auch cucchiaino!*
> **G** tries to make L understand that she has a spoon because she wants to eat some pudding, too, and so L should move.
> **L** [after several attempts on G's part]: *Was? Ich nicht versteh. Ich versteh nur Deutsch.* (What? I don't understand. I only understand German.)
> **G:** *Ich spricht nur Italienisch, wie Papi. Lisa, ich hat cucchiaino!!!* (I speak only Italian, like Daddy. Lisa, I have a spoon!)
> **L:** *Was sagst du? Ich versteh nur Deutsch ...*
> The girls continue this way until their mother moves L so that G can also eat some pudding.

The *Wie?* strategy never hurt their mother's credibility with the girls, partly because friends and relatives never made comments which might have raised doubts about the seriousness and importance of the tactic; they respected her reasons and were of the opinion that the end was worth the means. And just as the girls' mother explained her linguistic behavior with her daughters to her friends, so the girls explained theirs to their friends. For instance, when Lisa (3;11) saw that her friend Marco (4;6) did not understand what she was saying to her mother, she explained, "I speak German with my mommy, because otherwise she doesn't understand".

As the girls grew older, they began to interpret their mother's *Wie?* not only as a request for the usual code switch, but also as an invitation to be more explicit, and this contributed greatly to the improvement of their replies and explanations. For instance:

> **G** walks into her mother's study and takes the adhesive tape:
> **G** (6;6): *Meine **pagina** ist **strappata**.* (My page is torn.)
> **M:** *Wie bitte?*
> **G:** *Eine Seite von mein Heft in der Mitte ist abgerissen und ich mag sie wieder ankleben.* (One of the pages in my notebook is torn in half and I want to put it together again.)

By this age, the girls could not help making a wry comment now and then regarding their mother's well-known strategy:

**G** (6;7) speaks in Italian to her mother, who answers with *Wie?* and thus forces the child to repeat her statement.

**L** (7;8) [turns to G without looking at her mother, and with an overly serious expression on her face, speaks in German, instead of the usual Italian that the sisters adopt with each other]: *Ja ja weil die Mami doch kein Italienisch kann! Na sowas! Dann muss ich schon Esel zu ihr sagen. Nachdem sie 10 Jahre hier in Italien ist und immer noch kein Italienisch kann! Das hätte mir passieren sollen.* (Yes yes, because Mommy doesn't know Italian. Think of that! At this point, I have to say she's a bit thick. After 10 years in Italy she still doesn't know Italian. If that had happened to me ...)

### 6.2.2 A Natural Strategy

Studies on verbal interaction between mother and child have shown that the mother quickly begins to repeat her child's short or incomplete utterances, expanding or completing them. Mothers of bilinguals do the same thing, but also often translate, if necessary:

**G** (2;5) [drawing]: *Guck, ich macht piove.* (Look, I make rain.)
**M:**    *Ach, du malst Regentröpfchen.* (Oh, you are painting raindrops.)

This spontaneous strategy has been observed in the mothers of many bilinguals (see Cunze [1980] and Bizzarri [1978b]).

### 6.2.3 A Request That is Destined to Fail: "Say It in English"

Unlike Lisa and Giulia, who often did not obey their mother's request to repeat their sentence in the other language, Nicola, the boy studied studied by Bizzarri, [10] was more docile, and happily obeyed his mother when she said, "Say it in English!" But after two years, the boy's mother understandably grew tired of continually repeating this request. Unlike the *Wie?* strategy, the request to repeat does not condition the child to speak automatically in the other language. Nicola would wait for his mother's request before deciding to speak in English, and if the request was not forthcoming, it is likely that he did not think it necessary. With time, it becomes harder and harder for the adult to interrupt speech continually, doubling the amount of time needed for each interaction. In the long run, this request is acompanied by anxiety, unhappiness, and dissatisfaction, culminating in an overall state of frustration, and the parent feels he has failed in bringing up his child as a bilingual.

---

10 Personal communication.

## 6.3 The Third Stage: The Maintenance of Bilingualism

As the Child grows older, it becomes harder and harder to give him constant rich contact with the "foreign" language, i.e., the one that does not belong to his environment. This is not only because he begins to do more and more things which take him away from the family, but also because even when bilinguals are with other bilinguals, they usually end up speaking the language of the environment. Furthermore, the child chooses his friends on the basis of mutual interests, and it is impossible to condition these interests to meet linguistic or pedagogic purposes. And what adult wants to spend one boring afternoon after another for the sole purpose of teaching his child a second language?

The beginning of nursery school is an important moment for the child, as he begins spending a good part of his day in a social group which is very different from his family. Even if the school is bilingual, most of the children speak the local language instead of the "foreign" one. Such schools are usually attended largely by bilingual children, with some monolingual foreign children as well. The child who has been brought up in a bilingual family will undoubtedly find that the bilingual nursery school conforms more closely to his daily life at home, and this may be a highly important stimulus.

However, Lisa and Giulia went to Italian nursery school, and thus were not able to take advantage of such a situation. Despite this, the contact they had had until then with their two languages, plus their mother's *Wie?* strategy, had been enough to help them to become bilinguals.

By the time the child enters nursery school, he is a little more grown up and can use his memory more completely and visualize the past and future instead of only the here and now. These aspects have a positive influence on the child's bilingual acquisition. He no longer forgets about the progress he has already made, and the brief but intense contact he has with the "foreign" language lasts longer in his mind. Furthermore, he is now able to imagine what will happen in a few months' time, when, for example, he will go to visit and play with his cousins who speak only the "foreign" language. He can also remember how happy he was the last time he was able to speak with his "foreign" language grandparents, and can visualize how difficult it would have been if he had not understood them or they him. He is no longer so attached to the here and now, and his motivation for speaking two languages can be more than the immediate need to communicate. Thus, he now has a secondary motivation: he wants to be bilingual so that he can play with his cousins or understand his grandparents, and so forth.

This is demonstrated by the recovery of active English on the part of Neale, the child studied by El-Dash [1981]. The imminent arrival of his English-speaking grandmother was sufficient stimulus for him to pick up that language extremely rapidly, even before she arrived. At zero output at 4;4, Neale began inserting more and more English words into his Portuguese sentences, until at 4;6 he was capable of such utterances as [El-Dash, 1981, pp. 13, 14, 17]:

"When I wake up I wanna ride the bicycle"
"Santa Claus no gonna take my bicycle"
"I wanna give a kiss for you"

These are the reasons why the data for Lisa and Giulia no longer showed the highs and lows of the earlier period, when their bilingual production was directly proportional to the quantity and richness provided by the environment in both languages. This does not mean that there was suddenly perfect symmetry between the two languages; but the increases and decreases became more prolonged and less abrupt. At a point such as this, the "sole" interlocutor is somehow again able, despite the fact that he has less contact with the child than others, to establish a true linguistic environment, supported as the interlocutor now is by the existence of another monolingual society which the child remembers as a concrete setting instead of as a momentary contact.

This sort of change can be observed as early as at the age of 3. Thus, six months after her German-speaking aunt and uncle hade left, Lisa's output was still more or less the same in both languages, and was perfectly capable of telling a story in both:

> L (3;7) holds the book *Janko and His Sheep* and spontaneously tells her mother the story, turning the pages after each statement, and describing what she sees.

L:  *Und die Zicklein marron und klein klein . . . Es war einmal der Janko und ein Hut und der Himmel und der Hase ist da. Es war einmal der böse grosse Wolf! Ist schon weg, und der Janko ist schon weg! Der grosse böse Wolf! Das Zicklein frisst! Und das Zicklein sagt: ich hab Hunger, ich will essen, ham! Und der böse Wolf frisst! Ich will essen und das Zicklein ist nicht da! Sei mal lieb. Und die Hunde gelaufen und marsch marsch, wieder der böse Wolf! Und nun mein Zicklein und die Sternlein und der Mond ist da und ist dunkel.* (And the lamb brown and little, little . . . Once upon a time there was the Janko and a hat and the sky and the rabbit are there . . . Once upon a time there was the big bad wolf! He already left! The big bad wolf . . . The sheep eats! And the sheep says, "I'm hungry, I want to eat. Yum!" And the bad wolf eats! I want to eat and the lamb is gone! Be good . . . And the dogs walk and march and march . . . Again! The bad wolf! And now, my lamb, and the stars and the moon are there and it's dark.)

> L reaches the last page and closes the book.
> An hour later, with the book in hand, she tells the same story to her father, this time on request:

L:  *C'era una volta un pastore, le pecore che vanno sulla montagna. E lì un sole rosso rosso. E c'è nel bosco la casetta. Ecco **der Janko** e il cane. Pi piii piii. Ecco qui non c'è il flauto, c'è a casa il flauto. Quello è un bastone. E poi il sole, le montagne, due: uno per Lisa e uno per Lisa. Per Giulia no, niente. Ecco il lupo! Ecco ho fame!* (Once there was a shepherd, the sheep that went to the mountains. And there the red red sun.

And in the woods there's a house. Here's Janko and his dog. Pi piii piii.
Here there's no flute, there's at home the flute. That's a stick. And then
the sun, the mountains, two: one for Lisa and one for Lisa. For Giulia,
no, nothing. Here's the wolf! Here, I'm hungry!)
L looks at her father.

**F:** *Racconta la storia anche a Paola.* (Tell the story to Paola, too.)

**L** [looks at the book again]: *Ecco mi mangio arrosto! Ecco mi mangio
arrosto!* (Here, I'm eating me roasted! I'm eating me roasted!)

**F:** *E chi mangia, il lupo?* (And who eats, the wolf?)

**L:** *La pecorella. Mangia e te ne dò. Ecco ecco mangio! Mi mangio!* (The
sheep. It eats and I'll give you some. Here, here, I'm eating! I'm eating
myself!)

**F:** *Che, lui si mangia da solo?* (What, he eats himself?)

**L:** *Si, non c'è la pecora. Ecco le pecore fanno tam tam taram.* (Yes, there's
no sheep. Here's the sheep making tam tam taram)

**F:** *E poi?* (And then?)

**L:** *Il sole ha dormito, non ha sonno adesso. Finita la favola!* (The sun slept,
it's not sleepy now. That's the end of the story!)

During this period, Lisa's contact with the two languages resembled that
of the earlier period: her father spoke to her in Italian and her mother in German, and her friends were mostly Italian, with a few bilinguals and almost no
monolingual Germans. There were also short visits with her Italian relatives
from 3;6 to 3;6,15 and from 3;10 to 3;10,15 (see Table 6.3).

At the age of 4, Lisa spent two months with her German-speaking grandparents. Her speech in the recording made just before her departure (Table
6.4) was essentially the same as in the one made just after her return (Table
6.5). However, there were a few subtle differences. Before she left, there were
more Italian interferences in her German utterances, while the opposite was
true when she returned. There was lexical improvement in German, but
morphology and syntax remained basically the same, and Lisa made the same
"mistakes" as before, i.e., she used the double subject and failed to place the
verb in the final position (such constructions are marked with an asterisk in
the tables). Whereas before she had rarely spoken to her sister in German, and
switched languages automatically when she addressed her, they now also
spoke to each other in German (see Examples 15, 17, and 21 for Lisa and 17,
18, 19, 22, and 23 for Giulia in Tables 6.4 and 6.5).

As much as eighteen months after they returned from their stay with their
German speaking grandparents, the girls' linguistic output was still good in
both languages, despite numerous visits from their paternal grandparents in
the meantime and increased contact with the Italian nursery school, which
they were now attending all day instead of only in the morning. The maternal
grandmother's visit from 5;0 to 5;3 was very important for the maintenance of
German, as can be seen in the example (p. 216).

**Table 6.3.** Summary of the relationship between Lisa's linguistic contact and linguistic output from the age of 3;6 to 9;0

| Age | Linguistic contact | Linguistic output |
|---|---|---|
| 3;6 – 5;6 | M is the principal German interlocutor. | |
| | F, nursery school, neighbors, and friends provide the principal contact with Italian | |
| 3;6 – 3;6,15 | Intense contact with Italian | |
| 3;7 | | Output still equal in the two languages |
| 3;10 – 3;10,15 | Intense contact with Italian | |
| 3;11 | | Slight dominance of Italian |
| 4;0 – 4;2 | Intense contact with German | |
| 4;2 | | Slight dominance of German |
| 4;2 – 4;2,15 | Intense contact with Italian | |
| 4;3 | Begins to attend Italian nursery school in afternoon also | |
| 4;6 – 4;6,15 | Intense contact with Italian | |
| 4;10 – 4;10,15 | Intense contact with Italian | |
| 4;11 | | Slight dominance of Italian |
| 5;0 – 5;3 | Intense contact with German | |
| 5;2,10 – 5;2,25 | Intense contact with German | |
| 5;6 – 6;0 | F and G are principal Italian interlocutors. | |
| | M, nursery school, grandmother, and neighbors provide the principal contact with German | |
| | | Slight dominance in German |
| 5;6,05 – 5;6,12 | One week in a bilingual community | |
| 5;7 | | Equal output |
| 6;0 – 7;0 | M and German teacher are principal German interlocutors. | |
| | F, school, and friends provide the principal contact with Italian | |
| 7;0 | | Good output in both languages, lexically richer in Italian |
| 7;0 – 9;0 | M and domestic helper are principal German interlocutors | |
| | F, friends, and school, provide the principal contact with Italian | |
| 7;0 – 7;2 | Intense contact with German | |
| 8;1 – 8;3 | Intense contact with German | |
| 9;0 | | Good output in both languages, lexically richer in Italian |

**Table 6.4.** Excerpt from a recording made before Lisa's two-month stay with her German-speaking grandparents in Brazil. An asterisk denotes sentences with incorrect subject-verb inversion or a double subject

| Lisa | Giulia | Mother |
|------|--------|--------|
| 1. Ich will ein Kaugummi suchen. (I want to look for chewing gum.) | | |
| | | Du willst ein Kaugummi suchen? Ich habe aber kein Kaugummi. (You want to look for some gum? But I don't have any gum.) |
| 2. Ein Kaugummi wie Giulia ... (Gum, like Giulia ...) | | |
| | | Zeig mal, wo hast du den Kaugummi, Giulia? (Show me, where did you put the chewing gum, Giulia?) |
| | 3. Ich hab ... Ich hab *geperso*. (I have ... I have *ge*lost.) | |
| 4. Ach guck hier, das hier isses. (Oh, look here, this here is it.) | | |
| | 5. Ist mein (It's mine!) [she grabs the gum from L's hands] | |
| | | Was hast du in der Hand? (What are you holding?) |
| | Dieses? (This?) | |
| | | Hm? |
| | 6. So ist die Kastanie. (The chestnut is like this.) | |
| 7. Guck, tut weh die vaccinazione. (Look, the shot hurts.) | | |
| | | Hm. Lisa, hast du dein Brot schon gegessen oder habe ich's umsonst gemacht? (Lisa, have you already eaten your bread, or did I make it for nothing?) |
| 8. Lisa hat nicht gegessen weil, weil du bist du* in die Stube, wie Giulia. Und Giulia ist auch in die Stube gekommen und Lisa ist auch in die Stube gekommen. (Lisa didn't eat because, because you are you in the living room | | |

**Table 6.4** (continued)

| Lisa | Giulia | Mother |
|---|---|---|
| like Giulia. And Giulia also came to the living room and Lisa also came to the living room.) | | |
| | | Dann geh mal in die Küche essen. (Then go eat in the kitchen.) |
| 9. Und Giulia *rest* hier? (Is Giulia staying here?) | | |
| | 10. Und ich nein. (And not me.) | |
| | | Und Giulia bleibt hier, nicht *rest* hier. [M corrects *rest*, from the Italian *restare*.] |
| | 11. Nein ich … (Not me …) | |
| 12. Und warum? (And why?) | | |
| | | Warum nicht? (Why not?) |
| 13. Warum ja. (Why yes.) | | |
| | 14. Guck Mami, ich geh in der Küche. (Look Mommy, I'm going into the kitchen.) | |
| | | Ah, du gehst in die Küche? (Oh, you're going into the kitchen?) |
| | 15. Gulia nicht weint. (Giulia isn't crying.) | |
| | | Nein? Hast du Angst oder Courage? (Are you afraid or brave?) |
| | 16. Coraggio. (Brave.) | |
| 14. Nachher regnet, Mami, Mami. (Later it will rain, Mommy.) | | |
| | | Jetzt hat's schon aufgehört zu donnern. (Now it's already stopped thundering.) |
| | 17. [to L] Io vado ganz nackig, io vado alla casa, questa casa la sopra. (I'm going all naked, I'm going home, this house up there) [looking at things from the balcony] | |
| 15. E dovè? (Where?) | | |
| | 18. E'la su. (It's up there.) | |
| 16. Sono le case un po' più alte. Dentro le case sono un po' più alte. (They are a bit higher. Inside the houses are a bit higher.) | | |

**Table 6.5.** Excerpt from a recording made after Lisa's two-month stay with her German-speaking grandparents in Brazil. An asterisk denotes sentences with incorrect subject-verb inversion or a double subject

| Lisa | Giulia |
|---|---|
| 17. Hier ist mein Haus. (Here is my house.) | |
| | 19. Das ist dein Bett, das ist mein. (This is your bed, this is my bed.) |
| Ja, das ist meins und das ist deins. Okay. Hier ist mein Haus, du schläfst du* heute mit mir. Das ist dein Bett und da oben ist mein Bett. (Yes, this is mine and this is yours. Okay. Here is my house, you sleep you today with me. This is your bed, and up there is my bed.) | |
| | 20. Ja so, guarda come io sò fare. (Oh yes, look what I know how to do.) |
| 18. Adesso è schlafen, adesso ... Adesso è giorno. Adesso la nonna è sveglia. Ciao nonna come stai? Sapete che io vado oggi, vado nel Geschäft? Allora, sì, allora io devo mich anziehen. (Now is sleep, now ... Now it is day. Now grandma is awake. Hi Grandma, how are you? Do you know that I'm going to the shop today? Well, yes well I have to dress.) | |
| *Ten minutes later* 19. Das ist rot. (This is red.) | |
| | 21. Ich will rot warum ich bin gross*. (I want red why I am big.) |
| 20. Il tuo è weiss. (Yours is white.) | |
| | 22. Macht man so. (This is how you do it.) |
| 23. Jetzt muss ich ein bisschen schlafen warum ist Sonne.* Wenn du hast du* geschlafen dann tun wir das nehmen. (Now I must sleep a bit why there's the sun. When you've you slept then we'll take this.) | |

**L** (5;7) [to M]: *Ich kann es machen. Guck meins. Heute ist nicht mein Kleid schmutzig und dieses von Giulia ja.* (I can do it. Look at mine, today my dress is not dirty and Giulia's is.)

**L** [taking a book]: *Du kannst auch in mein Buch schreiben. Guck was schöne Augen.* (You can write in my book, too. Look, such nice eyes.)

**L** [points to a cat while M looks for a pencil]: *Ja du hast sie, aber du suchst sie, nicht? Du findest keine? Musst jetzt suchen. Mami, ich will das nicht dass Giulia mit meine Buntstifte schreibt.* (Yes you have it, but you look for it, no? Can't you find one? You have to look now. Mommy, I don't want this that Giulia writes with my colored pencils.)

**L** (5;7) [to G]: *Vuoi che ti tolga la paletta? Se la vedi la schiacci? Su, metti la macchina, vedi quanto posto c'è? Quella era la porta, sennò cascava. Poi non puoi uscire. Quando devi entrare fai così. Tu vuoi fare quello che faccio io vero? Io voglio andare in altalena, tu anche?* (Do you want me to take the shovel out for you? If you see it will you crush it? Go on, put the car there, see how much room there is? That was the door, otherwise it would fall. Then you can't go out. When you have to go in do this. You want to do what I do, right? I want to go on the swings, do you?

Lisa received a great deal of motivation from her winter stay in a bilingual Italian-German community in northern Italy at this time. The fact that the waitress spoke to her father in Italian, to her mother in German, and to her in both languages delighted her, and she had great fun walking through the hotel speaking with everyone in one language and then the other. When she got back to Rome, she told her sister, "Giulia, up there everyone speaks Italian and German, like we do!"

When Lisa was $5\frac{1}{2}$ years old, she spent five months in Germany with her mother and Giulia, then $4\frac{1}{2}$. During this time she went to German nursery school from nine to three o'clock every day. In addition, her German grandmother came to visit her for three months. Her contact with Italian came mostly from daily contact with her sister and with her father, whom she saw only every other weekend.

This prolonged stay in Germany gave her (and, of course, her sister) a richer lexicon, and their interaction in that language became more spontaneous and immediate. It took Giulia one month and Lisa three months to pick up the cadence used by the children of Heidelberg. Giulia was not happy until she was able to pronounce the uvular fricative German *r*, and in her attempts she went through a stage of pronouncing it as the postalveolar English *r*. [11] She was often seen practicing her pronunciation of words with an uvular fricative *r*. Nonetheless, even when she had acquired it, she never used it for Italian words. On the other hand, Lisa decided to use the German *r* only at the end of her stay, and he was never seen practicing it.

The girls also replaced the German negative *nicht* with the dialect pronunciation *net*; the pronouns *dies* and *das* ("this" and "that") with the more generic dialect equivalent *des*; *der, die*, and *das* with the dialect word *de*; and finally, *ein* and *eine* with the dialect word *a*.

While before they left for Germany most of their mistakes were in article gender and case, these decreased greatly during their stay abroad, at least to the extent that the dialect allowed them to make the distinction (see examples 1 and 2 below).

---

11 The girls' principal German interlocutor, their mother, uses the Italian polyvibrant alveolar *r* instead of the German *r*.

The words they used as such did not change so much as the way they said them. When they returned to Italy, German had become their dominant language, and their Italian dialogues began to be infiltrated with German (see example 3 below).

Example 1:

**G** (5;0):  *Also, dann, einmal war ein Nega mit Mama und Papa und Chiquita Banana, der Hund. Dann, als Chiquita Banana, hatte Husten, und dann hatta Medizin ğekriegt. Und dann issa wieda gesund geworden und dann sind die spaziern gegan, denn ham se Pilze gefunden und Erdbeeren. Und die Erdbeeren haben sie sofort gegessen. Zu Ende.*
(So, once upon a time there was a black man with Mommy and Daddy and Chiquita Banana, the dog. Then, when Chiquita Banana had a cough, and then he had medicine. And then he got better and then they went for a walk, then they found mushrooms and strawberries. And they ate the strawberries right away. The End.)

Example 2: L (6;1)

**M:**  *Lisa, erzähl du mal eine Geschichte.* (Lisa, you tell a story.)
**L:**  *Jetzt wieda die Geschichte von erst?* (The same one as before, again?)
**M:**  *Ja.* (Yes.)
**L:**  *Die weiss ich nicht mehr.* (I don't know it any more.)
**M:**  *Nein?* (No?)
**L:**  *Dann mach ich eben eine andere* (Then I'll tell another.)
**M:**  *Eine ähnliche?* (Like the other one?)
**L:**  *Eine normale. Dann, es war ein mal ein kleines Mädchen mit Vater, Schwester und Mutter, die sind in Wald spazieren gegan, das war doch herrlich. Habense Kirschen gefunden, Pilze und auch Erdbeeren und das alles was in den Wald war. Dann haben se ein Haus gesehn mit eine Wohnung drinn, da war Käse. Und da habense ein ganz lang Spaziergang, die ganze Nacht, und haben so Hunger, dann dann auch, warn auch die weichen Betten, vier Betten warn da und dann haben sie geschlafen und gegessen. Da kann aber, da kommen aber, die Räuber. Die Räuber von den Berg hinunter. Die Polizei aber ist neben die Räuber versteckt in den Baum. Versteckt hinter ein Baum. Aber der Jäger, der weiss was mit den Räuber machen, jetzt aber schiessen!* (An ordinary one. So once upon a time there was a little girl with a Daddy, sister and Mommy; they went to take a walk in the woods. That was wonderful! They found cherries, mushrooms and even strawberries and everything that was in the woods. Then they saw a house with an apartment in it, and there was cheese there. And there they took a long walk, all night long, and they were so hungry, then even then there were also soft beds, four beds were there and so they ate and slept. But there they came, ... the robbers came. The robbers down from the mountains. But the police are

nearby hidden in the tree. Hidden behing the tree. But the hunter, he knows what to do with the robbers. But it's time to shoot!)

L:      *Nein, bitte nicht! Und dann renn die weit!* (No, please no! And they run far away!)

L       [determined]: *Eh! Was macht denn ihr. Dast ist die Wohnung von die andern. Ihr habt Essen gestohlen!* (Hey! What are you doing? This apartment belongs to someone else. You robbed food!)

L       [fearful]: *Oh nee, da gehn wir den Wald hinauf!!* (Oh, no! Then let's climb the mountain!!)

L       [determined]: *Gut! Aber schiess ich. Pum pum! Räuber sind tot.* (Okay! But I'll shoot! Boom boom! Robbers are dead.)

Example 3:

**L** (6;1): *Dov'è la tigre hai **gemalt**?* (Where is the tiger you have drawn?)

**G** (5;0): *Ma io non l'ho **gemalt** perché non la voglio. L'avevo **wo andas gemalt**.* (But I didn't draw it because I don't want it. I had it drawn somewhere else.)

**L:**     *Giulia, vero che è **schade** che tu hai una guerra?* (Giulia is it true that it's a pity that you have a war?)

**G:**     *Sì. Io ho la guerra.* (Yes, I have a war.)

**L:**     *Quando vai nella guerra, Giulia?* (When are you going to the war, Giulia?)

**G:**     ***Kämpfen.** Io vado nella guerra!* (To fight. I'm going to the war!)

**L:**     *Sai che la guerra è molto brutta?* (Do you know that war is very ugly?)

**G:**     *Sò.* (I know.)

**L:**     *A me però piace.* (But I like it.)

**G:**     *Anche a me. Molto bella. Io ci vado.* (Me, too. Very beautiful. I'm going.)

**L:**     *Io ci vado pure e voglio vedere com'è la guerra. Se è brutta torno subito a casa.* (I'm going too and I want to see what the war is like. If it's bad I'm coming right back home.)

**G:**     *Io vado a **kämpfen.** Vuoi vedere come io **gewinnt**?* (I'm going to fight. Do you want to see how I win?)

Their attendance at German nursery school caused the girls no difficulties at all. They made friends with the other children right away and were happy to go. In fact, they liked it better than their Italian school, because the activities were more congenial and they had more freedom.

At 6;1, Lisa returned to Rome; two months later she began first grade. For the next year, her week was organized as follows: Italian school every morning except Sunday from 8;30 to 12;30, lunch with her mother and sister using German, homework with her mother's help and thus for this purpose using Italian, gym three times a week in Italian, and the other three afternoons spent with a German nursery school teacher and her sister. During this period, the friends she saw in what little free time she had were mostly Italian.

As much as a year after they returned from Germany, the two girls were still speaking excellent German. The only change had been a reversion to the Italian polyvibrant alveolar *r* for German, although they were still able to say the German *r*. They no longer used such expressions as *gell?* ("yeah?") and *net*, but had reverted to *okay* and *nicht*; they had again picked up their mother's pronunciation and dropped the cadence used by the children of Heidelberg. During this year, the triweekly visits of the German nursery school teacher played an important part in keeping their German good. In the beginning, the teacher and the girls' mother had worked out a teaching program. It included activities such as listening to short stories, writing short German dictations, copying pieces they liked especially, and doing exercises in books brought especially from Germany, such as *Rechenspiele für das erste und zwei Grundschuljahr,* by Ursula Lauster (1977).

But this program failed miserably: the third time the teacher came, the girls barricaded the door with all their strength to keep her out. It was urgent that a different way be found for them to spend time together, and the one which was found was very successful: the teacher simply played every imaginable game with them, from hide-and-seek to cards. In addition, she did arts and crafts with them, such as cutting and pasting, sewing, clay modeling, and so on. Both types of activities were integrated with intensive and correct use of speech, with the teacher describing her activities: *So, jetzt nehmen wir den gelben Pappkarton und schneiden ihn einmal in der Mitte durch* ... ("So, now we take the yellow cardboard and cut it in half ..."), and making sure that the girls did the same, asking questions if necessary:

G: *Ich will das da haben.* (I want that.)
T: *Was möchtest du?* (What would you like?)
G: *Ich möchte die Schere haben.* (I would like the scissors.)
T: *Wozu denn?* (What for?)
G: *Na, um hier doch zu schneiden.* (To cut here.)
T: *Wo schneiden?* (Cut where?)
G: *An dieser Ecke hier, vom gelben Pappkarton, wie du gesagt hast.* (In this corner here of the yellow cardboard, as you said.)
T: *Na gut, pass aber auf und schneide dich nicht. Nimm aber die kleine Schere, die hat keine Spitze.* (Good. But be careful not to cut yourself. Take the small scissors with no point.)
G: *Ja, okay, ich nehm die kleine aber die grosse schneidet besser.* (Yes, okay, I'll take the little ones, but the big ones cut better.)

The girls never barricaded the door again. In fact, they ran to open it, because they loved the afternoons they spent playing with their teacher.

At the end of the school year, when she turned 7, Lisa went to spend two months with her German speaking grandparents. When she returned, the family hired a full-time domestic helper who spoke German and stayed with them for the next two years. From 7;3 to 9;3, Lisa went to Italian school every morning, spent three afternoons at gym, two at music lessons and one playing with her schoolmates, mostly Italian monolinguals. Her mother continued to help her with her homework at times, and when she did, they spoke Italian. As always, Lisa saw her father mostly in the evenings and on weekends. She spent Easter and Christmas with her Italian grandparents, and her German relatives came to visit in the summer.

Over these two years, the girls saw their mother primarily at lunch and dinner, as she was quite busy. The presence of the monolingual German domestic helper was a positive factor in keeping Lisa and Giulia bilingual. In the meantime, they had also learned to read, and thus came into contact with their two languages in another way. Although they went to Italian elementary school, it was not difficult for their mother to teach them the few additional letters of the German alphabet and call their attention to the different ways of writing sounds. This reading instruction, which was given occasionally, during free time, was based upon reflections about the differences in writing between the two languages. Each time, one aspect was pointed out, as in the following example:

"The people who decided to put German into writing many years ago did it a little differently than those who decided to put Italian into writing. We have to remember both ways, so we won't be confused. So let's take the sound that's written *ghe* in Italian: in German it's written *ge*. The sound that's written *ge* in Italian doesn't exist in German. So: Italian *ga, ghe, ghi, go, gu* are the same as German *ga, ge, gi, go gu*." Or: "The German sound *ch* as in *ich* doesn't exist in Italian. Have you ever heard it?" (Trials.) "But it does in German. For example, *Bach, möchte,* and so forth. How is it written? Like this: *ch*. The German *ch* has nothing to do with the Italian *ch*. The Italian one is not pronounced soft but hard."

At ages 8 and 9, Giulia and Lisa are able to read German and Italian with no difficulty. The remarks made on contrasts between the two languages also helped them learn to write both. It should be pointed out that neither Lisa nor Giulia has ever had greater difficulties at school than their average schoolmates. Since the ages of 7 or 8, they have both been able to write in Italian with no spelling errors. They still make spelling mistakes in German, but these are due to their lack of practice and not to the influence of Italian. They tend to write as they speak:

**L** (9;0):  *Die Biaget hat von dea Schule angerufn ont gesacht du sollst wieder anrufn.* (Birgit called from school and said you should call her back.)

This short note left for her mother shows that Lisa has learned to write some words correctly (*die, hat, von, Schule, du, sollst,* and *wieder*) but has not yet mastered others (*Birgit, der, angerufen, und,* and *gesagt*). This may be because they have practiced more reading than writing in German.

Although Lisa and Giulia speak German fluently, they have always talked to each other in Italian, even when in a German monolingual community, and thus there has never been a period in which they had contact with only one language. On the few occasions when the girls spoke German to each other, there was usually a reason. Sometimes they wanted their mother to understand what they were saying:

**G** (2;7)    wants the wallet Lisa has.

**G**    [to M]: *Mami, dies ist meine Tasche, warum!* (Mommy, this is my bag, why!)

Instead of giving it to her, L makes various comments to G:

**L** (3;8):    *Das ist eine Geldtasche. Dieses ist nicht eine Geldtasche und Lisa hat die Bilder hier drinne.* (That is a wallet. This is not a wallet and Lisa has the pictures in here.)

Or:

L is wearing a poncho, which G wants. L doesn't want to.give it to her.

**G** (2;8)    [touching poncho]: *Bello il poncio.* (Nice poncho.)

L moves closer to M.

**L** (3;9)    [to G]: *Mein Poncho, weil Lisa friert.* (My poncho, because Lisa is cold.)

**G:**    *Auch Giulia friert.* (Giulia is also cold.)

**L**    [amazed]: *Auch du? Frierst du?* (You too? You're cold?)

At other times, it was reason enough if the three of them were together:

**M, G** and **L** are looking at a picture.

**G** (3;2):    *Diese Kakteen trinken alleine alleine und holen Wasser von Meer. Und die Bäume essen Gras. Auch das sind die Blumen, Mami ja? Nein die Sonne nicht.* (These cactures drink by themselves and take the water from the sea. And the trees eat grass. These are flowers, too, right Mommy? No, not the sun.)

**L** (4;3)    [to G]: *Doch, die Sonne doch! Die Bergen essen Bäumen.* (Yes, the sun, too! The mountains eat trees.)

Or:

Lisa has hurt her hand, so she is only watching as **G** draws. M is nearby.

**G** (3;2):    *Ein grosser Kopf und heisst Lisa. Und jetzt die Augen, cilien, der Mund und nachher der Mund. Ist die Lisalein.* (A big head and it's called Lisa. And now the eyes, eyelashes, mouth and then the mouth. It's little Lisa.)

**L** (4;3)    [to G]: *So ist nicht Lisa. Lisa hat ein kleines Kopf.* (Lisa is not like this. Lisa has a small head.)

**G**    [ to L]: *Dann ist Giulia. Ich hat ein ganz grosser Kopf. Ist Giulia das.* (Then it's Giulia. I have a really big head. This is Giulia.)

Or when they pretended to be their parents:

L (4;3) is the father and G (3;2) the mother.

**L:** *Questa è la frittata.* (This is an omelet.)
**G:** *Mache gnocchi, ich.* (Make gnocchi, I.)
**L:** *Wollen wir schlafen, nachher gehen wir zur spiaggia.* (We want to sleep and then we'll go to the beach.)
**G:** *Erst essen, Papi.* (First eat, Daddy.)
**L:** *Ich will nicht, Mami.* (I don't want to, Mommy.)
**G:** *Du musst, Papili.* (You must, Papili.)
**L:** *Und warum?* (And why?)
**G:** *Warum ja. Sonst kommt der böse Wolf.* (Why yes. Otherwise the bad wolf will come.)
**L:** *Okay. Ich gehe in mein Bett. Ciao Mami.* (Okay, I go to my bed. Bye Mommy.)

This game shows that the girls associated German so strongly with their mother that they have her speaking it in her interactions with their father, which never happened in real life.

By the age of 8 or 9, the bilingual child behaves more or less like the adult bilingual, in that he is easily able to switch codes according to the circumstances. Lisa and Giulia have no trouble speaking Italian with their mother or with anyone else. During their last brief stay in Germany, they were their father's interpreters, and they were obviously proud of their accomplishment.

It was also quite common, however, to hear them speaking with lexical interferences in both languages. At the ages of 7 or 8, at a time when the girls had been speaking both languages well and keeping them distinct, their mother had decided that it was perhaps not necessary to keep the two lexicons strictly separated, and she began using Italian words often in her German sentences. But less than a month later, almost all of the girls' utterances contained lexical interferences. Thus, if the adult wants the child to produce speech that is free of such interferences, he must speak without them himself; otherwise a habit will become established which is very hard to stop.

## 6.4 Summary

In this chapter we have seen that the same linguistic environment (in our case a bilingual family in a monolingual community) is experienced differently by the child, depending upon the level of social, cognitive, and linguistic development he has achieved. We have identified a first stage, during which the linguistic input within the family is sufficient to make him bilingual. During a second stage, the child is able to socialize more, and thus other interlocutors come to be very important. At this point, the linguistic input within the family is no longer enough to ensure comprehension and production in the "foreign" language. When this happens, the child becomes conditioned to think that the language which belongs to the environment is more effective, and thus he loses his motivation to speak both. It has been suggested that during this second stage efforts should be made to make the child see that both languages are equally effective. This can be done by creating the same conditioning for the "foreign" language; in other words, the person who speaks the "foreign" language should at appropriate moments pretend he does not understand what the child is saying in the "local" language.

Finally, during the third stage, the child has matured, and thus the linguistic contact he has with his family is once again sufficient for him to continue to acquire and maintain both languages. Now the child derives his motivation not only from the here and now as in the earlier stage, but also draws upon past experience and makes plans for the future. In this way he is able to place each language within a much greater context than that of his home, and will be moved to speak two languages instead of one.

I shall conclude by relating a lovely example of the girls' ability to express themselves in both languages and use creative games to reelaborate and reexperience their bilingualism. When they were 6 and 7, they both wanted very badly to fly, and this desire strongly conditioned their games for several months. During this time they created an imaginary world inhabited by the "Caratei", which they described as follows:

**L** (6;11):   *I Caratei vivono su una nuvola, volando e stanno così lontani che vedono la terra piccola come un punto e le stelle non le vedono neanche: Questo mondo si chiama Schwighit e si parla Auet. Gli italiani dicono Auèti, ma è Auet. Per arrivare a quel mondo basta saper volare.* (The Caratei live on a cloud, flying and they are so far away that the earth looks like a dot and they don't even see the stars. This world is called *Schwighit* and they speak *Auet*. The Italians call it *Auèti,* but it's *Auet.* To get to that world, all you have to do is know how to fly.)

**G** (5;10):   *I miei Caratei vivono a Anatra, ma si può dire anche Shanela, dove si parla Äneta. Tutti sono trasparenti a Shanela, hanno solo due occhi come i fantasmi. Anatra è un mondo ancor più lontano (di quello di Schwighit), di là non si vede neanche la terra. Uno ci arriva velocissimo volando, a volte con un razzo.* (My Caratei live in Anatra, but it's also called Shanela, where they speak Äneta. They're all transparent in Shanela, they only have two eyes, like ghosts. Anatra is even further away (than Schwighit) and you can't even see the earth from there. You get there very fast by flying, sometimes on a missile.)

When Lisa's mother asked her to tell the story of the Caratei, she refused, because otherwise the enemies would find out about them and that would be the end, the very end of the Caratei. A while later, she tried again with Giulia, asking her to write the story of the Caratei and giving her paper and pencil. But the child answered, *"Da in Anatra wo alle Äneta sprechen haben sie dis-*

*kutiert und gesagt: es gibt keine Geschichte!"* ("There in Anatra where everyone speaks Äneta, they discussed and said: 'there will be no story' ". So her mother asked her to dictate the story to her, and this time she agreed.

**G:** *Also, in Anatra gibt's Caratei. Wenn du, du die mit Hörner siehst, von ganz weit weg siehst, nehm die dich und tun dich in Feuer. Punkt. Feuer, hast geschrieben? Wenn du nicht in Feuer gehen willst, musst du hinter ein Baum gehen. Die klein Caratei sehen dich wenn du hinter den Baum bist. Du Mami, mein Carateo König der weiss Deutsch, ganz viel Deutsch, wie die Omi Măe. Mein Carateo ist immer böse mit den anderen, mit mir net. Dann essen die dich.* (Well, in Anatra there are Caratei. There you see them with horns, you see them from far away; they take you and they put you in the fire. Period. Fire, did you write it? If you don't want to go into the fire, you have to go behind a tree. The little Caratei see you when you're behind the tree. You know, Mommy, my Carateo King knows German, he knows a lot of German, like Omi Măe. My Carateo is always mad at the others, not with me. Then they eat you.)
**M:** *Die kleinen?* (The little ones?)
**G:** *Auch die grossen. Nicht schreiben. So. Dann musst du sagen: "Hau Hau Alanta." Punkt. "Carateo". Dann öffnet sich die Tür und du gehst drinne den Baum. In den letzten Baum ist mein König Carateo. Der hat ein ganz grossen Diamant und mir hat er gezeigt, den Diamant. Punkt. Aber da sind ganz viele Caratei, ja? Da kannst du dich aber ganz viel freuen. Punkt. Geschichte zu Ende.* (And the big ones. Don't write. Like this. So you have to say, "Hau, hau Alanta". Period. "Carateo". Then the door opens and you go in the tree. My Carateo King is in the last tree. He has a very big diamond and he showed it to me, the diamond. Period. But there are a lot of Caratei, yes? There you can be very happy. Period. End of the story.)

Half an hour later, Giulia dictated the story of the Caratei to her mother in Italian.

**G:** *Un Carateo ha fatto un guaio. Ha fatto così: Io stavo leggendo un giornale, mi son spaventata perché credevo che c'era un Carateo. Un Carateo è fatto con sei corna, col mantello e coi pantaloni e le mani e i piedi. E i baffi e la bocca. E la fronte con le rughe.* **So ist ein Carateo gemacht. Mami, die sehen ganz schrecklich aus.** *E hanno il barbone lungo.* **Mal ich hin.**
She takes a piece of paper and draws the Carateo.
**G:** **Ehrlich Mami, in Anatra sind alle ganz weiss, weisst du Mami? Da ist ganz viel Sonne.** *Il Carateo è verissimo e noi donne siamo bianche a Anatra. I Caratei mangiano anche le lampade perché hano i dentoni grandissimi, forti.* (A Carateo made a mess. He did this: I was reading a newspaper, I got scared because I thought there was a Carateo. A Carateo is made with six horns, with a cape and with pants and hands and feet.

And a moustache and a mouth. And a wrinkled brow. That's how a Carateo is made. Mami, they look very terrible! And they have a big, long beard. I'll draw it. Really, Mommy! In Anatra they're all very white, do you know, Mommy? There's a lot of sun there. The Carateo is real and we women are white in Anatra. The Caratei eat lamps, too, because they have big, strong teeth.)

L came by and called G to play. G asked to be excused and wanted to know if this was enough for her mother. "Yes", answered her mother, "I think that's enough".

# 7. Conclusions

The process of linguistic organization in the bilingual child is a complex phenomenon. It embraces the development of lexicon, sentence structure, morphology, syntax, and interferences, and is influenced by the linguistic environment in which the child has been brought up, his parents strategies, and his own procedures for distinguishing two distinct systems in his speech. In this final chapter, I will endeavor to relate these factors to one another and give an overall view of this process on the basis of the observations described thus far. At each age, there is a correspondence between the various stages of the aspects considered (see Table 7.1).

This study has shown that the development of speech is very similar in bilingual children and in monolingual children. Thus, if we add up the words which the bilingual knows in both languages, his lexicon is not much larger than that of the monolingual, and neither is it much smaller if we subtract the equivalents he possesses. Monolingual and bilingual children have nearly the same monthly rate of lexical growth, with the bilingual giving priority to the acquisition of words which express new objects and events rather than equivalents.

The gradual evolution of the principal sentence structures in Italian and German is the same in monolingual children as in the bilingual subjects studied here. There are certain structures which do not appear at the same time in the German and Italian of monolinguals, nor do these structures appear simultaneously in the bilingual's two languages. Moreover, certain structures having the same complexity of form in both languages do not appear at the same time in the bilingual child, because they are used differently by the adults who speak the two languages. The fundamental importance of the speech used by the adult when interacting with the child is also evident in morphology and syntax patterns. Some patterns appear in one language and not in the other, not because the bilingual child is not able to acquire them simultaneously, but because the input pattern in one of the two languages is not yet prominent enough in the child's perception.

But if the bilingual child acquires each language in the same way as monolingual children, does this not mean that he is acquiring two separate systems from the outset? Or, conversely, if there is initially only one system which gradually becomes two, what are the cues which show the child this distinction? These questions can be answered only by looking at the entire process of linguistic organization as performed by the child.

**Table 7.1**

|  | Lisa Giulia<br>1;1  0;11<br>First stage | Lisa Giulia<br>2;3  1;8<br>Second stage | Lisa Giulia<br>3;2  2;4<br>Third stage |
|---|---|---|---|
| Linguistic environment | Each parent speaks his own language with the child and understands everything the child says. | Each parent speaks his own language and understands everything the child says. But the environment is changing, because many of the monolingual interlocutors no longer understand all of the child's utterances.<br>The girls' mother begins to pretend not to understand their Italian and starts using the *Wie?* strategy. | The mother continues to use the *Wie* strategy and speaks only German with the children, even after this stage. |
| Child's cue for language choice | The child says words from both languages and uses them with everyone. | The child realizes that there are two different lexicons and begins to use the equivalent as a strategy to get his listener's attention. He begins to address each person in that person's language.<br>The girls had begun speaking only Italian, but two months after their mother starts her *Wie?* strategy, they speak only German with her. | The child sticks rigidly to the one person/one language principle, i.e., he always speaks the same language with each person.<br>Later, rigidity weakens considerably, and the child speaks to the interlocutor in the language in which he is addressed on each occasion. |
| Child's choice of language | The child's choice of language depends upon the pragmatic conditions in which he first learned to give a name to the particular object or event. | The interlocutor is not yet the child's cue to which language to use. He bases this choice on the phonology of the language used by the interlocutor. | The language is chosen based on the language of the interlocutor, who now serves as a cue for the child. Later, the child detaches the language from the interlocutor, and his cue becomes the interlocutor's entire language system, and not merely the phonological or lexical aspect of his speech. |

**Table 7.1** (continued)

| | Lisa 1;1  Giulia 0;11  First stage | Lisa 2;3  Giulia 1;8  Second stage | Lisa 3;2  Giulia 2;4  Third stage |
|---|---|---|---|
| Lexical development | The child's lexicon consists of words from both languages, but there are almost no equivalents. | Equivalents begin to be produced, and increase gradually, but are fewer in number than new words. | The child's lexicon develops in the same way as it did in the second stage. |
| Sentence structure development | The child goes from single words to vertical constructions to incomplete nuclear and a few complete nuclear structures. This occurs simultaneously in both languages. | Complete nuclear sentences are frequent, and incomplete ones disappear. All other sentence structures also appear (amplified nuclear, complex, and binuclear), but without the connective. This occurs simultaneously in both languages. | The most important complex and binuclear structures with the connective appear. |
| Morphology and syntax development | Morphological and syntactic patterns have not yet appeared in the two languages. | The first morphosyntactic markers appear and are learned in the same way as monolinguals learn them. Word order is correct, and halfway through this stage, there are examples of intra- and interlinguistic hypercorrection. | Word-order mistakes begin to appear, and many aspects of morphology and syntax are superextended incorrectly. Later, word order is again correct in sentences which were previously wrong. The same applies to previously incorrect morphology. |
| Interferences | There are no lexical interferences, because the child has not yet distinguished the two lexicons. | There are as yet no word-order interferences, but morphological interferences begin. Lexical interferences are also in evidence, because the child does not yet have equivalents for many words. | There are interferences in word order and in morphological markers. Later, these interferences decrease considerably. |

In the *first stage* of bilingual acquisition, the child's lexicon is made up of words from both languages, with no equivalents. In other words, he calls object X *Stuhl* ("chair") and object Y *tavolo* ("table"), but he does not call object X *Stuhl* and *sedia*, nor does he call object Y *tavolo* and *Tisch*. Because the acquisition of lexicon is not based on learning by equivalents, it is not possible to speak of bilingual lexicon acquisition in terms of two distinct systems. The child is acquiring one lexicon containing words from both languages.

During this initial stage, the child progresses in both languages from single words to vertical constructions to incomplete nuclear sentences, with a few rare complete nuclear structures. The morphological and syntactic patterns have not yet appeared, and because the child does not distinguish between the two lexicons, it would be inappropriate to speak of lexical interferences. Each adult speaks his own language to the child and understands what the child says. The child uses both languages with all of his interlocutors, basing his choice of words upon the pragmatic conditions in which he first learned to name a given object or event, and not upon such factors as the greater phonological difficulty of a word in one language as opposed to the other, or the person with whom the child is speaking (see Table 7.1, First Stage).

During *the second stage,* the child begins to produce equivalents. The equivalents gradually become more and more numerous, but never equal in number to the words used to express a concept in one language alone. Thus, the child begins to organize two distinct lexical systems during this stage. He understands that there are two different words to express one object or event and that adults sometimes use one group of words and sometimes the other. The child also learns that one group is called German and the other is called Italian. If he is asked, "What is this called in German (or Italian)?" he knows how to answer correctly.

During this stage, the complete nuclear sentences become more and more frequent, until the incomplete structures almost disappear. In addition, all of the other sentence structures make their first appearance, simultaneously in the two languages, but without the connective. As the main sentence structures evolve, the first morphosyntactic markers also begin to emerge, and the child learns them in the same way as the respective monolinguals do. But while it is true that certain functors and word orders appear at the same time as they do in monolinguals, this does not mean that the child has begun to use rules, or that these rules appear from the outset in the two systems. Rather the child has incorporated these structures without analyzing them first. In other words, the morphology and syntax of the two languages follow the same path as the lexical distinction which has already begun to take place, but have not yet taken the direction of true morphosyntactic distinction, which occurs later. Thus, morphology and syntax do not exist as such, as they do for the adult, but are as yet creative combinations of lexical elements.[1] During the

---

1 See Clark [1977] on the concepts of "coupling" and "shift to a new context".

second stage, interferences could be observed in lexicon and semantics, but not in morphology or syntax.

In this stage, each interlocutor is still speaking his own language with the child, but the environment is changing, because now that the child's utterances have become more complex, many of his interlocutors are no longer able to understand everything he says. The child has become aware of the existence of two lexicons, and has begun to use the equivalent as a means of gaining more attention. He is less bound to the pragmatic context in which he first learned to name a certain object or event, and he tries to adjust to his interlocutor by speaking the language in which he is addressed. At first glance, it would seem that the child understands which language to speak because of the interlocutor himself; as each adult always addresses him in the same language, the child has decided to use that language with that person. But this is in reality not the case, because I observed time and again that if an interlocutor switched languages, the child switched along with him, even within the same interaction.

A brief experience with Giulia Milli (1;8), an Italian-English bilingual, is interesting in this regard. Giulia had a lexicon which was very rich in both languages and contained many equivalents; she was in the stage when young bilinguals respond in the language with which they are addressed. Giulia had a favorite book, which she was often shown in both languages. When she was shown the book and addressed in English, the words which she imitated and spontaneously produced were almost exclusively English.[2] Even her comments on her own actions were in English, as in "down" when she threw the book on the ground, "sit down" when she sat down, or "thank you" when she gave the book to her interlocutor. Later, when she went through the same book and was addressed in Italian, she imitated and spontaneously produced only Italian words, saying *petea, seduta,* and *azie* in the above three contexts. Evidently, Giulia had not yet rigidly connected one language with one person, nor did she use previous experience in deciding which language to speak, as bilingual children do when they are older.[3] It would appear that Giulia used the phonological channel to decide how to adjust linguistically to her interlocutor. This hypothesis is supported by the fact that when the adult showed her the same book and said Italian words pronounced with an English accent and intonation, the child imitated the Italian words, but made spontaneous comments on the book and on her own actions in English. For instance, when she wanted the adult to take another book, she said, "Book?"; she put the bread she was eating on the table, saying "Up, up"; she repeated "Thank you" several times when giving and taking the book; and she said "Sit down" every time she sat down. Thus, in adjusting to her interlocutor, Giulia used

---

2  Giulia always imitated the adult's language. If she was told a single word, she repeated it entirely, and if she was told a sentence, she repeated the last part.

3  Even with her father, who always speaks Italian with Giulia, she answers in English when he speaks to her in that language.

something very concrete, something which is quite different and easily distinguishable in Italian and English, and something which she had come to know very well: the phonological channel, or, if you will, the two phonological channels. Therefore, although the interlocutor is an integral part of the context, during the second stage he is not yet a cue for the child in his choice of language (see Table 7.1, Second Stage).

In the *third stage,* the most important connected complex and binuclear structures appear, and for the first time the child expresses the relationship between two utterances verbally. At the same time, the child begins to use unorthodox morphological and syntactic structures such as Italian word order in German sentences or vice versa, or word orders which belong to neither language. He begins to practice hypercorrection in the use of functors, both intra- and interlinguistically. The fact that the child used certain word orders or morphemes correctly in the previous stage and now misuses them is an indication that he was using those structures without having analyzed them, and without a clear understanding of their meaning and/or function. He now appears to have realized that there are several linguistic rules, and to be under the impression that he may use these for both languages as he chooses. From this it becomes obvious that interferences are a manifestation of the interplay of procedures which have been activated at the interlinguistic level. As soon as the child has made some progress in his organization of the different rules, he no longer has these interferences.

There comes a time between the second or third stage when the child realizes that not everyone understands the two languages he speaks, and that he must therefore decide which to use. At this point, the child shows that he considers the other person's language to be one of the features which mark that person [De Lemos, personal communication].[4] It is also at this point that the child realizes that one of the languages is spoken by more people than the other, and begins to speak that language alone. Lisa and Giulia's mother, whose native language was not the one spoken by the majority, began to use the *Wie?* strategy at this point, and thus she characterized herself consistently with her language. As Karmiloff-Smith says [1979b, p. 15], "language learning is like problem solving with physical objects; language needs to be sorted, classified, compared, etc. ... and gradually organized into systems of relevant options". Bilingual children have different problems to solve than monolinguals, to the extent that they have more variables which must gradually be organized and grouped into two distinct systems. During the third stage, the child is actively occupied in organizing and arranging the various structures, which gradually acquire the status of morphological and syntactic rules. But he is also busy separating the various rules in the correct way indicated to him by the speech of his interlocutors. This is a delicate moment in the bilingual child's linguistic development, and it is only passed

---

4 For a study of the child's representation of his interlocutor and its importance in language acquisition, see De Lemos [1979].

successfully if the environment offers enough consistent input to enable the child to complete his arrangement of the two systems.

The consistency of the adult's linguistic behavior is thus a very important factor in the bilingual child's linguistic education, because it guides him in organizing and separating the two languages. When the child realizes that he cannot speak his two languages arbitrarily with everyone, he uses the language spoken by his interlocutor as the basis for his decision on which language to speak. Thus, it is during the third stage that the adult becomes a cue in this regard. Once the child has completed this process of distinguishing between languages and has decided to connect one language with a certain person, this connection must be permanent. The child may now become stubborn and intolerant if the adult switches languages.[5] An interesting example of this was the behavior of Andrea (3;0), a German-English bilingual who went to visit her aunt and heard her speak only English for two days. When the woman then addressed the child in German, she looked at her aunt in shock and scolded her with, "Don't speak like that!"

It is no coincidence that the child shows a strong need for consistency during this period, for he is working at applying several new procedures, i.e., the morphological and syntactic rules, to his organization of the two languages. In other words, he is starting to base his use of language on rules. During the previous stage, the child has reached a good level of equivalent production without great difficulty and even begun to speak the language spoken by each of his interlocutors. But now things begin to change. What once seemed to be a natural predisposition towards bilingualism suddenly becomes active monolingualism. Furthermore, if thanks to the correct communicative strategies of his parents, the child continues to be bilingual, he manifests a rigid attachment to the one person/one language principle. The reason for this is that he is now speaking less automatically, making fewer and fewer utterances by rote repetition, and trying to guide his linguistic behavior with the help of rules. But the child cannot base his choice of rules on lexicon alone. He may add Italian endings to German words, and vice versa, and his word order may be arbitrary. In the initial difficulties he experiences in seeking a path through the jungle of linguistic rules, the child tries to use his interlocutor as the reference point in the interaction so as to know which language to use and which rules belong to which language. It is likely that the monolingual child uses the same procedure, but he does not have to keep asking the adult to be consistent.

By permanently connecting each person with a specific language, the bilingual child saves himself the trouble of repeatedly having to choose a language. He cannot allow himself to have to make this decision at the beginning of each interaction or, worse still, before each utterance, because that would complicate the process of speaking even more; the art of speech is based upon

---

5 The application of the one person/one language principle has various degrees of rigidity and differs from subject to subject.

principles of efficiency, and the child knows he should strive to be as clear, rapid, and convincing as possible. In permanently connecting each person with one language, he makes an important part of language acquisition automatic, and thus frees his mind for the other aspects. This is what Karmiloff-Smith [1979b, p. 240] has called the dynamic process for handling the environment: "Only by seeking to conserve patterns and procedures can the child get a 'grip' on the environment and gain what Nelson (1977) has called increasing 'predictive control'. If the child were to take into consideration each new piece of information, constantly remodel his procedures, and slip to and fro between competing theories about the environment, he would not have the opportunity of consolidating the procedures in the first place. This consolidation allows the procedure to become automatic ... thus *freeing the representational processing space* for other developments." From this it becomes clear why the one person/one language principle is again and again propounded. The child must be given consistent input if he is to distinguish and reorganize the two different linguistic systems.

The following example clearly shows how "person-bound" Lisa's speech was. Not only did direct interaction with her mother make Lisa switch languages; her very presence was enough to produce the same effect.

> L is alone in the room, speaking Italian with her toys. When her mother comes in, she begins to speak German to her doll.
>
> **L (4;3):** *Mach den Fuss hoch. Ein Moment, nicht so! Ein, nur ein. So. Jetzt den andern! Ach, zu schwer, ach, zu gross! Könn wir das nicht anziehen. Dann womma besser nur das Kleid anziehen.* (Raise the foot. One moment, not like that! One, only one, like that. Now the other one. Oh, too difficult. Oh, too big! We can't wear these. Then it's better to wear only the dress.)
>
> **M** goes out of the room.
>
> **L:** *E anche le mutandine, quelle gialle e quelle bianche e anche le calze* ... (And your panties, too. The yellow ones and the white ones and your stockings, too ...)

With the one person/one language procedure the child does more than just ensure himself a consistent source of information. He organizes the world of his knowedge and shares it with the adult. In the bilingual, the one person/one language principle is a dialogic constraint of bilingual acquisition which leads to a better understanding between the child and his interlocutors.

Nevertheless, the attachment to the one person/one language procedure does not last forever. It gradually weakens during the period when morphological and word-order "errors" also disappear. The child's insistence on linguistic consistency diminishes considerably, and he becomes willing to speak either language with anyone. During the third stage, the interlocutor is an integral part of the linguistic system the child is learning to cope with, but by the end of this stage, language has become more and more detached from the individual. The child once again allows his interlocutor to change languages, although he would still prefer the language he is accustomed to speaking with that person. At this point, the entire linguistic system, and not merely words or sounds, becomes the cue upon which the child bases his choice of linguistic code.

Because bilingualism offers the child variables which are not always valid for both languages, it may give him the stimulus to reflect early upon language. As Vygotsky [1962, p. 110] observes, the use of two languages gives the child the chance to "see his language as one particular system among many, to view its phenomena under more general categories, and this leads to awareness of his linguistic operations". By now, he has reached the point of bilingual competence which Schönpflug [1977, p. 16] has described as follows: "Balanced bilingualism may also be achieved by means of the individual's ability to have different social identities exist side by side. The bilingual has learned to perceive his own role according to his interlocutor's linguistic background, and thus he has learned not only to speak two languages, but to be socially flexible."

In summary it may be said that just as a bilingual child recognizes the different meanings of two words and the different functions of a morpheme, so he also realizes that he is speaking two languages which gradually grow apart and whose differences and similarities increase with his competence. Thus the child begins to recognize lexical equivalents at an early period and equivalent morphological functions at a later one, and does so at a metalinguistic level, as in this lovely example:

**L** (9;5): *Mami, weisst du dass Deutsch und Italienisch ganz egal sind?* (Mommy, did you know that German and Italian are the same?)

**M:** *Ach ja?* (Oh yes?)

**L:** *Ja guck, man sagt doch: io ho smesso, tu hai smesso, egli ha smesso. Und in deutsch: ich bin gegangen, du bist gegangen, er ist gegangen! Ist immer dasselbe. Bemerkst du nicht Mami? Das ist doch klar! Käseleicht.* (Yes, look. [In Italian] you say: *io ho smesso, tu hai smesso, egli ha smesso.* [I have stopped, you have stopped, he has stopped] And in German: *ich bin gegangen, du bist gegangen, er ist gegangen.* [I have gone, you have gone, he has gone]. It's always the same, don't you see? It's so simple!)

**M:** *Ja, du hast recht. Das ist einfach käseleicht.* (Yes, you're right. It's really very simple.)

# References

Antinucci, F., Parisi, D. (1972): "Due fasi nello sviluppo iniziale della competenza linguistica"; Tech. Rpt. CNR, Institute of Psychology, Rome

Antinucci, F., Volterra, V. (1973): "Lo sviluppo della negazione nel linguaggio infantile: uno studio pragmatico"; Tech. Rpt. CNR, Institute of Psychology, Rome

Arsenian, S. (1945): "Bilingualism and Mental Development", Teacher's College Contributions to Education, Rpt. 712, Columbia University, New York

Asher, J. K., Garcia, R. (1969): The optimal age to learn a foreign language. Mod. Lang. J. **53**, 334 – 341

Baetens-Beardsmore, H. (1982): *Bilingualism: Basic Principles* (Tieto, Cleveland)

Bamberg, M. (1980): A fresh look at the relationship between pragmatic and semantic knowledge. Linguist. Ber. **62**, 23 – 42

Bamberg, M. (in press): Metapher, Sprache, Intersubjektivität. Muttersprache

Bates, E. (1976): *Language and Context* (Academic, New York)

Bates, E., Rankin, J. (1979): Morphological development in Italian: Connotation and denotation. J. Child Lang. **6**, 29 – 53

Bates, E., Camaioni, L. Volterra, V. (1975): The acquisition of performatives prior to speech. Merrill-Palmer Q. **21**, 205 – 226

Bellugi, U. (1971): "Simplification in Children's Language", in *Methods and Models in Language Acquisition,* ed. by. R. Huxley, E. Ingram (Academic, New York)

Benedict, H. (1979): Early lexical development: Comprehension and production. J. Child Lang. **6**, 183 – 201

Benelli, B. (1978): *Effetti del bilinguismo nell'evoluzione del realismo nominale,* Quaderni Cladil, 19/20 (Minerva Italica, Bergamo)

Bergman, C. R. (1976): "Interference vs. Independent Development in Infant Bilingualism", in *Bilingualism in the Bicentennial and Beyond,* ed. by. G. Keller (Bilingual, New York)

Berko, J. (1958): The child's learning of English morphology. Word **14**, 150 – 177

Bever, T. G. (1970): "The Cognitive Basis for Linguistic Structures", in *Cognition and the Development of Language,* ed. by. J. R. Hayes (Wiley, New York)

Bizzarri, H. (1977): L'acquisizione e lo sviluppo del lessico in un bambino bilingue che inizia il processo di verbalizzazione in ritardo. RILA **3**, 61 – 81

Bizzarri, H. (1978a): Il rapporto semantico in un caso di bilinguismo precoce. RILA **2/3**, 73 – 89

Bizzarri, H. (1978b): Alcune osservazioni sullo sviluppo della competenza comunicativa di un bambino bilingue durante e dopo un soggiorno negli Stati Uniti. RILA **2/3**, 51 – 73

Bloom, L., Lightbown, P., Hood, L. (1974): "Conventions for Transcription of Child Language Recordings"; Unpublished manuscript, Teacher's College, Columbia University

Bloomfield, L. (1935): *Language* (Allen & Unwin, London)

Bowerman, M. (1976): "Semantic Factors in the Acquisition of Rules for Word Use and Sentence Construction", in *Normal and Deficient Child Language,* ed. by D. M. Morehead, A. E. Morehead (University Park Press, Baltimore)

Bowerman, M. (1978): "The Acquisition of Word Meaning: An Investigation into Some Current Conflicts", in *The Development of Communication,* ed. by N. Waterson, C. Snow (Wiley, Chichester)

Braine, M. (1963): The ontogeny of English phrase structure: The first phase. Language **39**,1 – 14

238     References

Braine, M. (1976): Children's first word combinations. Monogr. Soc. Res. Child Dev. **41**, Serial No. 164

Brooks, N. (1960): *Language and Language Learning* (Harcourt Brace, New York)

Brown, R. (1979): *La prima lingua I, II* (Armando, Rome) [Italian translation of: Brown, R. (1973) *A First Language* (Harvard University Press, Cambridge, MA)]

Brown, R., Bellugi, U. (1971): "Three Processes in the Child's Acquisition of Syntax", in *Intellectual Development,* ed. by P. S. Sears (Wiley, New York)

Bühler, K. (1934): *Sprachtheorie* (Fischer, Jena, reprint: Fischer, Stuttgart 1966)

Burling, R. (1971): "Language Development of a Garo and English Speaking Child", in *Child Language: A Book of Readings,* ed. by A. Bar-Adon, W. F. Leopold (Prentice Hall, New Jersey)

Calasso, M. G., Garau, Z. S. (1976): Maia. RILA **2/3**, 117–138

Calasso, M. G., Garau, Z. S. (1978): La coesione interna di due versioni die 'Capucetto Rosso' raccontata in inglese da una bambina italiana bilingue. RILA **2/3**, 3–33

Camaioni, L., Volterra, V., Bates, E. (1976): *La comunicazione nel primo anno di vita* (Boringhieri, Turin)

Cancino, H., Rosansky, E. J., Schuhmann, J. (1978): "The Acquisition of English Negatives and Interrogatives by Native Spanish Speakers", in *Second Language Acquisition,* ed. by E. M. Hatch (Newbury, Rowley, MA)

Canepari, L. (1979): *Introduzione alla fonetica* (Piccola Biblioteca Einaudi, Turin)

Cazden, C. B. (1972): *Child Language and Education* (Holt, Rinehart and Winston, New York)

Celce-Murcia, M. (1975): "Phonological Factors in Vocabulary Acquisition: A Case Study of a Two-Year-Old English-French Bilingual", TESOL Conference, Los Angeles

Chomsky, N. (1971): "Deep Structure, Surface Structure and Semantic Interpretation", in *Semantics: An Interdisciplinary Reader in Philosophy, Linguistics and Psychology,* ed. by D. D. Steinberg, L. A. Jakobovitz (Cambridge University Press, London)

Clark, H. H., Clark, E. V. (1977): *Psychology and Language* (Harcourt Brace Jovanovich, New York)

Clark, R. (1974): Performing without competence. J. Child Lang. **1**, 1–10

Clark, R. (1977): What's the use of imitation? J. Child Lang. **4**, 341–358

Corder, S. P. (1971): "The Significance of Learners' Errors", in *New Frontiers in Second Language Learning,* ed. by G. H. Schuhmann, N. Stenso (Newbury, Rowley, MA)

Cunze, B. (1980): "Lo sviluppo linguistico di una bambina bilingue italo-tedesca"; Thesis, University of Rome

De Lemos, C. (1979): "Adult-Child Interaction and the Development of Aspectual Markers in Brazilian Portuguese", Child Language Conference, Max Planck Institut, Nijmegen

De Matteis, M. (1978): *Mehrsprachigkeit: Möglichkeiten und Grenzen* (Peter Lang, Frankfurt)

Doyle, A. B., Champagne, M., Segalowitz, N. (1978): "Some Issues in the Assessment of Linguistic Consequences of Early Bilingualism", in *Aspects of Bilingualism*, ed. by N. Paradis (Hornbean, South Carolina)

Dulay, H. C., Burt, M. K. (1974a): Natural sequences in child second language acquisition. Lang. Learn. **24**, 37–53

Dulay, H. C., Burt, M. K. (1974b): Errors and strategies in child second language acquisition. TESOL Q. **8**, 129–136

Durga, R. (1978): Bilingualism and interlingual interference. J. Cross Cult. Psychol. **9**, 401–415

El-Dash, G. L. (1978): "Study of Early Vocabulary Acquisition, Syntax and Language Mixing in a Portuguese-English Bilingual Child"; Unpublished paper, Unicamp, Campinas

El-Dash, G. L. (1981): "Second Language Learning/Acquisition in a Small Child, A Case Study"; Unpublished paper, Unicamp, Campinas

Emrich, L. (1938): Beobachtungen über Zweisprachigkeit in ihrem Anfangsstadium. Deutschtum im Ausland **21**, 419–424

Ervin, G., Osgood, C. E. (1954): Second language learning and bilingualism. J. Abnorm. Soc. Psychol. **49**, 139–146

Ervin, S. (1964): "Imitation and Structural Change in Children's Language", in *New Directions in the Study of Language,* ed. by E. H. Lenneberg (MIT Press, Cambridge, MA)

Ervin, S. M., Miller, W. R. (1964): "The Development of Grammar in Child Language", in *The Acquisition of Language,* ed. by U. Bellugi, R. Brown, Monogr. Soc. Res. Child Dev. 29.1

Ervin-Tripp, S. (1973): *Language Acquisition and Communicative Choice* (Stanford University Press, Stanford, CA)

Fillmore, C. J. (1978): "On the Organization of Semantic Information in the Lexicon", Parasession on the Lexicon, Chicago Linguistic Society

Fodor, J. A., Bever, T. G. (1965): The psychological reality of linguistic segments. J. Verb. Learn. Verb. Behav. **4,** 414–420

Foster-Meloni, C. (1978): Code switching and interference in the speech of an Italian-English bilingual child. RILA 2/3, 89–97

Francescato, G. (1970): *Il linguaggio infantile* (Einaudi, Turin)

Francesconi, C. (unpublished manuscript): "The Position of the Adjective in the Nominal in Italian"; Thesis to be submitted to Cambridge University

Fraser, C., Roberts, N. (1975): Mother's speech to children of four different ages. J. Psycholinguist. Res. **4,** 9–17

Funke, A. (1902): *Aus Deutsch-Brasilien* (Teubner, Leipzig)

Gleason, J. B. (1973): "Code Switching in Children's Language", in *Cognitive Development and the Acquisition of Language,* ed. by T. E. Moore (Academic, New York)

Glinz, H. (1961): *Die innere Form des Deutschen* (Bern)

Greenfield, P. M., Smith, J. H. (1976): *The Structure of Communication in Early Language Development* (Academic, New York)

Grimm, H. (1973): *Strukturanalytische Untersuchung der Kindersprache* (Hans Huber, Stuttgart)

Grimm, H. (1977): *Psychologie der Sprachentwicklung, I, II* (Kohlhammer, Stuttgart)

Grimm, H., Schöler, H., Wintermantel, M. (1975): *Zur Entwicklung sprachlicher Strukturformen bei Kindern,* Band I (Beltz, Basel)

Gumperz, J. J., Chavez, E. H. (1972): "Bilingualism, Bidialectualism, and Classroom Interaction", in *Functions of Language in the Classroom,* ed. by C. B. Cazden, V. P. John, B. Hymes (Teacher's College Press, New York)

Gvozdev, A. N. (1949): *Formirovaniye u rebenka grammaticheskogo stroya russkogo yazyka, I, II* (Akad. Pedog. Nauk RSFSR, Moscow)

Haugen, E. (1956): *Bilingualism in the Americas: A Bibliography and Research Guide* (University of Alabama Press, University, Alabama)

Helbig, G., Schenkel, W. (1969): *Wörterbuch zur Valenz und Distribution deutscher Verben* (VEB Bibliographisches Institut, Leipzig)

Hoyer, A. E., Hoyer, G. (1924): Über die Lallsprache eines Kindes. Z. Angew. Psychol. **24,** 363–384

Imedadze, N. V. (1967): On the psychological nature of child speech formation under conditions of exposure to two languages. Int. J. Psychol. **2,** 129–132

Itoh, H., Hatch, E. (1978): "Second Language Acquisition: A Case Study", in *Second Language Acquistion,* ed. by E. Hatch (Newbury, Rowley, MA)

Jarovinsky, A. (1979): On the lexical competence of bilingual children of kindergarten age groups. Int. J. Psycholinguist. **6,** 43–57

Jespersen, O. (1953): *Come si insegna la lingua straniera* (Sansoni, Florence)

Juhasz, J. (1970): *Probleme der Interferenz* (Max Huber, Munich)

Kalepky, T. (1928): *Neuaufbau der Grammatik* (Leipzig, Berlin)

Karmiloff-Smith, A. (1978): "The Interplay Between Syntax, Semantics and Phonology in Language Acquisition Processes", in *Recent Advances in the Psychology of Language,* ed. by R. N. Campbell, P. T. Smith (Plenum, New York)

Karmiloff-Smith, A. (1979a): Micro- and macrodevelopmental changes in language acquisition and other representational systems. Cognit. Sci. **3**, 91 – 118

Karmiloff-Smith, A. (1979b): *A Functional Approach to Child Language* (Cambridge University Press, Cambridge)

Katz, N., Baker, E., Macnamara, J. (1974): What's in a name? A study of how children learn common and proper names. Child Dev. **45**, 469 – 473

Keenan, E. (1978): "La competenza conversazionale nei bambini", in *Sviluppo del linguaggio e interazione sociale,* ed. by L. Camaioni (Il Mulino, Bologna)

Keenan, E., Schlieffelin, B. (1976): "Topic as a Discourse Notion: A Study of Topic in the Conversation of Children and Adults", in *Subject and Topic,* ed. by C. Li (Academic, New York)

Keller, G. D. (1976): "Acquisition of the English and Spanish Passive Voices Among Bilingual Children", in *Bilingualism in the Bicentennial and Beyond,* ed. by G. D. Keller, R. V. Teschner, S. Viera (Bilingual, New York)

Kessler, C. (1976): *The Acquisition of Syntax in Bilingual Children* (Georgetown University Press, Washington, D.C.)

Klima, E. S., Bellugi, U. (1966): "Syntactic Regularities in the Speech of Children", in *Psycholinguistic Papers,* ed. by J. Lyons, R. J. Wales (Edinburgh University Press, Edinburgh)

Lamont, D., Penner, W., Blower, T., Mosychuk, H., Jones, J. (1978): Evaluation of the second year of a bilingual (English-Ukrainian) program. Can. Mod. Lang. Rev. **34**, 175 – 185

Lauster, U. (1977): *Rechenspiele für das erste und zweite Grundschuljahr* (Ensslin & Laiblin, Reutlingen)

Lehman, W. P. (1973): A structural principle of language and its implications. Language **49**, 47 – 66

Lenard, A. (1970): *Die Kuh auf dem Bast,* 2nd ed. (Weiner, Vienna)

Lenneberg, E. (1971): *I fondamenti biologici del linguaggio* (Boringhieri, Turin)

Leopold, W. F. (1939, 1947, 1949a, 1949b): *Speech Development of a Bilingual Child: A Linguist's Record,* I: Vocabulary Growth in the First Two Years, II: Sound Learning in the First Two Years, III: Grammar and General Problems in the First Two Years, IV: Diary from Age Two (Northwestern University Press, Evanston, IL)

Leopold, W. F. (1956): Das Sprechenlernen des Kindes. Sprachforum **2**, 117 – 125

Leopold, W. F. (1971): "The Study of Child Language and Infant Bilingualism", in *Child Language: A Book of Readings,* ed. by A. Bar-Adon, W. F. Leopold (Prentice Hall, New Jersey) pp. 1 – 13

Leopold, W. F. (1978): "A Child's Learning Two Languages", in *Second Language Acquisition,* ed. by E. M. Hatch (Newbury, Rowley, MA)

Lindholm, K. J., Padilla, A. M. (1978): Language mixing in bilingual children. J. Child Lang. **5**, 327 – 335

Locke, L. (1981): "Issues and Procedures in the Analysis of Syntax and Semantics", in *Communication Assessment of the Bilingual, Bicultural Child,* ed. by J. G. Erickson, D. R. Omark (University Park Press, Baltimore)

Loprete, R. (1976a): Bilinguismo precoce: quando e come? RILA **2/3**, 139 – 151

Loprete, R. (1976b): Due casi: Maria Francesca e Delia. RILA **2/3**, 151 – 179

Lorenzer, A. (1976): "Zur Konstitution von Bedeutung im primären Sozialisationsprozess", in *Methodologie der Sprachwissenschaft,* ed. by Schecker, M. (Hoffmann und Campe, Hamburg)

McCarthy, D. (1954): "Language Development in Children", in *Manual of Child Psychology,* 2nd ed., ed. by L. Carmichael (Wiley, New York)

Mackey, W. F. (1956): Toward a definition of bilingualism. J. Can. Linguist. Assoc., March

McLaughlin, B. (1978): *Second Language Acquisition in Childhood* (Lawrence Erlbaum Associates, New Jersey)

MacNamara, J. (1967): The bilingual's linguistic performance: A psychological overview. J. Soc. Issues **23**, 58 – 77

McWhinney, B. (1980): "Levels of Syntactic Acquisition", in *Language Development: Syntax and Semantics,* ed. by S. Kucsaj (Lawrence Erlbaum Associates, New Jersey)

Manzotti, E. (1978): "Artikel und Stoffnamen: Eine kontrastive Untersuchung zum Italienischen und Deutschen", in *Kasusgrammatik und Sprachvergleich,* ed. by C. Schwarze (Gunter Narr, Tübingen)

Maratsos, M. P. (1974a): Children who get worse in understanding the passive: A replication to Bever. J. Psycholinguist. Res. **3**, 65 – 74

Maratsos, M. P. (1974b): Pre-school children's use of definite and indefinite articles. Child **45**, 446 – 455

Menyuk, P. (1964): Syntactic rules used by children from pre-school through first grade. Child Dev. **35**, 533 – 546

Mikés, M. (1967): Acquisition des catégories grammaticales dans le language de l'enfant. Enfance **20**, 289 – 298

Miller, M. (1976): *Zur Logik der frühkindlichen Sprachentwicklung* (Ernst Klett, Stuttgart)

Mills, A. (in press): "The Acquisition of German", in *The Crosslinguistic Study of Language Acquisition,* ed. by D. Slobin (Lawrence Erlbaum Associates, New Jersey)

Murrel, M. (1966): Language acquisition in a trilingual environment: Notes from a case study. Stud. Linguist. **20**, 9 – 35

Mussen, D. H., Conge, J. J., Kagan, J. (1976): *Linguaggio e sviluppo cognitivo* (Zanichelli, Bologna)

Nelson, K. (1973): Structure and strategy in learning to talk. Monogr. Soc. Res. Child. Dev. **38**, Serial No. 149

Nelson, K. (1974): Concept, word and sentence: Interrelations in acquisition and development. Psychol. Rev. **81**, 267 – 285

Nelson, K. (1977): "How Young Children Represent Knowledge of Their World In and Out of Language: A Preliminary Report", Symposium on Cognition, Carnegie-Mellon University

Nemser, W. (1971): Approximative system of foreign language learners. IRAL **9**, 115 – 124

Nickel, G. (1972): "Grundsätzliches zur Fehleranalyse und Fehlerbewertung", in *Fehlerkunde,* ed. by G. Nickel (Cornelsen, Velhagen & Klasing, Berlin)

Ochs, E. (1979a): "Introduction: What Child Language Can Contribute to Pragmatics", in *Developmental Pragmatics,* ed. by E. Ochs, B. S. Schieffelin (Academic, New York)

Ochs, E. (1979b): "Transcription as a Theory", in *Developmental Pragmatics,* ed. by E. Ochs, B. S. Schieffelin (Academic, New York) pp. 43 – 72

Ochs, E., Schieffelin, B. S. (eds.) (1979): *Developmental Pragmatics* (Academic, New York)

Oksaar, E. (1971): Zum Spracherwerb des Kindes in zweisprachiger Umgebung. Folia Linguist. **4**, 330 – 358

Oksaar, E. (1977): *Spracherwerb im Vorschulalter* (Kohlhammer, Stuttgart)

Ornstein, J., Valdis-Fallis, G., Dubois, B. L. (1971): Bilingual child acquisition along the United States-Mexico border: The El Paso Ciudad-Juarez-Las Cruces triangle. Word **1 – 3**, 386 – 404

Padilla, A. M., Liebman, S. (1975): Language acquisition in the bilingual child. Bilingual Rev. **2**, 34 – 35

Padilla, A. M., Lindholm, K. (1976): "Acquisition of Bilingualism: An Analysis of the Linguistic Structures of Spanish/English-Speaking Children", in *Bilingualism in the Bicentennial and Beyond,* ed. by G. D. Keller, R. V. Teschner, S. Viera (Bilingual, New York)

Parisi, D. (1977): *Sviluppo del linguaggio e ambiente sociale* (La Nuova Italia, Florence)

Parisi, D., Antinucci, F. (1973): *Elementi di grammatica* (Boringhieri, Turin)

Parisi, D., Giannelli, W. (1974): "Linguaggio e classe sociale a due anni", Tech. Rpt. CNR, Institute of Psychology, Rome

Park, T. Z. (1974): "A Study of German Language Development", Tech. Rpt., Psychological Institute, Bern

Park, T. Z. (1976): "Imitation of Grammatical and Ungrammatical Sentences by German-Speaking Children", in *Baby Talk and Infant Speech,* ed. by W. Raffler-Engel (Sveets & Zeitlinger, Amsterdam)

Pavlovitch, M. (1920): *Le language enfantin: acquisition du serbe et du français par un enfant serbe* (Champion Éditeur, Paris)

Peal, E., Lambert, W. F. (1962): The relationship of bilingualism to intelligence. Psychol. Monogr. **76**, Serial No. 27

Piaget, J. (1973): *La rappresentazione del mondo nel fanciullo* (Boringhieri, Turin) [Italian translation of *La répresentation du monde chez l'enfant* (Presses Univ. de France, Paris 1926)]

Preyer, W. (1882): "Die Seele des Kindes", in *Child Language: A Book of Readings,* ed. by A. Bar-Adon, W. F. Leopold (Prentice Hall, New Jersey 1971)

Raffler-Engel, W. (1964a): *Il pre-linguaggio infantile* (Paideia, Brescia)

Raffler-Engel, W. (1964b): L'influenza dei fattori ambientali nello sviluppo linguistico del bambino. Boll. Psicol. Appl. **65/66**, 109 – 114

Raffler-Engel, W. (1965): Del bilinguismo infantile. Arch. Glottologico Ital. **50**, 175 – 180

Raffler-Engel, W. (1966): Linguaggio attivo e linguaggio passivo. Orientamenti Pedagogici, **13**, 893 – 894

Ramge, H. (1975): *Spracherwerb* (Niemeyer, Tübingen)

Redlinger, W. E., Park, T. Z. (1980): Language mixing in young bilinguals. J. Child Lang. **7**, 337 – 352

Regula, M. (1951): *Grundlegung und Grundprobleme der Syntax* (Heidelberg)

Reilly, J., Zukow, P., Greenfield, P. (unpublished): "Transcription Procedures for the Study of Early Language Development", Dept. of Psychology, UCLA, CA

Richard, J. (1971): A non-contrastive approach to error analysis. Engl. Lang. Teach. **25**, 204 – 219

Rodari, G. (1978): *La gondola fantasma* (Einaudi, Milan)

Roeper, T. (1972): "Approaches to a Theory of Language Acquisition with Examples from German Children"; Ph. D. Thesis, Harvard University, MA

Roeper, T. (1973): "Connecting Children's Language and Linguistic Theory", in *Cognitive Development and the Acquisition of Language,* ed. by T. M. Moore (Academic, New York)

Ronjat, J. (1913): *Le développement du langage observé chez un enfant bilingue* (Champion Éditeur, Paris)

Rosch, E. H. (1973): "On the Internal Structure of Perceptual and Semantic Categories", in *Cognitive Development and the Acquisition of Language,* ed. by T. M. Moore (Academic, New York)

Rosch, E. (1978): "Principles of Categorization", in *Cognition and Categorization,* ed. by E. Rosch, B. B. Lloyd (Lawrence Erlbaum Associates, New Jersey)

Rüke-Dravina, V. (1965): The process of acquisition of apical /r/ and uvular /r/ in the speech of children. Linguistics **17**, 56 – 68

Rüke-Dravina, V. (1967): *Mehrsprachigkeit im Vorschulalter* (Lund, Gleerup)

Sachs, H., Schegloff, E., Jefferson, G. (1974): A simplest systematics for the organization of turn-taking in conversation. Language **50**, 696 – 735

Sachs, J., Devin, J. (1976): Young children's use of age-appropriate speech styles in social interaction and role-playing. J. Child Lang. **3**, 81 – 98

Schachter, J., Celce-Murcia, M. (1977): Some reservations concerning error analysis. TESOL Q. **11**, 441 – 451

Schmidt-Rohr, G. (1933): *Muttersprache* (Amt der Sprache bei der Volksbildung, Jena)

Schönpflug, U. (1977): *Psychologie des Erst- und Zweitspracherwerbs: eine Einführung* (Kohlhammer Taschenbücher, Stuttgart)

Scollon, R., (1976): *Conversation with a One-Year Old* (University of Hawaii Press, Honolulu)

Scollon, R. (1978): "Riassunto informale di uno studio sul linguaggio infantile", in *Sviluppo del linguaggio,* ed. by L. Camaioni (Il Mulino, Bologna)

Selinker, L. K. (1972): Interlanguage. IRAL **10**, 209 – 231

Shatz, H., Gelman, R. (1973): The development of communication skills: Modifications in the speech of young children as a function of the listener. Monogr. Soc. Res. Child Dev. **38**, Serial No. 5

Simoes, M. C. P., Stoel-Gammon, C. (1979): The acquisition of inflections in Portuguese: A study of the development of person markers on verbs. J. Child Lang. **6**, 53 – 69

Slobin, D. I. (1975): "Language Change in Childhood and History", Working Paper 41́, University of California, Berkeley

Slobin, D. I. (1978): "Universal and Particular in the Acquisition of Language", Workshop Conf. on Language Acquisition: State of the Art, University of Pennsylvania, May 19 – 22

Smith, M. E. (1935): A study of the speech of eight bilingual children of the same family. Child Dev. **6**, 19 – 25

Snow, C. C. (1972): Mother's speech to children learning language. Child Dev. **43**, 549 – 565

Stern, C., Stern, W. (1965): *Die Kindersprache: eine psychologische und sprachtheoretische Untersuchung* (Wissenschaftliche Buchgesellschaft, Darmstadt)

Swain, M. (1971): "Bilingualism, Monolingualism and Code Acquisition", Child Language Conference, Chicago

Swain, M. (1972): "Bilingualism as a First Language"; Ph. D. Thesis, University of California, Irvine

Swain, M. (1973): "Child Bilingual Language Learning and Linguistic Interdependence", Conference on Bilingualism and its Implications for Western Canada, University of Alberta, Edmonton

Swain, M., Wesche, M. (1975): Linguistic interaction: Case study of a bilingual child. Lang. Sci. October, 17 – 22

Tabouret-Keller, A. (1969): "Le bilinguisme de l'enfant avant six ans"; Ph. D. Thesis

Taeschner, T. (1976): Come definire la lingua dominante in un soggetto bilingue dalla nascita. RILA **8**, 139 – 151

Taeschner, T., Testa, C. (1978): "La frase subordinata", First Austro-Italian Meeting organized by SLI, Bressanone, Italy

Taeschner, T., Volterra, V., Wintermantel, M. (1982): "Un confronto tra lo sviluppo della frase in bambini bilingui e monolingui", Tech. Rpt. CNR, Institute of Psychology, Rome

Tesnière, L. (1953): *Esquisse d'une syntaxe structurale* (Librairie C. Klincksieck, Paris)

Titone, R. (1972): *Bilinguismo precoce e educazione bilingue* (Armando, Rome)

Titone, R. (1981): Educazione bilingue precoce e sviluppo cognitivo. Età Evolutiva **8**, 91 – 100

Viera, S. (1976): "Needed Research in the Fields of Psycho- and Socio-Linguistics as They Relate to the Instruction of Minority Children in the Bilingual Education Programs of North American Schools", Eric Document

Volterra, V. (1972): Il "no". Prime fasi della negazione nel linguagio infantile. Arch. Psicol. Neurol. Psichiatr. **33**

Volterra, V., Taeschner, T. (1978): The acquisition and development of language by bilingual children. J. Child Lang. **5**, 311 – 326

Volterra, V., Antoniotti, C., Pennavaja, A., Rivardo, M. (1979): "Le intenzioni comunicative espresse da bambini che frequentano il nido a da bambini che non lo frequentano", Tech. Rpt. CNR, Institute of Psychology, Rome

Vygotsky, L. S. (1962): *Thought and Language* (MIT Press, Chicago)

Walters, J., Zatorre, R. J. (1978): Laterality differences for word identification in bilinguals. Brain Lang. **6**, 158 – 167

Weinreich, U. (1974): *Lingue in contatto* (Boringhieri, Turin)

Weisgerber, L. (1933): Die Stellung der Sprache im Aufbau der Gesamtkultur. Wörter und Sachen **15**, 134 – 224

Wintermantel, M., Knopf, M. (1978): "Längsschnittuntersuchung der Sprachentwicklung von zwei- bis siebenjährigen Kindern aus verschiedenen sozialen Schichten"; Forschungsbericht, Heidelberg

Wong-Fillmore, L. (1976): "The Second Time Around: Cognitive and Social Strategies"; Ph. D. Thesis, Stanford University, CA

Zydatiss, W. (1976): *Tempus und Aspekt im Englisch-Unterricht* (Scriptor, Kronberg)

# Subject Index

## Verbal Processes in Children

Progress in Cognitive Development Research

Editors: **C. J. Brainerd, M. Pressley**

1982. 10 figures. XIV, 289 pages
(Springer Series in Cognitive Development)
ISBN 3-540-90648-7

**Contents:** Two Decades of Referential Communication Research: A Review and Meta-Analysis. – Bilingual and Second Language Acquisition in Preschool Children. – Cognitive Processes and Reading Disability: A Critique and Proposal. – Acquisition of Word Meaning in the Context of the Development of the Semantic System. – Memory Strategy Instruction with Children. – Children's Understanding of Stories: A Basis for Moral Judgment and Dilemma Resolution. – Verbal Processing in Poor and Normal Readers. – Growing Up Explained: Vygotskians Look at the Language of Causality. – Index.

## Children's Logical and Mathematical Cognition

Process in Cognitive Development Research

Editor: **C. J. Brainerd**

1982. 16 figures. XVI, 216 pages
(Springer Series in Cognitive Development)
ISBN 3-540-90635-5

**Contents:** Conservation-Nonconservation: Alternative Explanations. – The Acquisition and Elaboration of the Number Word Sequence. – Children's Concepts of Chance and Probability. – The Development of Quantity Concepts: Perceptual and Linguistic Factors. – Culture and the Development of Numerical Cognition: Studies among the Oksapmin of Papua New Guinea. – Children's Concept Laarning as Rule-Sampling Systems with Markovian Properties. – Index.

## Learning in Children

Progress in Cognitive Development Research

Editors: **J. Bisanz, G. L. Bisanz, R. Kail**

1983. 5 figures. Approx. 230 pages
(Springer Series in Cognitive Development)
ISBN 3-540-90802-1

**Contents:** Structural Invariance in the Developmental Analysis of Learning. – The Learning Paradigm as a Technique for Investigating Cognitive Development. – A Learning Analysis of Spatial Concept Development in Infancy. – Research Strategies for a Cognitive Developmental Psychology of Instruction. – Social Learning, Causal Attribution, and Moral Internalization. – Ordinary Learning: Pragmatic Connections Among Children's Beliefs, Motives, and Actions. – Learning from Children Learning. – Author Index. – Subject Index.

Springer-Verlag
Berlin
Heidelberg
New York
Tokyo

Springer-Verlag
Berlin
Heidelberg
New York
Tokyo